# Representing Autism

# REPRESENTATIONS:
## HEALTH, DISABILITY, CULTURE

*Series Editor*
Stuart Murray, University of Leeds

This series provides a ground-breaking and innovative selection of titles that showcase the newest interdisciplinary research on the cultural representations of health and disability in the contemporary social world. Bringing together both subjects and working methods from literary studies, film and cultural studies, medicine and sociology, 'Representations' is scholarly and accessible, addressed to researchers across a number of academic disciplines, and practitioners and members of the public with interests in issues of public health.

The key term in the series will be representations. Public interest in questions of health and disability has never been stronger, and as a consequence cultural forms across a range of media currently produce a never-ending stream of narratives and images that both reflect this interest and generate its forms. The crucial value of the series is that it brings the skilled study of cultural narratives and images to bear on such contemporary medical concerns. It offers and responds to new research paradigms that advance understanding at a scholarly level of the interaction between medicine, culture and society; it also has a strong commitment to public concerns surrounding such issues, and maintains a tone and point of address that seeks to engage a general audience.

# Representing Autism

## *Culture, Narrative, Fascination*

Stuart Murray

LIVERPOOL UNIVERSITY PRESS

First published 2008 by
Liverpool University Press
4 Cambridge Street
Liverpool L69 7ZU

British Library Cataloguing-in-Publication data
A British Library CIP record is available

ISBN   978-1-84631-091-1 cased
ISBN   978-1-84631-092-8 limp

Typseset in Iowan Old Style by R. J. Footring Ltd, Derby
Printed and bound by CPI Group (UK) Ltd, Croydon, CR0 4YY

*This book is for Lucas – never alone in any world, because he is always in mine.*

# Contents

# Figures

# Permissions

I am grateful to McGraw-Hill Education for permission to reproduce Thomas Balsamo's photographs from *Souls: Beneath and Beyond Autism* in chapter 3, and to the GRACE gallery for permission to reproduce the images (taken by Michael Gray) of Larry Bissonnette's work in chapter 2. I would also want to express my thanks to Ralph Smith for granting his permission to reproduce his photographic posters that I use in my conclusion, and to The Option Institute for permission to use the advertisement for the Son-Rise Program that appears in chapter 5.

Some parts of chapter 3 of this book originally appeared in 'Hollywood and the fascination of autism', published in Mark Osteen (ed.), *Autism and Representation* (New York: Routledge, 2008), and I am grateful to Taylor & Francis for the right to republish those here. In addition, some material in chapters 3 and 4 was part of my article 'Autism and the contemporary sentimental: fiction and the narrative fascination of the present', published in *Literature and Medicine* (volume 25, number 1, spring 2006), and part of chapter 1 appears in 'On autistic presence', published in the *Journal of Literary Disability* (volume 2, number 1, 2008).

# Preface: questions

The photograph on the cover of this book was taken by Jane Bown at The Lindens, a school in Surrey for children with learning disabilities, in March 1966. The school was one of the earliest institutions to have a specific focus on the education of children with autism, taking its first autistic student in 1960. The development of special education at The Lindens parallels the establishment of the National Autistic Society, itself formed in 1962, initially as the Society for Psychotic Children.[1] The photograph comes, then, from an early moment in the proper appreciation of the nature of autism as a distinct condition. Two girls are on a rudimentary seesaw or swing boat, probably used in the school to help children interact with one another. From their positions the girls seem to be at rest, though it is possible they are moving. They seem to be displaying no awareness of each other; the girl on the left has her forehead on her knees while the girl on the right appears to have her whole head covered, apparently resting it on the metal frame of the swing boat.

The choice to use the photograph was not an easy one; the very concept of an appropriate cover for a topic such as the representation of autism (or indeed any disability) is complex. Many, if not most, covers of books dealing with issues of disability or exceptionality feature abstract designs, attractive patterns that might point to the text's seriousness or that seek to engage its audience through the use of specific colours. Nevertheless, given that this book deals with representing autism, I thought it was appropriate to have an example of such representation on the front. Indeed, the selection of *which* representation to use on the cover became, in itself, a microcosmic form of the overall challenge of writing the book. In addition, I realized, having a photographic representation of autism offered an opportunity to convey a sense of what the crucial elements in the depiction of the condition might be, to give an idea of the various forms and functions such representation takes. I felt that the cover needed to signal both a sense of autism in and of itself, an idea of what the condition is, and that it also should draw some attention to its own methods of portraying such an idea. When I look at Bown's photograph I think of the two children who are represented, and I also think of the mechanics through which the image is produced, the values at work in the taking of the picture.

In part, the photograph was chosen for the cover because it offers a series of immediate challenges and questions. My sense is that these come not in any particular order, but rather as a group, all pushing at one another during the time that the picture takes to register its effects on the viewer. What are the two girls doing? Are they in the middle of something, or is an activity over or possibly about to start? Are they interacting with each other and is such a question in any way important? Is there anything in the photograph that conveys to viewers how the girls might be feeling? What appears to be the attitude of the photographer to her subjects? Is this an intrusive picture? Does it seek to spectacularize the girls because of an assumed idea of their difference? Or is it maybe a photograph that catches two girls being themselves, one that pays testimony to the selfhood of each of these two individuals? Crucially, how does the photograph make us, its viewers, feel? Does it raise issues about how we react to the sight of those different from ourselves? Does it seek to work on our instinctive reactions to the sight of disabled children?

These are only some of the initial questions prompted by Bown's photograph, but even to mention them here is to begin to enter into the debate that is at the heart of this book, a debate that asks how we read and respond to the varying representations of those with autism. My sense is that, for many, the photograph might convey a sense of tiredness or even sadness. Sadness is usually read in terms of facial expression, and here the faces of the girls are almost totally hidden, but their bodies appear to be slumped and inert. The fact that an instrument of interactive play seems not to be being used for the purposes for which it was designed suggests that possibly something that should have happened has not; that the girls cannot, or will not, participate in the activity planned. Potentially their body positions suggest something even worse: that the activity or even the idea of it has caused both of them to become upset. For many viewers who have a general knowledge of autism, the girls may appear to have 'retreated' or 'withdrawn', closed themselves off. The photograph catches the moment when, because of their autism, the girls simply stop because their immediate environment has become too much for them to bear.

It may well be that the above observations are all either correct or convey a truth that existed at the time at which Bown's photograph was taken, in which case we might feel that the picture gives us a window upon the sadness we feel it communicates. In this formation it becomes, at heart, sentimental, transmitting a sense of the girls' difference, which becomes reinforced by the way it makes those who are not autistic reflect upon themselves. Here the precise framing of the photograph might work to stress such thoughts. The girls and the swing boat fill the frame; viewers have no choice to look away. The invitation to look, possibly stare, at the two girls and to conjecture upon their autism, their futures, their lives, seems obvious enough.

I want to suggest that such a reading of Bown's picture, however, is simply a version of the moment being captured and that, even in promoting the possibility that it might be a version, the photograph works to challenge a number of the orthodox conceptions of what autism is and how it functions in the world. In part, this is a question of how we might read the evidence the photograph offers. After an initial glance, we might feel it offers up a second set of potential questions: Why *should* the girls' body positions convey sadness, or upset, or tiredness? Can we automatically assume that, just because the girls are not looking at each other, they are not interacting? What values and terms inherent to our own processes of looking are being queried by the picture? If we know that autism carries with it a strong element of difference, why should we assume that we can map any instinctual sense of the girls that we might produce when looking at the photograph on to them without trying to recognize that difference? In other words, it is possible to read Bown's photograph as a document that actually asks its viewers to interrogate their own systems of critical reading and judgement, to pause and think through any immediate supposition that the girls have 'retreated' into themselves.

Seen in this way, the photograph offers other possibilities. Maybe it captures a moment of pleasure for both girls, where those particular positions on that object create sensory satisfactions. Many children with autism are over-sensitive to touch and movement, and are upset by certain tactile experiences or by excessive motion; but equally many are under-sensitive, and delight in physical sensory stimulation. Perhaps Bown captures the end of an activity that has been deeply pleasurable, with the girls' body positions indicating their desire to hold the moment of pleasure for as long as they can. Key to this potential interpretation is the question of recognizing what actually might be constituted by the difference that autism undoubtedly contains. Any disabled difference is, within the economies produced by contemporary societies and cultures, traditionally seen in terms of a lack or an absence. As the neurologist Oliver Sacks has written: 'Neurology's favourite word is "deficit"', 'its only word, indeed, for any disturbance of function'.[2] The medical framework that surrounds ideas of impairment dominates perception to such an extent that its model of presumed physical or neurological integrity is taken as orthodox in the public consciousness: bodies and minds either work or they contain flaws that prevent such function. To seek to understand and respect the difference of autism is necessarily to challenge such a view. It involves a reconfiguration of what we might think of as a 'working' spectrum of humanity. It calls for the revision of processes by which we read and judge the autistic subject. It requires us to look twice at Bown's photograph.

The dominant arc of most disability narratives is a movement from the representation of an impairment to the overcoming of the difficulties that are seen to come from it. Such a trajectory provides all manner of resolutions: individuals prove their integrity in the process of the struggle; communities learn from the dignity of the afflicted; humanity as a whole triumphs and we are all rewarded. It is impossible to tell if the girls in Bown's photograph 'overcome' anything. They are not in the business of such an act. Crucially, the photograph implicitly asks us, its viewers, what exactly there might be to overcome in the first place and why we might make such an assumption. While on a first viewing we might presume we have an instinctual knowledge of the issues the picture raises, the longer we look at it, the more we realize that possibly we don't.

The 'overcoming' narrative is so dominant in the representation of disability that it almost seems that there is no alternative. If those with disabilities *don't* struggle against the limitations their conditions impose and make us all the richer for it, then what exactly *is* the story? As seemingly the most enigmatic of conditions, autism fits the demands of such popular narratives perfectly. There is, we are led to believe, such a space to travel between autistic otherness and full neurobehavioural normality, and it is precisely all the unknowns that populate that idea of the enigmatic that make the journey towards its erasure so compelling. But, as always with disability, there is a curious catch. If a majority culture wishes to champion the overcoming of disability, it also can't help but dwell upon the fascination of the strange nature of the condition that has to be overcome. Even as all that is good about human behaviour is felt to surround the exertions to transcend the problems of impairment, the impairment itself becomes compellingly attractive in the way it presents human otherness. Because it is seemingly beyond current scientific knowledge, and because it evades a popular idea of the rational, autism appears to be such otherness in the extreme and, as a consequence, the source of endless fascination.

To return to Bown's photograph, another reason behind my choice to use it on the cover lies in an idea connected to this notion of fascination. The picture was in part chosen because of its age. Images of children with autism (and it is particularly children who are the subjects of portrayals of the condition) have become increasingly common in recent years, across a range of media. And the increase can be explained by the escalation of fascination and wonder that autism has produced in modern audiences. As a consequence, the invitation to look and conjecture upon the nature of the autistic child in the very contemporary period is wrapped within this idea of the condition's present profile. In the UK in the 1960s, such a scenario did not exist. Autism, though a diagnosable condition, had no real public profile; many autistic children were still officially labelled 'psychotic' or as suffering from 'childhood schizophrenia'. The condition was even in an ambiguous position in terms of political and educational policy. Autism itself was not mentioned in any parliamentary legislation until the Chronically Sick and Disabled Persons Act in 1970, and before 1971 children with disabilities not listed in the specifics of the 1944 Education Act had to undergo tests, before the age of five, to determine whether they would benefit from being taught. Those considered 'non-educable' might be forced to remain at home or placed in centres for the 'severely subnormal', where staff were not qualified to teach. The girls in Bown's photograph probably had diagnoses of 'classical' autism, which would have allowed them access to educational resources that would have been denied to the many autistic children without diagnoses. Equally, the condition had no discernible presence in the cultural narratives of the 1960s, precisely because of the wider ignorance of autism within the society of the time. Bown's photograph is thus an anomaly, an intervention into 1960s conventions of looking at children. It is not overlaid by the complex public apprehension of autism that we find in our present. As such, its status as a black and white image, and the details of the girls' clothes, shoes and the swing boat on which they sit, remove us from the contemporary realm of fascination autism occupies. Instead, I felt, the picture had to some degree created a freedom to think about autism without being locked into its present formations. It allowed for a different type of concentration.

Above all, and this is central to the text that follows, the girls in Bown's photograph are *present*, and it is the fact of their presence that needs to be reckoned with, understood and listened to. It is autistic presence, in all its many forms, that is the core of all attempts to discuss agency and legitimacy in those subjects for whom autism is in some way part of their representational existence. It is also autistic presence that resists the many discourses that would simplify or ignore the condition. The material nature of such presence, the excess it creates when confronted with any idea of what 'normal' human activity or behaviour might be, stubbornly refuses to be reduced to any narrative – medical, social or cultural – that might seek to contain it without reference to its own terms. In the chapters of this book, such a conception of presence underpins all my discussions of how autism is represented in the various cultural forms in which it features.

So, when I look again at Bown's photograph, I see the two girls in their own time and space, even as the many narratives that autism inevitably produces tumble in upon them. I see the potential for the sentimental reading but I also see the possibility of advocacy; I see a lack of interaction but also the suggestion of difference that undermines the theoretical grounds on which such an idea of lack might be based. Ultimately, I see two girls who may well be oblivious to the photographer's presence, but who nevertheless can set the agenda for the interpretation of the photograph. And I see a need to let that happen.

### Notes

1 Following its January 1962 foundation, the Society changed its name in that same year, from the Society for Psychotic Children to the Society for Autistic Children. It became the National Society for Autistic Children in 1966 and finally the National Autistic Society (NAS) in 1982. The Lindens itself appears not to have been a NAS school. The first of these was the Sybil Elgar School, opened in 1965. My thanks to staff at the National Autistic Society in London, and also to Michael Baron, for help in establishing these details.

2 Oliver Sacks, *The Man Who Mistook His Wife for a Hat* (London: Pan Books, 1986), p. 1 and p. 81.

# Introduction: autism and narrative

I

Listening to the radio while driving into work one morning in 2006, I heard an advertisement for a new breakfast show that was about to start on BBC's 6 Music, one of the Corporation's digital channels. The ad itself was mainly a monologue by one of the presenters – I missed the name – full of rapid-fire speech that captured what seemed to be an intended manic personality. I presume the idea was that the programme could be sold by getting any potential audience interested in the personalities of the hosts – pretty much the idea behind any breakfast show. The words didn't make any real impression until I suddenly heard the voice say: 'I've got OCD and he's got ADHD, so how can you not tune in and listen?' My response was to be quite startled. As I took that trip to work, I was thinking, in a general sense, through the issues of this book, namely how narrative representations of autism are becoming increasingly common in contemporary culture, and how there seemed to be a public awareness of the condition and others like it that had formed but had not, as yet, really been analysed. Suddenly, listening to the radio, I felt that I was being far too slow in my considerations. Here was a programme in part being sold, quickly and in an almost throw-away manner, precisely *because* of an assumed public knowledge of neurobehavioural difference, using acronyms that would have been meaningless just a few years before. In addition, I realized that the conditions mentioned were here being used not as indicators of medical difference or personal difficulty, but as badges of personality, signs of eccentricity that a public culture could, and would, recognize. Clearly, there were more narratives, and they were doing more, than

I had grasped. People might now know more about the relationship between the brain and behaviour, might speak of 'cognitive impairment' instead of 'mental retardation', but for the BBC to advertise itself in such a way was obviously something else altogether.

The general public awareness of autism and other neurobehavioural conditions invites a number of considerations. If there has been a consensus within disability studies in the last twenty years or so to attempt to move beyond a medical model, and to point to social and environmental factors and the ways in which they affect the lives of those with disabilities, then much of the public sense of disability still focuses upon the idea of the 'personal tragedy' that, it was hoped, such a transition would help to eradicate. Increasingly common, as autism has become the subject of sustained mainstream media discussion, has been the representation of the individual or family story where the condition has impacted on lives. As part of the research for this book, I set up a Google alert, just using the word 'autism', and each morning, as I scrolled through the results, it was noticeable that the stories the alert threw up were often accounts of individual coping, or of families unable to access needed resources. Time and time again, and especially in the news media, autism is seen to be something that 'affects' people, a condition that produces personal stories.

The other frequent narrative that was thrown up by the Google search concerned the reporting of medical investigation into the possible causes of autism, along with the increased rate of diagnosis and the potential treatments available. The following, from my alert of 5 May 2007, was typical:

> It's the fastest growing developmental disability in the US, autism. One in 150 kids now have the neurological disorder and doctors are not yet clear on what causes it and there is no cure but a treatment now done here in Rockford is making significant strides....[1]

This, from the homepage of wifr.com, a news service serving northern Illinois and southern Wisconsin in the US, is the kind of headline currently being repeated over and over again across countries and continents. This narrative is a blend of features – the increase in diagnoses, the unknown origin, the commitment to tackling the problem, the hope inherent in the new development – that then leads on to the specific news story. Within it, autism is both a pressing issue of current concern and a somewhat abstracted, unsourced, alien phenomenon, something that seems to have come from nowhere. As is usual, the wifr.com story picks up on the incidence of autism in children, and it is an adult concern over the health of children that drives many such reports. More than anything else, autism emerges from these multiple daily stories as a worry, an unknown fear and threat, that needs to be addressed as soon as possible.

This 'fact' of autism as a worry and a fear is possibly best seen as an example of the ways in which disability disrupts the majority, non-disabled, worldview. As numerous critics and theorists working within disability studies have noted, the disabled body or exceptional mind works to demand explanation or invite correction. Its status as a difference from the norm is itself a 'worry', a clear embodiment of what can and does 'go wrong'. Autism appears as a peculiarly silent and pernicious version of this disruption, an object difficult to identify and too problematic in its range (from the non-verbal to the garrulous, from severe sensory and environmental experiences to small character 'eccentricities') to regulate precisely. One possibility that always seems to provide unease is that the spectrum of autistic subjectivity might be as wide as the spectrum of non-autistic subjectivity. This inability to *locate* autism properly is common to many of the news stories in which it features, though played out in different forms.

But it is precisely because autism works as a specific form of contemporary disability disruption that we need to understand the ways in which disability and narrative interact. At the very beginning of their seminal account on the topic, *Narrative Prosthesis: Disability and the Dependencies of Discourse*, David Mitchell and Sharon Snyder posit the idea that the imaginative or fictional narrative that represents disability often offers a revisionist version of more conventional accounts of the place of impairment or disability in society. Noting that their book 'analyzes literary works as *commentaries* on the status of disability in other disciplines', they go on to assert that 'imaginative literature takes up its narrative project as a counter to scientific or truth-telling discourses. It is productively parasitic upon other disciplinary systems that define disability in more deterministic ways'.[2] Such a view of literary or artistic narratives as being productive in this way has a long history, of course. The celebration of the flexibility of imaginative narrative, with a stress on the truth that can be found in its fictions, has been central to critical reading practices ranging from new criticism to Marxism and beyond. In terms of disability, such fictions can, Mitchell and Snyder assert, 'expose ... an artificial, and thus resignifiable relationship' between cultural narrative and its production of images and stories that focus on impairment. And, they acknowledge, 'literary representation bears on the production and realization of disabled subjectivities', in the manner in which those representations are disseminated and consumed.[3]

Given autism's place within an overall spectrum of disability, and especially given the rise of interest in autism in recent years, it is understandable that the above ideas have a number of relations to the representation of the condition within cultural narratives, the issue that is the subject of this book. Often the relationship between depictions of autism in the media and the condition itself is highly artificial, something I will explore in detail in the pages that follow. Equally, fictions representing autism can be correctives to the kind of 'deterministic' accounts of which Mitchell and Snyder speak, and release the condition from its often pejorative subject positions in, say, the case studies of medical research or the sentimentalizing narratives of mainstream news media. At the same time, however, it would be wrong to say that imaginative accounts of autism are regularly 'productively parasitic'. The incredible increase in autism narratives in contemporary culture, from novels and films to radio phone-ins and magazine articles, has arguably not led to a profitable revision of public knowledge about what autism is. Rather, we might feel that such narratives have overlaid the condition not with understanding but with the complex desires of a society that wishes to be fascinated with a topic that seems precisely to elude comprehension. Certainly, the majority of the analysis that follows will be of stories, accounts and versions that *create* an idea of autism rather than try to reflect one, and in seeking to explain why this is so there is a real need to look at the place of the condition, and disability more generally, within contemporary culture and the stories we tell ourselves.

But Mitchell and Snyder are correct to point to the centrality of narrative when seeking to understand how disability operates in the world. The point that they make about a specific US context, that 'Americans learn perspectives on disability from books and films more than from policies or personal interactions', is true of non-American locations as well, and is an observation that can be extended to the wider media.[4] Though this might seem an obvious reflection, its full force is something that has been recognized only relatively recently. All disabilities, autism included, have histories of discussion and analysis within the fields of medicine, psychology, sociology and education. The library shelves in these subjects are now stacked with works of reference exploring the forms impairment takes and how these impact upon people and the world in which they live. But we are novices when it comes to thinking how specifically *cultural* versions of disability influence their various subject matters, for all that such versions are increasingly popular. It is as if the use of disabled characters in novels or films or on television has somehow crept upon us by stealth, without the kinds of analysis of such use that we might expect.

With specific regard to autism, it is – in one sense – only one condition among many that needs to have its place within cultural narratives explained. Even though the developmental psychologist Uta Frith wrote in 1989 that 'because its scientific study has barely begun, we still only know a fraction of what there is to know about Autism', that scientific study has, by this point in the first decade of the twenty-first century, produced large numbers of papers, articles and studies.[5] Yet disabilities of all kinds continue to be subjects that many would sooner not discuss in the public arena, because of the threat they are perceived to display to ideas of bodily or mental integrity. These are still topics that can inspire fear. At the same time, much of the force of this study's critical focus stems from the belief that autism is in some way a condition that has acquired a particular and specific emphasis, and indeed popularity, in the very contemporary period. It is, we might say, the condition of fascination of the moment, occupying a number of cultural locations that reflect a spectrum of wonder and nervousness – the allure of potentially unquantifiable human difference and the nightmare of not somehow being 'fully' human. This study will explore this fascination in full, seeing it as a manifestation of a number of contemporary moments. These range from a popularization of medical discourses, especially surrounding ideas of cognitive impairment and health, to the ever complex embedding of modern social life in new technological forms, where ideas about the brain circulate in the language of hard drives or 'wiring', and other, multiple, occasions where autism enacts a public enthralment. As the psychologist Laura Schreibman suggests in the title of her 2005 study of the condition, *The Science and Fiction of Autism*, autism is prone to representations that vary from the seemingly hard business of scientific enquiry to the more fanciful accounts of speculation.[6]

All these representations are narratives of differing forms. Some are fictions while others appear in the language of more officially informative discourses, such as news media or the medical journal. What the discussion of Jane Bown's photograph in the Preface also suggests, however, is that autism may in some way supply narratives of its own, stories and versions of life and its events that differ from those produced from within majority culture, what Donna Williams has termed an 'inside-out approach'.[7] Possibly it is here that Mitchell and Snyder's idea of the 'productively parasitic' might pertain, with a specific kind of disability narrative that – if it is read or seen or heard – can reorient ideas about what autism might mean. This book respects the idea that autistic presence contains its own logic and methods, and that these have to be understood, and if possible understood from within, if a full idea of the place of the condition in the world is ever to be gained. As we shall see, these expressions can be found across a range of cultural productions, from written life stories to the visual arts, and – more and more frequently – in the cyberspaces provided by the freedom of the internet, spaces that have become crucial to autistic expression.[8]

The idea that autism suggests its own narratives, and that these are not simply somehow erroneous or mistaken versions of other, more orthodox stories, raises the question of the difference of disability and how it might be quantified or recognized. Such difference is, for many, primarily a point about the politics that accompanies such a question. December 2006 saw the United Nations (UN) adopt a new Convention on the Rights of Persons with Disabilities, with signatures and ratification following from March 2007 onwards. The UN website describes the Convention as a '"paradigm" shift in attitudes and approaches to persons with disabilities', and the key question of rights is central to many of the advocacy movements that campaign to improve the lives of those who have disabilities.[9] Communities of those with autism and others who support them seek to articulate these rights in efforts to widen the understanding and acceptance of the condition. These articulations are themselves narratives of autistic presence, and in the chapters that follow I will look at the formations these narratives take, especially from those groups which advocate that autism is a way of being in the world that does not require 'treatment' or 'correction'. The traditional idea of disability as an absence is challenged by the assertion of difference as positive and not as a lack. At the same time, for some, such advocacy denies the very real complexities that come with autism and refuses real engagement with the condition – public conversations about autism are full of arguments between activists expressing a rights-based agenda and others, often parents, who see such expression as an avoidance of the suffering that they witness on a daily basis as carers.

Such debates, about the integrity of human worth and the 'quality of life', are seminal to our thinking about autism. The passion with which they take place reminds us that, in a contemporary world of vaccine scares, differences of medical opinion and discussion of an autism 'epidemic', the condition occupies contested ground in an arena in which it appears as if little is agreed upon. It is precisely because of such uncertainties that the cultural narratives that depict autism require analysis more than ever, because they function at a time when what is known about the condition is open to debate. In the free world of narrative interpretation, autism can, and does, become an open topic for representation, in part because of the lack of scientific consensus on the condition.

On the whole, most factual writing on autism has little to say about its place in narrative. Frith's *Autism: Explaining the Enigma* has a chapter entitled 'Beyond enchantment', which analyses classic fairy tales such as *Snow White* and *Sleeping Beauty*, as well as Russian 'blessed fools' and Arthur Conan Doyle's characterization of Sherlock Holmes, as possible cultural forms by which encounters with autism before twentieth-century medical pronouncements were mediated. Equally, psychiatrist Lorna Wing starts her short history of ideas on autism, a journal article which was the first piece in a new periodical, *Autism: The International Journal of Research and Practice*, in July 1997, with a page that considers changeling children and other 'legends and myths'.[10] But such thinking and exploration are rare, and even occupy little space in the specific book or article in which they might be found. Rather, much of the writing on the condition for lay (as opposed to medical or academic) audiences concentrates on making diagnostic criteria intelligible for a wider readership and then exploring the personal or social consequences of this, or the ideas of neurology and humanity that extend from such considerations. Oliver Sacks, possibly the most well known writer of popular accounts of clinical neurology, uses a number of literary parallels and analogies in *Awakenings*, his account of post-encephalitic patients first published in 1973, but there is less of this method in his two texts that feature discussions of autism, *The Man Who Mistook His Wife for a Hat* (1985) and *An Anthropologist on Mars* (1995).[11]

There is a vast amount of what we might term 'parents and professional' writing on autism, with publishers specifically targeting family and carers as a market. To pick just a single title, Nancy D. Wiseman's 2006 *Could It Be Autism? A Parent's Guide to the First Signs and Next Steps* is typical of the hundreds of books that seek to educate and advise parents concerned about their children's development.[12] Intriguingly, such texts have nothing of substance to say about the multiple popular narratives of autism and cognitive difference that surround any parents seeking more information on the condition, despite this being an obvious context in which their search might take place. The very title of Wiseman's book and its various chapter headings – 'Early signs', 'The path to diagnosis', 'Helping yourself, helping your child', 'Second steps and beyond' – point to its trajectory in explaining the paradigms of social care, education and especially therapy. As we shall see in chapter 5, the narrative that surrounds the 'catastrophe' of a parent discovering their child to have autism is one of the most prevalent in contemporary culture, whether found in fiction or the non-fiction exemplified by Wiseman's book. In such texts, autism is often portrayed as a condition open to treatment and remedy precisely because it is seen to have a base psychiatric component that allows for intervention and change. The notion that the child with autism can be 'saved' from the condition follows as a logic that says more about social fear and desire than it does about neurobehavioural difference.

If many of the books that do exist on autism have little to say about narrative, then it is possibly even more of a curiosity that the emerging field of disability studies, within an academic humanities context, which has a frequent and specific focus on narrative, has next to nothing to say about autism. Despite an obvious focus on the wide idea of disability, Mitchell and Snyder's *Narrative Prosthesis* contains more index entries on Nazis than it does on cognitive impairment, and though that text calls for a greater emphasis on the issues of neurological (as opposed to physical) difference, their follow-up monograph, *Cultural Locations of Disability* (2006), has little to say about cognitive exceptionality generally, and has a single paragraph on autism in a book of some 250 pages. The centrality that the *body* occupies in contemporary disability studies that focus on narrative is nearly ubiquitous. Mitchell and Snyder's 1997 edited collection of essays has *Discourses of Disability* as its subtitle, and is full of an attention to the subject of 'human disability', but its main title – *The Body and Physical Difference* – is a clear indicator of where its emphasis lies.[13] In a similar vein, *Disability/Postmodernity*, Mairian Corker and Tom Shakespeare's 2002 collection of essays that uses a variety of poststructuralist approaches to the questions surrounding disability studies, has as its subtitle *Embodying Disability Theory*, in a clear nod to the primacy of physical issues thought to lie at the heart of the subject.[14] Seminal figures in the field such as Lennard J. Davis and Rosemarie Garland-Thomson, who have produced excellent influential studies that have shaped the emerging forms of current critical disability scholarship, often make the linguistic slip whereby 'disability' in their writing comes to mean physical impairment.[15]

Such evasions and ignorance are odd, for it is increasingly clear that many conditions of cognitive or neurobehavioural difference, autism included, are produced to one degree or another by the physical structuring of the brain. For all that we need to think of autism, or conditions such as attention deficit disorder (ADD) and attention deficit hyperactivity disorder (ADHD), as having central manifestations that are behavioural or produced by the environment, recognizing the difference inherent in neurology is vital and the subject of much medical research. And, of course, seen in these terms the brain is as physical, if not as markedly visible, a part of the body as a limb. Indeed, it is intriguing to think of the seeming indifference paid to autism by disability studies scholars as being a point about *visibility*, considering the centrality of such a concept to the idea of disability as a whole. It does appear impossible, given the evidence, not to construct the ignorance and evasion of the topic in such terms. Equally, the life stories of many of those who have autism return to the frequent observation that one of the manifestations of the condition comes in the way in which it produces a need to *control* the body; the way the autistic body functions in space is part and parcel of what autism is and how it works – autism is a condition with a strong physical component.

One text that does have a sense of a narrativized idea of autism is Majia Holmer Nadesan's *Constructing Autism: Unravelling the 'Truth' and Understanding the Social* (2005). With a viewpoint grounded in medical sociology and health studies, Nadesan points out that, whatever the nature of its biogenetic origins, autism needs to be seen as a condition that rose to prominence in the twentieth century because of specific social factors that aided its identification and understanding. The practices and institutions that thus dictate such issues as diagnosis and treatment emerge not from a neutral space of scientific or medical knowledge but rather as a consequence of the ways in which science and medicine find themselves implicated in social debates. For Nadesan, autism, the idea of the spectrum and of Asperger's syndrome and so-called 'high functioning' autism, are all part of a crisis surrounding ideas of child development.[16] In this last emphasis her insight fits the concerns of a number of the cultural texts I will look at in this study, where the idea of what constitutes autism is frequently explored through the figure of the child, and in which a notion of a personal future is consistently stressed.

Nadesan's insight helps in the understanding of a wider point. Her stress on the 'use' of autism to explain complex contemporary social issues aids in thinking through the ways in which the condition has become an almost ubiquitous frame of reference for recent notions of difference. The label 'autistic' today is not necessarily always a description of an individual with a clear neurological difference. It is, in many ways, and as I shall explore fully in the pages that follow, a word that is increasingly used to describe both people, and indeed situations, as generically 'odd' or even dangerous. Such usage is the product of a slippage of terminology, a widening of meaning, which displays the manner in which an *idea* of autism has spread through public culture. So, any act of human behaviour that might be seen as obsessive, or concerned with difficulties in social interaction and expression, is increasingly thought of as 'autistic'. Equally, through processes of a retrospective diagnosing, historical and contemporary figures – from Isaac Newton and Albert Einstein to Andy Warhol and Stanley Kubrick – are 'outed' as individuals with autism through a reading of their characters and actions.[17] Psychiatrist Michael Fitzgerald is the writer most associated with this phenomenon. In books such as *Autism and Creativity* (2004) and *The Genesis of Artistic Creativity* (2005), Fitzgerald analyses a myriad of philosophers, writers, artists and musicians, through a variety of criteria, before arriving at a diagnostic pronouncement: 'George Orwell meets the criteria for Asperger's syndrome', or 'It would appear that Kant displayed the criteria for Asperger's syndrome'.[18] There is a clear danger in such processes, namely that the word and all it implies can be diluted to a point where its meaning becomes increasingly difficult to pinpoint; however, it should also be recognized that any desire to see autism as a viable, and not uncommon, part of the human spectrum requires an understanding of the condition that moves beyond a scientific or medical categorization. And, given that there have always been people with autism, there is an arguable logic to re-reading narratives in search of those people from periods before the condition had any diagnostic criteria or public dimension. The difficulty lies in establishing how extending an idea of autism that respects the nature of the condition might find expression at a time when it also has to be read in terms of its increased use as a metaphor, and how it interacts with the knowledge prevalent at a time before the category of autism itself came into being.

## II

In the *London Review of Books* in May 2006, Ian Hacking wrote, 'Over the past fifteen years everyone has got to know about autism.... Autism will figure this year in dozens, maybe hundreds of cheap novels, thrillers, and maybe a good book or two'.[19] He might have added that the condition would be featured in television dramas and be the subject of numerous documentaries, on both the small screen and the large. Equally, getting 'to know about autism' was, for many, a consequence of the huge media coverage surrounding vaccine scares, which have been a feature of recent public health discussions in both the US and the UK. Fears over the use of mercury in vaccines in the US, as covered by David Kirby's 2005 book *Evidence of Harm*, paralleled the intense media discussion of the possible relationship between autism and the measles, mumps and rubella (MMR) vaccine in the UK.[20] In all these different contexts, autism was an urgent topic, one dramatic and novel. Indeed, its novelty in the media itself has become a topic for discussion. 'Autism: the new Black?' asked American blogger Katherine

Riley on The Hum celebrity gossip website in October 2007, noting that: 'We're not poking fun (or making light of the fact that 1 in 166 kids are diagnosed with autism). We just couldn't help but notice that it's become *the* cause célèbre lately.'[21] Here, the prevalence of autism in the popular cultural narratives of the US especially is seen to be akin to some sort of fashion.

It is worthwhile stating the obvious: that all the discussion of autism in the last ten years, all the focus and concern, comes only sixty years since the condition first received its initial explication in the diagnostic systems outlined by Leo Kanner and Hans Asperger in the early 1940s; and that autism arguably moved out of the scientific/medical sphere into a wider public consciousness only in the 1980s. I shall examine in detail Kanner's system in particular at the start of the following chapter, but the point has to be made that any current preoccupation with autism comes relatively early in the history of its recognition (the general acceptance of the distinctive nature of Asperger's syndrome is, similarly, something that dates only from the 1980s). Seen in these terms, it has to be admitted that autism has rushed into the *public* realm comparatively soon after its first diagnostic formations (this may, indeed, explain the lack of clarity over the vaccine scares). At the same time, given that it is now understood to be a neurologically based condition, we know that autism has always been part of human diversity, and its current status should be seen in light of centuries when it belonged to the general categories of 'idiocy' or 'retardation'. So, as a subject matter, autism is both timeless and totally contemporary. It is part of human life, as it always has been, and yet today it is represented in certain formations that exist only because of the peculiar contemporary inflections that discussions of the condition have been given. When we speak of the representation of autism we need to bear in mind this dual positioning: the unique nature of its constellation of symptoms *as a condition of being human* and yet also the specific place it occupies because of the huge amount of contemporary interest it has generated.

With this in mind, this book has as its primary focus the study of contemporary narratives and texts, many taken from the last twenty years or so. The main reason for this is to seek an understanding of the nature of autism in terms that are themselves contemporary, and to enter into the immediacy of the debate. I am more interested in understanding these formations than in outlining a general cultural history of autism, partly because any attempt to do the latter could itself be understood only as a project dominated by the way autism exists in the present. On the occasions that I do look at texts or events from before the contemporary period, such as the analyses of works by Herman Melville or Charles Dickens in chapters 1 and 2, or in ideas that link autism back to constructions of 'idiocy', it is, in part, to explore autism in the knowledge that it has always existed; but it is also meant to suggest the methods by which the contemporary place of the condition offers new critical practices and reading strategies by which we might revise our cultural knowledge. In this sense, this study, overall, is part of that move in disability studies which seeks, in Snyder and Mitchell's phrase, to 'destabilize our dominant ways of knowing disability'.[22] It does not seek to unambiguously 'rescue' an idea of autism that is uniformly positive, as that runs the risk of replacing one scheme of misrepresentation with another, but it does aim to work with the consequences of understanding autism on its own terms, including the possibility that this can, and does, lead to conclusions that are on subjects other than autism itself. Like any other disability, autism is not endlessly self-referential. To talk of Melville's Bartleby or Dickens' Barnaby Rudge as having autism, as I do in the chapters that follow, is not simply to place a new variable in for the consideration of criticism. It is, rather, to suggest different possibilities as to what these stories might *mean*. This is, at heart, a critical process that has its origins in the contact with autism that stems from the contemporary moment. It is a consequence of thinking about activism, rights and the outcomes of representation and how they extend into the field of cultural criticism and public debate. I hope that it also indicates a way of respecting the fact of autism in previous centuries, whatever the difficulties we might feel lie in discussing such a fact. The heart of the enquiry, however, lies in a self-aware mobilization of contemporary criticism; this book is necessarily a part of the 'autism debate' and cannot be seen to stand outside it. We are not in a time for the assumption of such a perspective.

The texts that are examined here vary in their types of representations and constitute a flexible notion of the idea of the text itself. Because I sense that much of the current interest in autism stems from a general public and non-specialist awareness of the condition, I am drawn to look at those representations that emanate from popular media. In the last twenty years, texts such as Barry Levinson's film *Rain Man* (1988) and Mark Haddon's novel *The Curious Incident of the Dog in the Night-Time* (2003) have served as foundational explanatory markers of autism for different generations. Both hugely popular and critically acclaimed, Levinson's film and Haddon's book are what we might think of as autism 'events', fictions that almost achieved the status of sociological documents in the ways in which their presentation of the condition was received. At the time of their respective releases, there is no doubt that viewers and readers alike felt as though they were experiencing a specific insight into the nature of autism, because of the novelty of the narrative each contained. This idea that a text might constitute an event is only partially a point about the success of the fiction it contains; it is also a way for us to understand how a particular representation can engage in a zeitgeist moment. Haddon's novel especially appeared to be the book that the culture didn't know it needed until it appeared, and then it automatically became the focus for a wide social knowledge of autism that had not cohered up until that point. Both *The Curious Incident of the Dog in the Night-Time* and *Rain Man* are analysed across the various chapters, as different aspects of their fiction become the focus of different moments of enquiry.

A particular form of fascination with autism operates in the workings of forms such as television, the news media and popular cinema and fiction. As the following chapters will show, it is a fascination that functions as a combination of a number of overlapping features; there are, it seems, distinct narratives of autism and its effects that occur in the broad range of 'fiction'. From the 1990s to the present, a period when neuroscientific research has begun to understand more fully the genetic aspects of autism, and when the subtleties of the autistic spectrum have been further defined, there have been numerous examples in film, television and literature of narratives concerning autism operating within a discourse of knowledge of the condition. What unites the majority of these narratives is that the representations they contain are characterized by a focus on ontological and 'human' difference that frequently depicts an individual with autism in relation to an individual with ostensibly typical (non-impaired) behaviour and mediates an idea of the human by a refractive comparison of the two. Often the individual with autism takes the form of what we might call the 'sentimental savant', especially in the realms of creativity and an understanding of supposedly core human concerns, which are seen to inform and enrich the non-disabled and which work towards what Davis terms 'the construction of normalcy'.[23] In effect, within narrative, autism works to create a space, figured precisely because of how the condition is perceived to function, that, rather than allowing for the presentation of autism within the terms of the autistic individual (or indeed in any way connected to the autistic individual), reflects back upon the non-autistic world. The fascination with the subject must always be in the terms of the majority audience, of course, and it is by such methods that the processes of enquiry and fear and desire can be allowed to coexist. With autism, it is especially the imagined place of savantism that appears to exercise public imagination. Time and again in this study we shall see the figure of the autistic savant presented as the normative mode of autistic subjectivity, with all the complex ideas of fascination this brings for consideration.

This kind of formation is an example of the narrative prosthesis central to Mitchell and Snyder's theory of disability narratives in general, in which disability works as a 'stock feature of characterization' or 'an opportunistic narrative device' in the stories in which it is used.[24] The worry that the disabled body or mind produces ultimately lies in the ways in which it might pervade the non-disabled spaces it encounters, and narrative is a key element in this process. In this sense, autism parallels other disabilities as they are represented from without in cultural narrative, being part of a dualistic process by which an idea of the 'normal' or 'abled' is produced. As Davis has shown, the idea of the normal or normalcy (and therefore cognate terms such as 'abnormal') is surprisingly recent, dating from the mid-nineteenth century, when an idea of the 'norm' began to supplant an earlier conception of the 'ideal'.[25] The ideas of normal and abnormal therefore are, and have always been, bound up with ideas of both health and the popular that stem from the processes of social change that specifically come with recent modernity. Just as crucial notions of psychiatry – which made the medical identification of autism possible – coalesce in the nineteenth century, so a sense of the popular reception of cultural texts exists in a time line that stretches from that period to the present. The American freak shows of the late nineteenth and early twentieth centuries, so well examined by Garland-Thomson in her 1997 study *Extraordinary Bodies*, have as their contemporary equivalent the television documentary that focuses on an idea of the 'extraordinary person'.[26] Ostensibly narratives about the 'triumph' of the human, such programmes are all too frequently invitations to voyeuristic engagement from a majority, non-disabled audience. These ideas of the relationship of the defined 'normal', especially in popular forms, with that which falls outside its terms are spread across all the chapters that follow. They are a core concern of this book.

At the same time, important as the above realization is in the presentation of autism, the ways in which the condition is represented in the various 'inside' narratives that communicate a sense of its meaning offer a parallel category of potential interpretation. Here it is vital to focus upon the accounts produced by those with autism themselves, whether in the form of fiction, artwork, memoir, blog, internet chat room discussion, or the politicized pronouncements of those disability activists seeking to improve the lives of autistic individuals. The terms of these representations differ markedly from the fictions that construct the condition. Often directly related to what are perceived as misrepresentations, they are – as we shall see from the discussion of autistic presence in chapter 1 – frequently assertions of agency and demands to be heard, and they occupy a contested space in the wider discussion of autism.

A counterpart to those narratives produced from within autism comes from the vast literature from a variety of specialisms that purports to inform and advise on the nature of the condition. Texts like Wiseman's, mentioned above, present a particular form of the 'overcoming' narrative, usually that of families, in which autism is seen as a potential destroyer of the family unit, but emerges as an affliction that can be fought (the idea of conflict is often central to such formations) through perseverance and love. In chapter 5, I examine this kind of narrative, with a concentration on how ideas of family and morality are frequently the content of its concerns. It has been a number of decades since the Austrian psychoanalyst Bruno Bettelheim's theories of parent causation of autism were discredited, but it is still intriguing to see how parents are frequently the targets of much of the literature based around 'treating' autism. The focus on parents and families is one with a long tradition, from memoirs written in the 1960s, such as Clara Claiborne Park's 1967 *The Siege: A Family's Journey into the World of an Autistic Child*,[27] to many of the most recent representations of autism on television. *The West Wing*, *ER* and *House* are all examples of high-profile US series that have introduced autism either through characters or as a topic in a more general way. In the UK, while there have been similar 'additions' to long-running programmes, the tendency has been to feature autism in a number of one-off dramas (including fictionalizations of the MMR debates), nearly all with a family focus. The thesis that 'autism ruins families' appears to be as strong as any other currently in circulation about the condition's effects. It is a strange kind of social narcissism that produces such representations, as if (again) the 'difficult difference' of autism can be fully understood only through external parameters focused on majority concerns: an examination of what it means to be a mother, or how a marriage copes with a disabled child.

The majority of the representations analysed in this book are taken from UK and US contexts. I find that there is no little irony in this, because, as an academic who has been trained and who largely specializes in the field of postcolonial studies, my main areas of intellectual enquiry have always stemmed from outside American and European sources, and if pushed I would always want to represent myself as someone who saw cultural processes as being inherently global, even as they require located and specific analyses. This scope should be true of all aspects of disability studies as well of course, and I am frustrated that there is not more of this dimension to this book. A reason for this is, I think, that organized thinking about autism and culture is still very much in its infancy and, to some degree, to know about autism in different cultures in the contemporary moment requires the experience of the condition in those cultures, and this is something that is not always possible. Anthropologist Roy Richard Grinker's recent study *Unstrange Minds: Remapping the World of Autism* (2007) covers issues of autism as Grinker finds them in France, India, Korea and South Africa, and arguably begins the process of thinking about autism globally.[28] This is a necessary development that will hopefully proceed. As things stand, my sense is that autism is configured, understood and discussed in vastly different ways in different parts of the world, and to know the condition properly we will have to work through many examples of its various manifestations.

Two overriding concepts dominate the ways in which the representations that do feature in this book are framed. The first is that to discuss autism is necessarily to discuss the condition of being human. All roads lead back to this point. It is the most crucial and vital of all the observations made on the subject, and a reminder of the importance of the topic and the analysis that goes with it. The second is that any attempt to account for the place of autism in the world needs to deal with the fact of autistic presence. As I stressed in the Preface, presence is, indeed, the key category in discussing contemporary representations of autism and therefore the focus of my attention in the chapter that immediately follows. It is a sense of the increased presence of autism in the contemporary world that has created such popular interest in the condition. It is often a *misapprehension* of autistic presence in the various narratives this book will look at, albeit through a desire to capture the difference of that presence, which leads to its frequent refraction and distortion within the logics of majority storytelling. But presence cannot, and will not, ultimately be removed. It is the presence of the person with autism, in whatever form, that stops the condition being *only* subject to the workings of metaphor and fascination. Those autistic individuals who speak, write or communicate in some other way make their presence felt through their entry into the domain of cultural representation, and they inform everyone who makes the effort to listen what living with, and in, the condition can be like. And, of course, those who do not communicate in these ways are no less a presence. Their individuality is a narrative of its own; their physicality and character are statements of human integrity. To write on autism as it is portrayed in the contemporary world is to engage with this centrality.

## III

In thinking through the business of writing on disability, it is an obvious suggestion that the job of the critical practitioner overlaps with that of his or her medical counterpart when it comes to an idea of diagnosis. Reading, watching, judging and evaluating – all are common broad features in both spheres. But the critic seeking to write on representations of disability needs to be aware of the force that diagnosis often exerts in the lives of those with impairments. For some, proper diagnosis is welcome, allowing both self-understanding and access to support and resources. For others, however, diagnosis functions to convey the cruelty of misunderstanding and stigma, to separate individuals from one another and to classify them as being in need of 'special' services. The history of abuse of those with disabilities is real and painful. Autism, because of its seeming 'invisibility' and its manifestations in terms of behaviour, has had more than its fair share of examples of such abuse, often emanating from sources of medical or social power. Many observers have shown how the processes of medical categorization and institutionalization have ended up producing some of the parameters of the very conditions they ostensibly wish to 'treat'. With specific regard to autism, Hacking has suggested that medical 'classifications' work to 'interact' with the individual so classified in a form of 'looping', with the result that the complexity of the condition is forever reduced to the terms that dominate any given period's sense of what constitutes 'best practice' in terms of treatment and knowledge.[29] Autistic cyberspace is full of personal accounts pointing to how hospitals or schools have inflicted great damage on individuals and their sense of self.

There is no doubt that such processes take place. Possibly we like to feel that they do so less now, in an era of – for example – inclusive practices in education, but the classifying of the disabled constitutes the darkest of histories and it is best to remember that such histories project into the present. At the same time, classification in both medicine and criticism must and will continue. The diagnostic process that is common to both is the method by which knowledge and understanding are produced, and the productive or insightful or groundbreaking piece of research can come only through some kind of methodology that works within the parameters of the relevant subject area at the time.

All critical work that has any kind of claim to be worthwhile needs to be aware of its positioning, and here it becomes important to situate this study in such terms. It is a noticeable feature of much of the emerging work on autism in the humanities that it comes from scholars who have a personal connection to the condition, usually as parents of a child or children with autism. Indeed, those who do not have this connection are in a minority position, one upon which they frequently comment. My youngest son was diagnosed with 'classical childhood autism' in 2002, and my eldest with Asperger's syndrome in 2004. At the time of the first diagnosis, one of my many reactions was connected to the processes of writing academic criticism. I asked myself what I thought was a reasonable question: Given that I live with someone whose appreciation of all aspects of the world, from how things looks and sound and smell to what gives pleasure or pain, is so different from my own, how can I continue to write and publish analysis or commentary on this book or that film in which I advocate that it has certain meanings that I have the capability to discern? From where do I get such authority? What consensus operates that allows for such partiality and calls it knowledge? For the summer of 2002 I remained stuck in the loop produced by such self-investigation. Not much work was done.

The answer to this question emerged, as it had to, in its own time, as it became obvious that the *only* way to write, comment and analyse is to work from such a position of partiality. The naivety of my question was, I hope, explicable, and of course there is an argument that no cultural critic should write anything without having a good position on this issue before starting. My understanding of this, that something I took to be specific and personal was, in fact, only a version of the conditions that had always surrounded my writing, was nevertheless something more than recognition of the obvious. It prompted an immediate realization that if it was not possible to communicate somehow, when writing academically on autism, what I had learned from living with the condition, then there was not much point in continuing. This realization was automatic, a feeling that this revision of my writing position (even if it was only substantiating and translating something that was already, I hope, at work) was inevitable. Any work I did on the topic could only issue from such a context, and it is fair to say that when I make the claim in the pages that follow that a character or an action is autistic, it is because I am *recognizing* it as such. This is obviously partial, but it is, I hope, partial in the best sense. The readings are personal, as the book is as a whole, but that does not, I would assert, mean it cannot be scholarly.

The ironies of the situation are not lost on those who find themselves thus positioned. It is strange to be part of a zeitgeist moment, to talk of the 'explosion' in diagnoses of autism at the same time as witnessing the processes of such diagnosis at first hand, or to seek to critically interrogate the centrality of the family in contemporary representations of autism while being part of such a family oneself. In addition, scholars coming into the study of autism, or disability more widely, because of personal contact with any diagnosed condition, may well have spent many hours in the seminar room discussing the premise that it is not necessary to be black to discuss black writing, or a woman to discuss feminist filmmaking, noting that such positions may have had historical moments of application but that we as a critical community are now beyond seeing such affiliation as obligatory. And now, teaching disability studies in the classroom, like writing on the topic, is a process of negotiating with the personal and wondering exactly what the extent is of its involvement.

Shuttling back and forth between these various positions – subjective engagement and critical distance – and openly declaring such movement is only a transparent version of the critical process anyway, a declaration of origins. And, as a consequence, the anecdote emerges as a tool every bit as useful as the studied analytical insight – not simply in the ways in which it provides *material* for commentary, but often in the very shape in which it emerges. Take just two examples. First, as the computer on which he is working in a different room to mine makes a succession of alarming sounds, I ask my eldest son, 'Is that you making that noise?' 'No', he replies, 'it's the computer'. Second, as I deliberately move down to the level of my youngest son and make sure he looks at me as I talk to him, his eyes naturally move to look at my mouth, a movement he follows by placing his fingers on my lips. My mouth is where the words are coming from, so what better place to assume their meaning might be found? Certain manifestations of autistic difference are amazing in their logic and simplicity, as rational – we might say – as the desired end product of the kind of critical writing that seeks to preserve the integrity of scholarly distance. But more important than this is the sense that it is the *structure* of observations such as these that it is vital to understand, that to talk of characters with autism in fiction is not simply to engage in some simple process of spotting. I take from the anecdotes above an idea of how it is possible to see autism reordering the narratives in which it is found, giving different stresses and inflections to responses that might seen familiar, and as a consequence quite possibly changing their meaning altogether.

If there are huge differences of opinion in the public discussion of autism, then it is fair to say that there are equally debates and divisions within scholarship itself on the topic. I have sought to avoid taking sides in the various controversies, mainly because in my own reading I have found elements of value in a number of different positions on the issues of what autism is and how it might be engaged with. To give an example, in *The Science and Fiction of Autism*, Schreibman is highly critical of Douglas Biklen and his advocacy, from the 1990s onwards, of the use of facilitated communication (FC) for some people with autism. FC involves the use of a facilitator, usually a teacher, parent or carer, who aids the person with autism to type or point to letters on a keyboard in order to communicate. FC works by a gradual reduction in the physical help given by the facilitator as the individual using the keyboard becomes more independent. A number of studies of the efficacy of FC showed that it was the facilitator, and not the person with autism, who was doing the communicating. For a psychologist like Schreibman, committed to the rigorous use of experimental evidence, FC was a 'bogus' method that was harmful in the ways in which it raised hopes about the possibility of hidden powers of articulation in often severely autistic subjects.[30] Biklen, a professor of special education at Syracuse University in the US, was pilloried by the scientific establishment when he defended FC and claimed it did indeed help provide a mode of expression for some with severe autism.

Schreibman's book is one of the best single-authored volumes that discusses and analyses all aspects of autism, from current thinking about causes to ideas surrounding treatment. Her work is rooted in the disciplinary practices of scientific testing. At the same time, Biklen's own book, *Autism and the Myth of the Person Alone* (2005), is one I found invaluable for helping to outline a sense of autistic agency. Schreibman is right that the majority of studies dismiss FC as mistaken, if not fraudulent, and she makes her case with impressive clarity, but it is noticeable that her book contains not a single comment from anyone who actually *is* autistic. Biklen's study, on the other hand, is largely given over to the thoughts and words of those with autism (often through FC) and, for all that it is necessary to be sceptical about much that is said of FC, it is difficult to conclude that every word written is being produced by someone other than the named autistic person.

Arguments such as these are possibly best seen as specific academic examples of the wider division of opinion that any discussion of autism appears to provoke. As someone fundamentally interested in cultural *representations* of the condition, I found that I could, to some degree, look on these particular scholarly debates as an observer. Psychology and education are not my disciplines, and I read material in both because of my interest in what they had to say. So I see both Schreibman and Biklen as valuable in helping the process of mapping out how autism exists in cultural narratives, despite their clear differences. It is also worth making the point, however, that their dispute is a peculiarly American one, and that this specific context is one that frames much of the controversy surrounding all discussions of autism. To read about autism in the US is to confront an often bewildering array of medical and therapeutic methods and acronyms, put forward and contested with evangelical zeal by proponents and detractors alike. Everything to do with autism in an American context appears at times to be driven by argument, with no consensus on any aspect of the condition, from the terminology of diagnosis to the place of vaccination or special education, and from the nature of disability advocacy to the provisions made by charities and the politics that surrounds them.

Such a vociferous debate points to real issues surrounding the place of healthcare and education in the US but, amidst the animosity, the difference of opinion also highlights something that is more fundamental, namely, that which is known about autism – by anyone, in any field – is probably in its infancy. It is good to be able to be specific about the neurological nature of the condition and to dismiss the psychology-based theories that blamed parenting. It is helpful to understand that autism has a genetic component, and to invest in research that will pursue something that is almost certainly foundational to the formation of autistic subjectivity. But for every piece of insight, there are countless unknowns, and many of these seem to dwarf that which has been agreed upon. Even the idea that autism is a single entity is one that is easily challenged. The much-used notion of the 'triad of impairments' – the highly influential diagnostic tool of problems in social interaction, social communication and behavioural patterns, developed by Lorna Wing and Judith Gould in the late 1970s – may mask the fact that such impairments are, in fact, separate and come together in different forms and to differing degrees in any individual thought to be 'classically' autistic. Equally, this idea of a matrix, of a series of overlapping phenomena, may well encompass both genetic and environmental arguments of causation, the possibility being that a genetic predisposition could interact with an environmental trigger at a certain point in the brain's development. Autism could be a set of coordinates, rather than a case of X marking the spot. As Biklen argues, global theories of the cause of autism – those that seek a single explanatory trigger – may well be mistaken in the way they seek to map out how 'central' neurological problems work. In addition, he notes, many of these global theories – he cites 'mind-blindness', central coherence and executive function – actually revert to metaphor to make their case. Even in the most clinical of medical prose, the subjects of case studies 'suffer from', or are subjects of, a deficit model. 'Metaphor operates as reality', Biklen observes, and it is possible that the majority of official discourses – medical, educational, institutional – create a singularity, when discussing autism, that is simply not there.[31]

One consequence of this is that we should not expect uniformity in the representations of autism that follow, especially when we are look-ing at representations produced from those with the condition. Where there *is* uniformity, it is likely to be because of media impressions of autism that desire to construct the condition in certain ways and for certain effects. If the creators of commercial cultural products wish to represent autism within narrative for consumption by a large audi-ence, it is not in their interests to present the condition as a complex overlapping of stark and subtle behaviours, itself bound into a specific personality. It is, it appears, far easier to have a static character, a recog-nizable shorthand for the presentation of this specific form of cognitive difference. There appears to be a place for autism in the minds of con-temporary audiences, and a number of cultural practitioners are more than happy to fill it with representations that owe little to any current genuine understanding of the condition. It is an irony, but probably not particularly surprising, that a condition so debated in the professional world achieves a consistency of presentation in the ways in which it is turned into stories, fiction and non-fiction alike.

## IV

At the start of the research that ultimately became this book, I did consider that it might be possible to work on all, or certainly most of, the various non-medical or non-scientific narratives of autism. The field seemed relatively small and unexplored, and I found myself mull-ing over the fact that I was consistently coming across characters in fictional narratives, or picking up the odd newspaper story, in which autism was being narrativized, but that there seemed no especial awareness of this being the case, and no outside frame of reference that could unpick the ways such narratives were put together. Over the course of five years, such an ambition became relegated to the realm of the ludicrous. The sheer proliferation of autism narratives, across all sorts of media, has made any desire to be comprehensive all but impossible. This is especially the case in trying to keep up with the terms of the public debate, as opinions on causation and treatment fly round the airwaves, and the print and virtual worlds, with the voicing of what seems to be every opinion imaginable. So, by way of necessity, this study became one of preference, in which the texts I touch upon and the arguments I make are those that it seems to me are the most revealing and pertinent. So, the concentration on idiots and savants in chapter 2, the questions of visualizing autism that are the focus of chapter 3, of age and gender in chapter 4, and the focus on families in chapter 5 formed themselves because of my sense that these were the best ways through the representations I had gathered together. Reflecting upon this, it struck me that such preference is not only the obvious methodological system for a book such as this, but it is recognizably an autistic system as well. In thinking through autism both as I encounter it on a daily basis and as it appears in the most subtle and illuminating of the texts in which it is represented, I realized that preference is an affirmative mode through which autistic presence can be gauged. In chapter 1, I make much of Herman Melville's character Bartleby in the story 'Bartleby the Scrivener', whose preference is central to his assertion of selfhood. More generally, preference, and the pleasure which can come from it, allows for a series of moments when those with autism show us how they determine the tenor of their lives, and in so doing ignore and escape the many narratives that would contain and define them, and turn them into something else.

So it is both my preference and my recognition of how an *idea* of preference might work that have guided what follows. I am perfectly happy that my choices will be contested. Indeed, autism being what it is, it seemed to me to be an impossibility that this would not be the case, and this realization has also shaped some of my arguments. Invariably there will be more critical studies of the way autism is represented in cultural narratives, and in the future doubtless all such work will be seen as being the products of a time when a particular and peculiar fascination with the condition dominated the ways in which it was talked about. Thought and work will be ongoing, but there have to be certain moments when ideas come together, and I hope that this book serves as one such occasion.

Like all others who work on autism, or in disability studies more widely, I am sensitive to the ongoing debates that exist over terminology and naming. For some, this is a trivial concern, especially when so much remains to be done in order for those with disabilities to be given the rights and respect they are properly due; but it seems to me that precisely because there is a need to continually revisit questions of subjectivity and agency, the decision over terms is not a purely semantic one. In thinking about the words we use, we also think about the kinds of spaces the disabled occupy in the social and the cultural spheres in which all people exist (Davis' excellent work, discussed above, on ideas of the 'normal' is, of course, the best example of this). So, to talk of 'being autistic' or 'having autism' is meaningful beyond what might seem a certain pedantry in the business of names.

In the various places in which autism is discussed, the concept of 'having autism' is the more popular of the two possibilities. It signifies an awareness that the person with autism is not just the sum of his or her condition, that there is an independence from the disability. This terminology is especially dominant in the professional areas of education, psychology, charity work and care. Within the same logic, 'being autistic' is criticized because of the ways in which it conflates the person and the condition, and assumes that there is no possibility to move out of such a conflation. For those interested in relegating the impact of autism, or moving beyond it, it is important not to see the disability defining the individual. Such thinking is sensitive to the many ways in which those with disabilities are all too often seen only in terms of that which disables them. At the same time, however, there are reasons to see the limitations of the idea of 'having autism'. It does suggest the possibility, perhaps too easily, that one might *not* have it, that it is like some sort of cold or other infection, and that it might go away; and this does have implications when we think of both the suggestion that the condition is in truth pervasive, and that for many the potential for a 'cure' is a real one. It also, by implication, suggests that to *be* autistic is necessarily negative, that the word 'autism' itself is, indeed, a marker of disability. I would like to think it is acceptable to be autistic, that it in fact illuminates a way of being human, and that there is much for those who are not autistic to learn from such illumination. In writing the book, I found myself alternating between the two phrases, seeing both as enabling. I have not been precise about this usage, so it may well be the case that one features more than the other, but they both appear here as positive terms that help us to think better. Ultimately, that is the goal of everything in this book.

## Notes

1 See http://www.wifr.com/home/headlines/7302411.html. Accessed 5 May 2007.
2 David T. Mitchell and Sharon L. Snyder, *Narrative Prosthesis: Disability and the Dependencies of Discourse* (Ann Arbor, MI: University of Michigan Press, 2000), pp. 1–2.

3 Mitchell and Snyder, *Narrative Prosthesis*, p. 9.
4 Mitchell and Snyder, *Narrative Prosthesis*, p. 166.
5 Uta Frith, *Autism: Explaining the Enigma* (Oxford: Basil Blackwell, 1989), p. 50.
6 Laura Schreibman, *The Science and Fiction of Autism* (Cambridge, MA: Harvard University Press, 2005).
7 See Donna Williams, *Autism – An Inside-Out Approach* (London: Jessica Kingsley, 1996).
8 In part, my idea of presence is taken from my reading in postcolonial fiction and theory, especially that pertaining to issues of material culture and agency in Indigenous populations. The key text defining such ideas is Gerald Vizenor's *Fugitive Poses: Native American Scenes of Absence and Presence* (Lincoln, NE: University of Nebraska Press, 1998).
9 See http://www.un.org/disabilities/default.asp?navid=12&pid=150. Accessed 15 October 2007.
10 Lorna Wing, 'The history of ideas on autism: legends, myths and reality', *Autism: The International Journal of Research and Practice*, vol. 1, no. 1 (July 1997), pp. 13–14.
11 Oliver Sacks, *Awakenings* (London: Duckworth, 1973), *The Man Who Mistook His Wife for a Hat* (New York: Simon & Schuster, 1985), and *An Anthropologist on Mars* (London: Picador, 1995).
12 Nancy D. Wiseman, *Could It Be Autism? A Parent's Guide to the First Signs and Next Steps* (New York: Broadway Books, 2006).
13 Mitchell and Snyder, *Narrative Prosthesis*; Sharon L. Snyder and David T. Mitchell, *Cultural Locations of Disability* (Chicago, IL: University of Chicago Press, 2006), paragraph on p. 11; David T. Mitchell and Sharon L. Snyder, *The Body and Physical Difference: Discourses of Disability* (Ann Arbor, MI: University of Michigan Press, 1997).
14 Mairian Corker and Tom Shakespeare (eds), *Disability/Postmodernity: Embodying Disability Theory* (London: Continuum, 2002).
15 To give one example, Davis writes in his introduction to *Enforcing Normalcy* that 'Disability exists in the realm of the senses. The disabled body is embodied through the senses' – two sentences that clearly display the conflation of a foundational idea of disability with that of its bodily presence. See Lennard J. Davis, *Enforcing Normalcy: Disability, Deafness and the Body* (London: Verso, 1995), p. 13.
16 Majia Holmer Nadesan, *Constructing Autism: Unravelling the 'Truth' and Understanding the Social* (New York: Routledge, 2005). See especially pp. 45–80.
17 Wikipedia's various entries on this subject included a 'List of people on the autistic spectrum' that had as its subdivisions 'People with unspecified forms of autism', 'People with Asperger [sic] syndrome', 'People with high-functioning autism', 'Autistic savants' and 'People with severe autism'. There was also a section entitled 'Speculation of autism in famous people' in the entry on the autism rights movement. See http://en.wikipedia.org/wiki/List_of_autistic_people and http://en.wikipedia.org/wiki/Autism_rights_movement. Accessed 16 May 2007.
18 Michael Fitzgerald, *The Genesis of Artistic Creativity: Asperger's Syndrome and the Arts* (London: Jessica Kingsley, 2005), p. 96 and p. 125. See also his *Autism and Creativity: Is There a Link Between Autism in Men and Exceptional Ability?* (Hove: Brunner-Routledge, 2004).
19 Ian Hacking, 'What is Tom saying to Maureen?', *London Review of Books*, vol. 28, no. 9 (11 May 2006), p. 3.

20 David Kirby, *Evidence of Harm – Mercury in Vaccines and the Autism Epidemic: A Medical Controversy* (New York: St Martin's Press, 2005). For a rebuttal of the idea that the MMR vaccine causes autism in a UK context, see Michael Fitzpatrick, *MMR and Autism: What Parents Need to Know* (London: Routledge, 2004). This issue is discussed in detail in chapter 5.

21 See http://www.eonline.com/gossip/hum/detail/index.jsp?uuid=56b9f664-f0e8-4092-80dd-0715ede58eb6. Accessed 8 October 2007.

22 Snyder and Mitchell, *Cultural Locations of Disability*, p. 4.

23 Davis, *Enforcing Normalcy*, p. 23.

24 Mitchell and Snyder, *Narrative Prosthesis*, p. 47 and p. 51.

25 Davis, *Enforcing Normalcy*, p. 24. See also Waltraud Ernst (ed.), *Histories of the Normal and the Abnormal: Social and Cultural Histories of Norms and Normativity* (London: Routledge, 2006).

26 Rosemarie Garland-Thomson, *Extraordinary Bodies: Figuring Physical Disability in American Culture and Literature* (New York: Columbia University Press, 1997). In this book Garland-Thompson does not hyphenate her surname, but she does throughout her later work. For simplicity, I have chosen to hyphenate her name throughout.

27 Clara Claiborne Park, *The Siege: A Family's Journey into the World of an Autistic Child* (Boston, MA: Little, Brown, 1967).

28 Roy Richard Grinker, *Unstrange Minds: Remapping the World of Autism* (New York: Basic Books, 2007).

29 Ian Hacking, *The Social Construction of What?* (Cambridge, MA: Harvard University Press, 1999), pp. 109–15.

30 See Schreibman, *The Science and Fiction of Autism*, pp. 202–13, for her full discussion of FC. See also Ralph James Saverese, *Reasonable People: A Memoir of Autism & Adoption* (New York: Other Press, 2007), pp. xx–xxv, for a sympathetic account of FC use.

31 Douglas Biklen, *Autism and the Myth of the Person Alone* (New York: New York University Press, 2005), pp. 35–45. The metaphor quote is on p. 37.

CHAPTER 1

# Presences:
# autistic difference

I

To seek out the details of autistic presence in the very contemporary
period might seem in some ways to swim against the tide. There is
a precision to the term 'autism', in what we might think of as clinical
terms, within the language of medicine, education and social care. As
a diagnostic label, the condition is judged by set criteria. Those set out
in the fourth (1994) edition of the American Psychiatric Association's
*Diagnostic and Statistical Manual of Mental Disorders* (*DSM–IV*) are possibly
the most well known. Here, impairments in social interaction and communication, language delay and repetitive behaviour are all put forward
as characteristics necessary for the diagnosis to be arrived at.[1] *DSM–IV*
is a yardstick in the discussions of autism. Both accepted and contested,
it aims for a degree of specificity in establishing what autism is. Yet the
word (and label) has increasingly become untethered from this kind of
attempt at precision. 'Unfortunately', Douglas Biklen writes in *Autism
and the Myth of the Person Alone*, 'metaphor is ubiquitous in the field of
autism'.[2] Biklen's observation is one arrived at after studying the work
of autism specialists – neurologists and psychiatrists – but his comment
is even more true of the wider world of commentary on the condition,
where analogies abound. In one morning's casual browsing of autism-
related stories on the internet, I found an article on toxins that linked
autism to the terrorist attacks on the US of 11 September 2001, and
another protesting against the location of a new all-Ireland centre for
the study of autism in Northern Ireland.[3] Both pieces were, in their own
ways, commentaries on specific issues, but each also practised the kind
of cultural linkage which is becoming increasingly common whenever

autism is discussed. 'America has Asperger's', historian Niall Ferguson wrote in the *Daily Telegraph* in May 2004, in one of the most explicit examples of this. 'You may not yet have heard of Asperger's syndrome', Ferguson wrote, 'But you can be sure that someone will sooner or later offer it as an excuse for his own bad behaviour, for it is the height of hypochondriac fashion in New York'.[4]

Ferguson's article was about what he felt was the failure of American foreign policy in George W. Bush's first presidential term – 'a Bush re-election will look to the rest of the world like evidence that Asperger's syndrome is no longer a treatable condition in America, but has become the national norm', he wrote – but whether autism is linked with politics, or an idea of national health following terrorist attacks, or the fallout from the peace process in Northern Ireland, its status as a contemporary metaphor is undeniable. There is no particular specificity in these examples. Rather, there is a process of creep, through which a perceived association between autism and a general notion of difference is articulated, or the condition starts to parallel other central news stories because of its seemingly inherent newsworthiness. Odd, strange, difficult and even dangerous (increasingly autism and Asperger's feature in the media profiles of those accused of crime – the claim that Virginia Tech killer Cho Seung-Hui was autistic is only the most high-profile example),[5] autism is diffuse in these commentaries, a floating term working through loose generic association.

The effects of such media portrayals of autism need to be understood. It is not quite the kind of 'hysterical epidemic' that Elaine Showalter discusses in her 1997 study *Hystories*, but the notion of a 'hysterical hot zone', as Showalter terms it, or the spread of an epidemic through stories, and an idea of contagion, seems relevant and germane.[6] Autism is physical and neurological in a way that hysteria is not, but it does seem to be a condition caught up in the fictionalizing and metaphorization of the modern of which Showalter speaks – the fixation on recovered memory or chronic fatigue syndrome and other associated 'conditions'. To extract autism from such association – to properly look for its presence – is a process that requires an understanding of its formations that *precede* the kinds of public metaphors that exist in the examples given above. Neurologically and somatically, autism is constituted primarily in terms of the individual and with differing individual emphases. It is the presence of the person with autism, rather than an abstracted idea of the condition itself, that needs to be starting point of any enquiry.

As a specific medical term, 'autism' was first used by Swiss psychiatrist Eugene Bleuler in 1908, not in relation to the condition as we understand it today, but rather in connection to schizophrenia. Bleuler was a pioneer in the development of psychiatric approaches to schizophrenia, a figure who became committed to the implementation of the use of psychological treatment. Ian Hacking has said of Bleuler:

> He was totally committed to the organic basis of mental illness, yet self-lessly dedicated to establishing personal and social relationships with schizophrenic patients. At a certain stage in his career, he lived with them night and day.... He believed in organic psychiatry, but practiced dynamic psychiatry.[7]

As part of Bleuler's dynamic method, his sustained observation of patients led to a series of descriptions of their behaviour. In using the word 'autism', Bleuler was, in Laura Schreibman's words, emphasizing 'the idiosyncratic, self-centred withdrawal into an active fantasy life exhibited by schizophrenics'.[8] The ideas at work here, especially of a supposed break from the real characterized by a perceived retreat into the self, would later translate into the notions of being 'closed off' or 'shut away' that would come to typify many descriptions of autism as we know it today.

Bleuler's term was adopted in 1943 by child psychiatrist Leo Kanner, in the research article that has come to be seen by many as the foundational document for modern understandings of autism. Kanner's 'Autistic disturbances of affective contact' was written as a consequence of his study of eleven children – Donald, Frederick, Richard, Paul, Barbara, Virginia, Herbert, Alfred, Charles, John and Elaine – in his clinical practice at Johns Hopkins University in Baltimore in the US. Observing the children, and working with documents produced by their parents, Kanner noticed a number of what he considered to be seminal traits: the children rarely interacted with adults in any physical way; they nearly all had delays in establishing communications and language, and especially struggled with the use of personal pronouns; language, when it did come, was often literal and repetitive, something he termed 'delayed echolalia'; their behaviour was often methodical and obsessive; and the children saw their environment, in terms of external noises and activities, often as a source of fear and stress. In a number of key phrases, Kanner wrote that the children's 'fundamental disorder' was their *'inability to relate themselves* in the ordinary way to people and situations', that they displayed an *'anxiously excessive desire for the maintenance of sameness'* and, in a revision of Bleuler's notions of a 'withdrawal', he felt that the children did not retreat or depart from relationships into the self but rather exhibited 'from the start an *extreme autistic aloneness* that, whenever possible, disregards, ignores, shuts out anything that comes to the child from the outside'.[9] In his 'Comment', the section that accounted for the last two pages of the article, Kanner noted that, despite some relationships with the idea of childhood schizophrenia as it was then understood, the condition he was describing displayed substantial differences from accounts of the schizophrenic. Autism was, he suggested, something new, a 'pure-culture example' of a distinct condition.[10]

Kanner's observations outline a specific sense of an autistic presence, one we might think of in terms of classic autism. The hand-flapping, self-stimulating, echolalic young child displaying no interest in others and obsessed with rituals is possibly the most obvious personification of the condition, the 'pure' example of which Kanner speaks. It is nevertheless worth commenting on this delineation, for despite being the product of clinical observation it is still clearly a characterization, and the formation of a type with specific characteristics. Firstly, in the language of Biklen, Kanner's definitions led to the idea of 'autism-inside-the-person', a notion that the condition is inherently internal, a 'collection of traits' *within* and bounded by the individual concerned.[11] The representation of autism as being a form of interiority in this way has, as we shall see, a number of repercussions for its depiction within cultural narratives, especially in the way it suggests the possibility of metaphor. Secondly, as Majia Holmer Nadesan has observed, the recognition of autism in the mid-twentieth century was possible only because of the emergence and evolution of specific medical disciplines, especially the development of psychiatry and the clinical and social institutions that surrounded childhood, in the late nineteenth and early twentieth centuries. As a *child* psychiatrist, Kanner himself practised a profession that needed specific category distinctions to come into formation before it became a viable, delineated role.[12] Two key consequences of this are that we can see the diagnostic dimension of autism thus emerging as a twentieth-century phenomenon, surrounded by cultural and social narratives that the contemporary period has clearly inherited, and also that the condition came to be associated with *children*, a preoccupation that very much continues into the present. From novels and films to the fears of the vaccine debates, it is the figure of the child that takes centre stage in our current thinking about autism.

Equally, Kanner's clinical *method* introduced a foundational dimension to our understanding of autism. For obvious medical reasons, Kanner's eleven children became objects of enquiry, figures subject to testing and surveillance, to the whole set of processes of determination from without, which then came to constitute the clinical parameters of the condition. The 'autism-inside-the-person' model seemingly allows and invites an interrogative approach by which the person is – appropriately – viewed as the complex *host* of the condition. This voyeuristic dimension, the idea that the person with autism is open to study (and study of all kinds), is a phenomenon that reaches beyond its medical origins. As we shall see later, in the commentary on the many films that portray autistic children in particular, ideas of staring, observing and witnessing are central to the contemporary ways in which the condition is apprehended and its fascination conveyed. As such objects of enquiry, of course, those with autism become part of the larger group of disabled subjects for whom exposure and labelling are daily facts of life.

The first notion of autistic presence that emerges from Kanner's work, then, is precisely one that is internal, and is then studied, recorded and (literally, as in the title of Kanner's final section of his article) commented upon. Presence is here about an idea of interiority and then one of exposure and distance, something that can be itemized and then subjected to the full regime of diagnostic terminology. From early forms of quantitative enquiry that produced such categories as 'defective', 'feebleminded' or 'subnormal', to the plethora of acronyms that abound in the contemporary period – ASD, OCD, ADHD, ADD, PDD[13] – the presence of the person with autism produces all manner of outside labels.[14] The ideas of 'treatment' that follow are conditioned by the recognition of the terms that are in use.

And yet, even within the clinical processes of Kanner's observations and all the differing descriptions of 'aloneness', there is still an alternative presence of the children he examines that resists eradication. 'He just is there', writes Kanner near the end of his article, generalizing about the autistic child after he has given a number of accounts of how the children in his study failed to interact with one another.[15] The phrase almost seems to slip out amidst the surrounding prose detailing the carefully considered study. For all that the exceptionality of the eleven children he observed can be viewed as symptoms, and for all that their behaviour is carefully analysed with a view to constructing a profile of their being in the world, Kanner's words here point to a central fact even as they occupy what seem to be the margins of his own thinking: the presence of the autistic person cannot be disavowed. As with the discussion of the girls in Jane Bown's photograph in this book's Preface, the child – Donald or any of the other boys Kanner worked with – here resists all the attempts at producing a version of his subjectivity that is constituted only in terms of the space between his actions and how those actions are read.

Intriguingly, Hans Asperger's work, conducted at the same time as Kanner's but on the other side of the Atlantic, in Vienna, and though published in German in 1944 not fully accessible in English until the 1990s, contains a similar term denoting presence. Asperger's study reflected Kanner's in its concentration on such features as mobility, facial expressions, obsessions and compulsions, environmental threats and problems with social interactions, and – uncannily – also used the word 'autism' to describe the children he studied. Like Kanner, he saw what seemed to be a contradiction between severe impairment and yet some markers of clear intelligence. As he wrote up his findings, he sought phrases that might encapsulate the situation he saw before him. 'The autist is only himself', he wrote, seeking to explain the personification of the condition.[16] As another 'inside-the-person' commentary, the description seems clear and direct; yet the force of the words escapes this logic even as they exemplify it. They mark a clear idea of presence – the figure in the room that any study cannot fully explain away.

'He just is there'/'The autist is only himself': in the ways in which these comments escape from the orthodox prose of medical description, Kanner's and Asperger's phrases invite an exploration of how the processes of cultural representation do or don't record such an idea of presence. The words themselves provide multiple possibilities that conform to the many subject positions characters with autism are given in fictional and non-fictional narratives alike. If the 'just' or 'only' is seen in a pejorative way, then the character is barely present, a prosthetic figure in the margins used only to make other aspects of the narrative work. As we shall see, such usage is common in many of the recent novels or films featuring autistic characters. If the emphasis in Kanner's and Asperger's observations is different, however, with a stress on the last words – 'is there', 'himself' – then we have the possibility of centrality and agency, of the occupation of the narrative foreground, and – potentially – that the person with autism might have some say in the definition of terms through which he or she is seen. It is this kind of presence we see in the many life accounts of those with autism, whether they be the printed narratives of high-profile figures such as Temple Grandin and Donna Williams (discussed below) or the proliferation of blogs and videos on YouTube that stress the familiarity that those with autism feel their lives encompass. In these narratives, life stories become the means both to counteract the misrepresentation inherent in 'able-ist' discourses and to show the nature of living as an autistic individual. In so doing, they wrestle an idea of the normal away from the conception of normalcy as illustrated by Lennard J. Davis (see Introduction), promoting a model of lived experience in contrast to the construction of disability central to normalcy's organizing method.

Those who come to disability life stories as interested readers of autobiographical writing, or who want to engage with the rising profile of such narratives on the web, probably see in these stories the possibility of an engagement with disabled difference. But there is more to such accounts than the straightforward notion of their being a window on to autistic lives. In the ways in which we read these narratives there is the real potential to form a conception of autism that extends beyond the ways in which the condition is labelled in medical and other institutional contexts. In *Autism and the Myth of the Person Alone*, Biklen makes a strong case for such an understanding of life narratives:

> The field of autism, by which I mean professional experts, researchers, parents, teachers and others who contribute to autism literature, inhabits a different location vis-à-vis people classified as autistic than do the people themselves. The outside perspective can never definitively know what the other person experiences or understands. The outsider is always in the position of having to ask, 'What am I seeing here? What does this mean?' The tendency in the field to frame a response to such questions has been deficit-oriented. Within this deficit model, the outsider develops hypotheses or theories … from a normate perspective and applies them to and tests them on people defined as disabled, in effect saying: What does the person labeled autistic lack that the 'normal' person possesses? An alternative stance would be to identify individual subjective understandings or assumptions by eliciting perspectives of people classified as autistic, and to interpret multiple meanings of autism with an eye to placing the perspectives of labeled people in the foreground.[17]

Biklen's theory that the subjective expression of those with autism can counteract the condition's primary public associations with lack and loss is a vital one. It is an observation underpinned by the sense of autistic presence that comes through the processes of such expression, the writings, films and statements of those autistic individuals who seek to represent themselves. The 'multiple meanings' of which Biklen speaks illustrate what is the very real complexity and range of this presence, characteristics that defy the perception that autism is best understood in terms of limits or restrictions. Life narratives as a genre invite an engagement, in part because of the ways in which they display their details, and there is no doubt that, in the context of disability, this can be a contentious issue. But even as this is acknowledged, these same narratives present a version of subjectivity and agency that can operate on the terms of those who create them. In terms of written life accounts, the requirements of publishing might seem to stress the need for disclosure and the overcoming narrative – such stories are those that sell – but this has to be balanced against the profile of the individual achievement contained within the story itself.

Such concerns do not exist when discussing life accounts that exist on the internet. Amanda Baggs' eight and a half minute video 'In My Language', posted on YouTube in January 2007, opens with a succession of humming and other noises produced by Baggs and her interaction with what she terms 'assorted objects' – a hoop around a doorknob, hands rubbed across surfaces, the flapping of a piece of paper. All these sounds are, in Baggs' voiced words (the majority of her communication is through typing) that open the second section of the video, part of her 'native language', her daily sense of her articulated self. 'It is about being in a constant conversation with every aspect of my environment, reacting physically to all parts of my surroundings', Baggs says of her communication, as the video displays further images of her flapping and interacting with objects around her. As she neatly observes in the 'translation' of her actions she offers the majority audience in the video's second section, it is an irony that this complex set of reactions to the multiple elements of her surroundings is characterized by many as evidence of her being in a world of her own. Such observers, Baggs notes, 'judge my existence, awareness and personhood on which of [*sic*] a tiny and limited part of the world I appear to be reacting to'.[18]

'In My Language' extrapolates from the personal in order to address how mainstream cultural narratives misrepresent autism. It does so in its pivotal move from the presentation of Baggs' everyday habits to a discussion of a wider autistic selfhood, especially the ways in which that sense of self is judged by others. Well aware that it is *difference* that is central to her argument, Baggs makes herself the subject of her wider political statement. It is her own pleasures, preferences and modes of communication that become the source of her articulation of what autistic subjectivity might be. The first section of the video, that entirely devoted to the various manifestations of Baggs' language, offers no explanation for the images and sounds being communicated. The flapping, humming and assorted other noises exist firstly in the individuality of their own presence, and then in relation to the video's title, which suggest their importance as a form of primary communication. The temptation to see Baggs isolated and 'locked away' here, somehow lost in her sensory experiences, is one that the video implicitly understands and then undercuts with the 'explanation' of her actions in the second section. Here, the assertion of the normativity of Baggs' world is, at heart, a statement about *rights*, a demand that her life is seen and comprehended on her own terms. For all of the brevity of the video, it is remarkably effective in its presentation of a viable and legitimate adult autistic self, and in its construction of a powerful argument about the need for such a self to be understood.

Baggs' autistic presence is one that achieves much of its profile through the internet. As well as her video work, she is also a blogger, writing (as Ballastexistenz, a word she deliberately adopts from Germanic eugenics movements) on all aspects of life on the autistic spectrum, and is the central figure behind the 'Autism: Getting the Truth Out' website, a narrative constructed through a series of still photographs of Baggs (although she is not identified) that expertly plays on the assumptions of viewers concerning autism.[19] 'Getting the Truth Out' begins with a succession of photographs of Baggs – curled up, sitting, flapping her hands – accompanied by a descriptive prose which talks of the limitations and difficulties of autism. As the viewer is encouraged to click on each successive page, the descriptions continue to outline Baggs as a generic figure, lost in her own world and unable to care for herself. But, in the same manner as 'In My Language', 'Getting the Truth Out' then turns expectations inside out by giving the 'voice' of the prose descriptions over to Baggs herself and then revisiting the photographs to comment upon them in the personal terms of subjectivity and agency. So, in the second half of the narrative, Baggs is seen to be curled up in a ball, not as some indicator of a 'retreat from the world' but because it provides sensory pleasure for her; sitting immobile is not evidence of 'retardation' but of preference. 'There's nothing to understand, nothing to figure out; nothing to figure out, nothing to fix', Baggs writes of the self in these photos. Rather, she asserts, she is simply being herself.

As a disability rights advocate, Baggs has been caught up in the often furious debates that exist, particularly in the US, over the nature of autism and especially the vaccine fears and the call for a 'cure' for the condition ('Getting the Truth Out' is itself an explicit riposte to the Autism Society of America's 'Getting the Word Out' campaign, a series of words and images about autism that many in the advocacy movement found disquieting). I will look at some of these arguments more fully in chapter 5, especially in relation to families, but it is worth noting here that, for some, Baggs' campaigning for the legitimacy of her individuality is a manipulation of a position that denies the damage done to many by autism. In describing 'her' world, Baggs knowingly extends her commentary to a more generalized idea of a life with autism. There are those who see such a move as, in itself, a misrepresentation of many lives lived with autism, and even those who doubt Baggs' representation of her own condition. The numerous autism blogs are full of claim and counterclaim as to the ethics and politics of such representation.

Baggs' presence here, then, is one that can be read as deeply provocative, even to those 'within' the various autism debates; yet in one sense her writing and films are a continuation of the tradition by which individuals with autism represent themselves. To date, such a tradition has been most frequently seen in published life writing – like that of Grandin and Williams – and it is intriguing to conjecture whether these written representations have a marked difference from those of advocates such as Baggs that might influence the ways in which they are received. Certainly there is a strong tendency in most published life writing by autistic individuals to address a non-autistic audience and to seek to 'explain' the condition, and this might offer a context for its difference, in that it is less challenging and more palatable to a mainstream audience. Yet, as we have seen, 'In My Language' also fulfils such a purpose, given the direct nature of its address to a majority audience and movement from 'my' to 'your' in its narrative. If Baggs seems a radical figure, are the earlier writers of autism less political and confrontational, for all that they might still be noticeably 'different' to a majority audience?

## II

Temple Grandin's *Thinking in Pictures*, updated in 2006 after an initial publication in 1995, offers a direct, first-person account of how being autistic creates a specific worldview. Grandin had first come to public attention through the 1986 publication of *Emergence: Labeled Autistic*, an autobiographical account co-written with Margaret Scariano.[20] In both texts, Grandin makes herself the subject of a personal story in a self-reflexive narrative move that uses the description of her experiences as the foundation for a more general discussion of autistic subjectivity; but if *Emergence: Labeled Autistic* outlined an initial sense of an autistic subject in terms of a traditional idea of personal growth and behaviour, *Thinking in Pictures* provides a more complex account of what such an autistic identity might be, by interweaving the life story with reflections on the nature of the condition. In the later book Grandin acknowledges a division between autism and what she terms 'normal', noting about her own methods of learning that 'More knowledge makes me act more normal. Many people have commented to me that I act much less autistic now than I did ten years ago'. Indeed, she ends the first chapter of her book with a section entitled 'Becoming more normal'.[21] For Grandin, the conception of 'normal' is not the kind of organizing power category it appears to be in the work of Lennard Davis or Rosemarie Garland-Thomson; rather it describes a series of engagements with the world, from which she knows she is distanced by the way her mind works. There is no doubting the centrality of Grandin's autistic difference – 'The more I learn, the more I realize more and more that how I think and feel is different', she writes – but such difference is always held in a defining relationship with the 'normality' that surrounds it.[22] The normal is a set of attitudes and behaviours that she acknowledges have to be learned if she is to participate in human and social communication in the way she wishes.

It is in analysing Grandin's sense of the process of learning, and in her figuring of how the difference of autism manifests itself, that we might move towards an understanding of her own presence as a *writer* of a certain kind of narrative of autism. Grandin's centrality to the idea of what it means to be autistic, especially in North America, has been apparent for over a decade now. As Ralph James Savarese has noted, she is 'the most famous American with autism and someone from whom we've perhaps extrapolated too much'.[23] Her books do contain what is, in truth, a quite specific, for all that it is widely accepted, account of how the condition functions, one that juxtaposes the exceptionality of autism with a potential integration of its methods within majority culture. For Grandin, learning how to mediate between what she calls 'my place along the great continuum' and the wider world is key not just to being accepted by others, but also for her sense of what it means to be autistic.[24]

Throughout her writings, Grandin stresses the *abilities* of those with autism. She notes how her own skills in visualization and thought processing made possible the pioneering radical designs of cattle-handling facilities for which she has become famous. 'One third of cattle and hogs in the United States are handled in facilities I have designed', she writes in *Thinking in Pictures*, in what reads like a statement of pride but which is, as well, the announcement of a fact.[25] She also writes of Albert Einstein, Ludwig Wittgenstein, Vincent van Gogh and Charles Darwin as figures with autistic characteristics, individuals without whose abilities the modern world would be unthinkable – 'Without autism traits we might still be living in caves', she notes.[26] Such abilities are, for Grandin, unique and special – 'I would never want to become so normal that I would lose these skills', she writes of her capacity for visualization.[27] At the same time, such uniqueness is not the delineated exceptionality that Baggs elevates to the status of a *separate* mode of expression and communication in her work. In Grandin's writing, autism, as with the other disabilities she comments upon, is arguably foundationally *negative* in its effects, unless it can be understood in terms of the wider spectrum of humanity:

> I believe that there is a reason that disabilities such as autism, severe
> manic-depression, and schizophrenia remain in our gene pool even
> though there is much suffering as a result. Researchers speculate that
> schizophrenia may be the evolutionary price that has to be paid for
> abilities in language and social interactions.... The gene that causes
> schizophrenia may confer advantages in a milder form. This may also be
> true for manic-depression and autism.[28]

For Grandin, the idea of autism as a 'price that has to be paid' can be
bridged by the proper use of autistic exceptionality. The value of autistic
difference is thus best observed when it can be aligned with the non-
autistic world. So her designs for the handling of cattle, or her claims
about Einstein's research, are most meaningful because of the ways in
which they add to and enrich the majority, non-disabled, culture.

It is clear, then, that Grandin's narrative construction of autism as a
condition, and the positioning of herself as a subject in her writings, in
part function in terms of the ways in which she presents a *negotiation*
between the disabled and abled worlds; indeed, it is an arguable,
though contentious, point that this is the primary function of her
prose. For all that she cites the skills of those with autism, and indeed
for all that she herself (crucially) becomes an exemplar of those skills,
the ultimate trajectory of her account is that of the happy and viable
autistic subject who, through difficulty, has learned to adapt and contribute to the world at large. As such, there is a common tendency in
her writing to move from an explanatory mode to an instructional one,
to point to how such a process of adaptation might be best undertaken,
as in the following example about the need for early intervention in the
education of autistic children:

> Autism and PDD [pervasive developmental disorder] are highly variable
> and the methods that work for each child should be used. Dr. Koegel
> [author of *Overcoming Autism*] found that some little children respond well
> to a highly structured Lovass-style program and other types of autistic
> children, who are more socially engaged, may make more progress with
> a less structured program. Do not get too single-minded on one method.
> Use things that work and eliminate things that do not work. Sometimes
> a combination of methods is best. For older high-functioning children,
> highly repetitive programs are boring and they need lessons that will
> stimulate their minds. In elementary school children a child's fixation
> can be used to motivate learning. If a child loves trains, then read a book
> about a train or do a math problem involving trains.[29]

What starts out here as descriptive becomes, by the end, the writing of
the teacher, and Grandin's prose in this mode is like the multiple texts
by those parents and professionals offering advice in the education and
care of children with autism (she has written a career advice book –

*Developing Talents*[30] – which is firmly located in this genre). If there is a sense here of Grandin's *own* presence as a woman with autism, it is as a figure who can read through the prism of her experiences to then communicate with others. Engaged in communication in this way, Grandin becomes a particularly vital exponent of the core concerns of the wider autism publishing industry – an 'insider' who can explain the nature of the condition to others, a privileged negotiator whose abilities are all the more remarkable because of the difficulties she is seen to have overcome.

Such presence differs from that of those activists and advocates, like Baggs, who seek to outline autism as a condition of being in the world in its own right that does not require correction. 'When I daydreamed, my teachers yanked me back to reality', Grandin writes of her time at school, in a phrase that makes clear the lack of reality of her childhood autistic reveries.[31] The need here to break out of the confines of autistic behaviour seem clear, though it is exactly such a view that many of the new generation of online autism advocates seek to overturn.

The complexities of such positions illustrate the heated nature of the arguments concerning the identity politics of autism. A cynical view of Grandin is that she acts *fundamentally* as an interpreter, a figure who is read and has become successful precisely because of her ability to allow the curious majority a window into her autism, through which they can practise their fascination with difference and muse on the nature of the human condition. David Mitchell and Sharon Snyder have observed that, for all that is positive about disability life writing, there is still an inherent aspect to the form that means it appears to require legitimizing from a majority audience:

> The autobiographical narrative of disability tools [*sic*] disability as a private and 'minority' concern, one that requires the attention of the culture because the social arena has proven inadequate to the task of responding – both legislatively and morally – to a population located on the fringes of institutional access. Nonetheless, first person narratives of disability have historically fed a public appetite for confessional writing that promises the revelation of personal catastrophe as the evidence of a more truthful access to secreted lives. The confessional mode places physical and cognitive limitation and difference on display to be consumed, and the mainstream parading of personal misfortune inevitably assures the reader/viewer of his or her comparative good fortunes or assuages a shared societal sense of guilt and insensitivity.[32]

Using these terms to locate Grandin's writings stresses the tension her prose produces. *Thinking in Pictures* undoubtedly conforms to the broad shape of Mitchell and Snyder's argument: it *is* a form of confessional writing that works in terms of consumption, as the reviewers' comments on the cover of the new edition make clear ('Grandin's window on to the subjective experience of autism is of value to all of us who hope to gain a deeper understanding of the human mind', noted the *Washington Times*). At the same time, however, Mitchell and Snyder are possibly too sweeping in their assertion that 'personal misfortune' takes the form of a 'catastrophe'. Grandin's writing is explicit in its stress on her specific achievements as a figure who can *only* function through her autism. Her career working with cattle, for example, is distinctive and unique precisely because of what is added by the autistic lens of her mind. 'Autism is part of what I am', she writes in *Thinking in Pictures*; it is not a removable element to her being, and as such she stands as an advocate, in her own right, of the possibilities of autistic achievement.[33] In these terms, her writing is not about the overcoming of her condition or the repair needed to heal damage.

Rather than try to resolve what might seem like an impasse, it is better to think that Grandin's position as a subject is contested because the meaning and value of autism are themselves contested. She is a high-profile figure who has discussed the difficulties of autism and written of the journey away from its most problematic excesses. In this she is like others with autism, such as writer Tito Rajarshi Mukhopadhyay and Sue Rubin, the subject of the 2004 Oscar-nominated documentary *Autism Is a World*, who have equally recorded the pressures that come with the limits placed upon them by their condition. That they do this even as they convey their own exceptionality, often through characteristics produced *because* of their autism, is part of the contestation that surrounds the representation of disability, and which is central to the questions posed by the disability rights movement as to how disability should be understood. Grandin's achievements and 'success' belong both to her ability to live independently – a point that might seem to make concessions to majority notions of disabled 'overcoming' – and to her articulation of the individual strengths of her autism and the ways in which they enrich her existence.

Seen in this way, Grandin's writing becomes emblematic of the ways in which much life writing on autism presents its subject matter. Donna Williams is Grandin's contemporary and the other major figure associated with published autistic life writing, though she has a strong online presence as well, as one of the organizers of the 'autism friendly' website www.auties.org and through her own blogs. Williams develops in her print volumes of autobiography a 'two world' system similar to Grandin's delineation of 'autistic' and 'normal'. 'This is a story of two battles', Williams writes in the 'Author's note' to *Nobody Nowhere*

(1992), the first of her four volumes of autobiography, 'a battle to keep out "the world" and a battle to join it. It tells of the battles within my own world and the battle lines, tactics used and casualties of my private war against others'. Describing her childhood, she goes on:

> 'The world' still seemed like either a battlefield or a stage, but I was forced to keep trying to 'play the game', if for no other reason than to survive. I would have been happy to 'let go' and retreat into my own world were it not for my belief that my mother and older brother seemed to thrive on my strangeness and inability to cope. My hatred and my sense of injustice were my driving force to prove them wrong. At the same time, my fear of feeling kept calling me back into myself. Both drives were intense and had a shattering impact, both on the real 'feeling me' within and the characters whom I threw at those who tried to reach me.[34]

Williams' autism, which in her childhood went undiagnosed and took the form of visual and sensory fragmentation as well as difficulties with social interaction, led to years of abuse at the hands of her family. The 'nowhere' she describes inhabiting as a child is, as one of her poems terms it, a space into which one might 'run and hide' in the 'corners of your mind'.[35] For Williams, the retreat into 'her' world was inevitable when the pressures around her became too difficult, and when the characters she created to cope with the social world (she talks in detail of two – Carol and Willie – who became the personae with which she engaged with those around her) could no longer function. The 'battles' and sense of an ongoing 'war' of which she speaks in her opening note to *Nobody Nowhere* became the inevitable outcome of a childhood when her very being was fundamentally misunderstood.

Yet the Donna Williams who was initially 'nowhere' became the subject of *Somebody Somewhere* (1994), the title of her second volume of autobiography and a book that charts an escape from what she terms in the earlier volume the 'trap' and 'blackness' of the space 'between "my world" and "the world"'.[36] The subtitle of *Somebody Somewhere, Breaking Free from the World of Autism*, gives a clear indication of the journey Williams undertakes, continuing the metaphor of battle and struggle she established in her first book. The trajectory of Williams as a subject here mirrors, in broad terms, that of Grandin: the escape from the 'unreality' of the world of autism into a functioning maturity. Equally, Williams parallels Grandin in the ways in which she has achieved the status of being a specialist in a chosen field – in Williams' case as a consultant on autism. In 1997 she founded her own consultancy service for people with autism, and between 1997 and 2002 she was employed in such a capacity by the National Health Service and Department of

Education in the UK. In addition – again like Grandin – she has become known internationally as a high-profile speaker on autism issues. And as a writer she has added to her autobiographical works with a number of instructional textbooks aimed at professionals and carers working with those who have autism.

As with Grandin, Williams makes her own experiences the basis of her instruction on issues of autism. Her 1996 study *Autism – An Inside-Out Approach*, for example, begins with a chapter entitled 'A bucket full of jigsaws', which maps out the details of her own autism as a base for the various strategies on and approaches to the condition that follow.[37] Such a process conveys an obvious sense of authority and the right to speak. It is also, however, a crucial example of the kind of connection that is often said to be impossible for those with autism to make. Writers such as Grandin and Williams clearly demonstrate, in the ways that they expand from their awareness of their own conditions, that autism cannot be seen as static or fixed. Their accounts of their lives display any number of occasions on which they learn, process, adapt, develop interests and renegotiate information in order to continue day-to-day life as individuals. As Biklen observes, such actions 'render the notion of the "autistic person alone" unrealistic, even mythical'.[38] Williams' journey from abused child with fragmented sensory responses to the world to university-educated international public speaker and acclaimed writer is one that can invite any manner of readings. But it cannot be denied that it is a social journey, one of engagement and progress, and one that has to be seen in terms of the evolution of autistic presence.

It is interesting to conceive in critical terms of Grandin and Williams specifically as *writers*. It is not disparaging to say that Grandin's prose has a certain functionality to it. In her books, sections and chapters regularly seem to stop rather than conclude, often when a specific point has been made and discussion thereby finished – as if the text were a form of manual. Such a writing style is entirely in keeping with the kind of self-presence that is described in Grandin's life writing and fits with the way she outlines her sense of the function of communication. Williams' writing style, on the other hand, is more self-consciously literary: 'If there was anything I was good at, it was the ability to create pictures out of words to explain what might otherwise have been disjointed strings of black print on white paper', she writes of her encounter with English as a subject at high school, and as her autobiographical writing progresses the increase in use of symbol, simile and metaphor is noticeable.[39] Discussing her return to Australia after living in Europe, at the start of *Somebody Somewhere*, she writes:

I had come back because I needed to go forward, and before fear and compulsion would let me walk free, I had to pick up the pieces of my twenty-five year war. Those pieces were scattered everywhere at the feet of so-called friends, in the faces of so-called family, and in the bedrooms of so-called lovers. I had 'the world' dictionary of control disguised as caring, of lust disguised as love, of uselessness disguised as charitable martyrdom, and of cheap entertainment disguised as accept-ance. I couldn't go forward with the old definitions. But to build new ones – *my* definitions – I would have to face the old ones and tell it like it was. I had to shatter the myths that had tied me in knots upon knots until my selfhood was immobile within a mental, emotional, physical and social straitjacket.[40]

Prose such as this has a real feel for the evocative potential of words, an understanding beyond the sense that they can communicate individual thoughts or feelings. As Williams' autobiographical writing matures, she not only develops this feel in the construction of phrases and sentences – 'Trying to make me stay present in company had been like trying to touch a fairy' she writes in *Somebody Somewhere* in a typical example[41] – but she is also increasingly assured in the ways in which she *characterizes* herself in her writing. Her third volume of life writing, *Like Color to the Blind* (1996), contains accounts of Williams' fame – pro-motional tours to North America, media interviews – in which she deftly recreates the pressures and difficulties that came with such exposure.[42] It is worth making an obvious point here: the ways in which Williams performs such a written version of herself is an obvious mani-festation of exactly the kind of self-reflexivity that those with autism are stereotypically said to lack. Such self-awareness is true of Grandin's evaluation of her past as well, and if we might at times see her writing as a mode that *does* appear to mirror her condition in the terms of its structure and expression, then we also need to admit that the work of both Grandin and Williams challenges many of the received stereotypes concerning autistic presence. For Williams in particular, the flexibility of writing – its sense of possibilities and a lack of fixity – is exactly part of its appeal. For all that her work does return to and repeat tropes and ideas (especially in the early volumes of her autobiography), her clear love of language's multiplicities and open suggestiveness necessitates a revision of the idea that individuals with autism always require stable continuity and precise answers in all that they do.

In July 2007, Williams interviewed Amanda Baggs for the online magazine *American Chronicle*. Because of her YouTube documentary and presence on the internet (especially through the 'Autism: Getting the Truth Out' sequence discussed above), Baggs has been elevated to the status of autism celebrity, with appearances on mainstream television and a central place in the politics of autism debates. 'Putting autism on trial' ran the title of the interview, accurately capturing the sense of controversy surrounding Baggs and her views. The exchange between the two is a virtual catalogue of the complex issues that make up autistic agency: both describe what Williams terms their 'systems', the often dizzying collection of physical, sensory, behavioural and emotional realities that make up their autism; both also outline the ways in which they have been required to position themselves with regard to what constitutes 'normal' in the environments in which they have found themselves. But possibly most interesting in the dialogue is the discussion of having to conform to mainstream ideas of what might, or might not, constitute autism itself. In framing one of her questions, Williams notes:

> As a 'famous' autistic I have found myself torn between those who would expect me to 'appear' more autistic and those proud of me for defying the stereotypes and seeing my selfhood as more important and sacred than my condition.

In response, Baggs makes a telling point about this interaction between autism and self:

> My strategy is to find what I need to do, then find a way to do it. If what I do seems to fit an autism stereotype, then so be it. If what I want to do seems to fit a stereotype of not being autistic, so be it too. I have had it with being controlled mindlessly by a set of requirements. I view 'autistic' as a word for a part of how my brain works, not for a narrow set of behaviours, and certainly not for a set of boundaries of stereotype that I have to stay inside.
>
> It so happens that my best strategy for words looks 'autistic' because it is not speech. Many of my strategies for managing and responding to sensory input look 'autistic' because they involve unusual movements of my body. I do not resist these things, I do not have the energy to, I have to streamline things.[43]

Baggs' articulacy here allows for an understanding that, for all of her role as an autism rights advocate, her sense of her own autism is not one that involves any straightforward acceptance of terms. The 'set of requirements' of which she speaks reminds us of a central contradiction, that although we acknowledge that autism as a condition is far from understood, there exists nevertheless a coherent public conception of how those with the condition should behave. For some, a figure such as Baggs (and indeed Williams as well) is 'impossibly' articulate for a person with autism. As she makes clear here, Baggs will make claims for the viability of her life without having to perform disability for those who expect it to come in a certain package.

## III

Grandin, Baggs and Williams are only the most familiar of those figures involved in autistic autobiography. Between 1985 and 2004, there were some fifty-five published autobiographical texts, in English, by autistic writers.[44] Equally, the many online sites devoted to autism, whether related to advocacy or not, feature numerous blogs and postings that convey impressions of autistic lives. The idea of presence that emerges from such accounts is anything but uniform. If we can recognize broad patterns associated with impairment in the various writings – issues of social interaction and communication, and of complex environmental responses, in particular – then we also have to admit that what Williams terms the 'jigsaw' or 'fruit salad' of autistic experience also displays manifest differences. For some, as mentioned before, the recognition that the autistic spectrum may be as wide as the non-autistic spectrum may appear worrying – it disturbs convenient ideas of 'autistic' or 'disabled' – but time and again life writing by those with autism illustrates this kind of variation. Williams, with a need for openness in her learning and dislike of categorized 'truly right or wrong answers',[45] is a world away from the more supposedly conventional autistic/Aspergic scholarly concentration on mathematics and science, such as that found in Daniel Tammet's memoir *Born on a Blue Day* (2006).[46] Likewise, Grandin's accounts of the personal relations in her life are nothing like those of Kamran Nazeer's *Send in the Idiots* (2006), in which Nazeer tracks down former classmates from his childhood special school and writes of them with an empathy that makes his memoir more a collection of biographies.[47]

The places where autistic lives do *not* show this kind of range are, of course, those created from outside the condition itself. In the mainstream news media and in the majority of fictional representations (across different media), autism is far more fixed and coherent than in the life accounts described above. In these narratives, autistic presence is predictably characterized by a succession of stereotypes, aspects of characterization and narrative function that work by reducing the multiplicities of the autistic subject to the portrayal of a type that is repeated, sometimes with subtle variations and occasionally with additions, across stories. From reading and watching the representation of autism in fictions, we might surmise that such narratives are simply unable to handle the spectrum of autistic subjectivity and presence. Instead, we have a characterization of both the autistic individual and the condition itself that, like the use of so many other forms of disability in narrative, is ultimately about issues only tangentially connected to autism itself.

Consider a couple of examples from novels. In David Lodge's *Thinks*
(2001), Oliver, an autistic teenage boy, is a minor character, obsessive
('He never forgets a name. Especially anyone who's been on television')
and – stereotypically – one who can only tell the truth ('Oliver doesn't
tell lies…. He doesn't understand the concept').[48] In Vikas Swarup's
*Q&A* (2005), Shankar – another minor character – is a young boy with
'friendship and curiosity and warmth and welcome' in his 'expressive
brown eyes', but who has a particularly unique form of expression.
When asked for directions by central protagonist Ram Mohammad
Thomas, Shankar replies 'Ykhz Sqpd Hz. Q Fiks X Ckka Lgxyz', while
'flapping his hands'.[49] In both texts the characters' autism is straight-
forwardly used, both to define the individuals in question in a form of
totality (all their characteristics relevant to the plot extend from their
autism) and to act as refractive points of comparison for the novels'
central characters and plot concerns. In *Thinks*, the central character,
Ralph Messenger, is a cognitive scientist, pursuing research into the
mind, who is also serially unfaithful to his wife. Oliver, in his brief
appearance, provides both source material for Messenger's musings
on the brain as well as, in his fidelity to the truth, an unfortunate
witness to Messenger's philandering. In *Q&A*, Mohammad Thomas
avoids arrest by the police by mimicking Shankar's speech, prompting
his would be arresting officer to observe 'We won't get anything out
of a lunatic' as he is released. At the end of the novel, Shankar himself
dies a 'horrible death' after contracting rabies.[50]

These are only two of the many instances of fictional characters
with autism who feature in contemporary fiction as minor diversions,
flitting across readers' attentions to work in terms of metaphor and
analogy. Such moments work to confirm autism as the current cultural
condition of choice when some marker of fascination or difference is
required to make a narrative enact a particular twist. This kind of use
seems a long way from the claims many disability studies theorists
make for the subversive presence of disabled characters in fiction. In
contrast, there seems little distinction in the sorts of characterization
exemplified by Lodge and Swarup from the stock use of impaired
and 'idiot' characters of previous centuries (on which see chapter 2).
Autism is always an exposed, intelligible phenomenon in such stories,
always readable and capable of translation, and always packaged for a
certain kind of consumption as a result.

What such narratives remove, of course, is the agency of the individual with autism, exactly the issue that is so crucial to the life
stories. Making such agency a possibility involves placing the autistic
character at or near the centre of the fiction, a process which is at

odds with the metaphoric usefulness of autism so common to the majority of narratives that employ representations of the condition. The one work of contemporary fiction that does go out of its way to establish such a centrality is Mark Haddon's *The Curious Incident of the Dog in the Night-Time*, a book so successful that it can be held to be indirectly responsible for the surfeit of autistic characters that have appeared in novels since its publication in 2003. Haddon's novel is about many things – masculinity, family, the social make-up of modern Britain – some of which will be explored in the chapters that follow, but it is driven by the power of its central narration – the voice of fifteen-year-old Christopher. Interestingly, at no point in the narrative does Haddon (or indeed Christopher himself) inform the reader that Christopher is autistic, but it is a point made on the jacket of most editions, with Oliver Sacks praising the novel's 'great insight into the autistic mind' on the cover of the first hardback edition. Equally, Christopher's descriptions of his own behaviour, his likes and dislikes, are clearly suggestive of an autistic presence to anyone with even a passing knowledge of the condition.

Christopher is clear about how he wishes to assert his presence and sense of self. Early on in the novel he discusses his own name in terms of a specific agency:

> My name is a metaphor. It means *carrying Christ* and it comes from the Greek words χριστος (which means *Jesus Christ*) and Φεριν and it was a name given to St. Christopher because he carried Jesus Christ across a river.
>
> This makes you wonder what he was called before he carried Christ across the river. But he wasn't called anything because this is an apocryphal story which means that it is a lie, too.
>
> Mother used to say that it meant Christopher was a nice name because it was a story about being kind and helpful, but I do not want my name to mean a story about being kind and helpful. I want my name to mean me.[51]

In wanting 'my name to mean me', Christopher is asserting his desire to be singular and to resist metaphor. He does not want to be 'explained away' or translated. As such, implicitly the novel makes a similar claim about his autism. It, too, does not 'mean' that which is beyond its various manifestations, and much of *The Curious Incident of the Dog in the Night-Time* carefully plots the ways in which Christopher's autism is first and foremost about his own character. Loosely, the novel's chapters alternate between those that advance the story and those that give us information about Christopher's various likes and dislikes – the colours of cars, timetables, Sherlock Holmes, the colours brown and yellow – and his particular way of reading the world: 'I see everything', he asserts in a tone both factual and superior, 'But most people are lazy. They never look at everything.... And the information in their head is really simple'.[52] By way of contrast, Christopher's world is complex and his autism, which he takes for granted because it is the basis of his self, is folded into his character as a natural element that resists the kinds of external interpretations that reduce the condition to the status of metaphor.

Haddon's creation of Christopher's presence is itself complex. Because *The Curious Incident of the Dog in the Night-Time* is a fiction, it does not conform to the kind of formations we observed as being central to the life writing. As a successful *novel*, Haddon's book does offer opportunities to be read metaphorically, but there is a crucial difference between this and creating a use of autism in such a mode. Indeed, part of the novel's achievement is that, for all it appears to come from a 'limited' singular viewpoint, it can be read as being 'about' all manner of topics genuinely unconnected to autism, or disability, or ideas of neurobehavioural difference. Readers might see the book as an account of the atomization of people in contemporary British society, or a subtle investigation of the pressures within a modern family, and these readings can be made without *necessarily* seeing them only in the light of an autistic narration. To this end, *The Curious Incident of the Dog in the Night-Time* is that rare thing in a disability text, a book both suffused by a disabled viewpoint but one that normalizes that viewpoint to the extent that, it can be argued, the disability vanishes. Intriguingly, such a position becomes possible precisely because Haddon's novel is a *fiction*; the rules of creative licence allow for a neatness in the presentation of Christopher's life that is absent from the real lives of Grandin or Williams. The imaginative fiction of the book also facilitates the presentation of a disability that can cohere in terms of the ideological arguments it wishes to make.

We might observe, especially in the light of reading autistic autobiography, that Christopher's created presence is too uniform: his tone and outlook rarely deviate, and he possesses a consistency as a narrator that no text written by someone with autism can rival. In part, this is because Haddon creates Christopher to resonate with the public's general awareness of what autism is and how it works. So, if we can say that the non-specialist idea of the condition in the general cultural environment is that an individual with autism is over-literal, 'emotionless' or 'robotic', then the novel mirrors this in aspects of its narrative voice. In the same way, Christopher's interests in cars, space, maths and timetables, and his assertion that 'my memory is like a film', fit with public stereotypes of autistic 'topics', and Haddon is careful to include aspects of the condition that will be familiar in this way.[53] Christopher is not a savant, but he is close enough to such a characterization to remind readers of what they might think they know about those with autism. This is, of course, a very delicate balancing act. Overstressing the stereotypical elements would tip the novel into the kind of exploitation of the condition that Haddon clearly wishes to avoid; yet to make Christopher work as a character, he needs to be recognizable enough to a readership that has only the passing relationship with autism that comes with the general cultural (mis)representation of the condition. Perhaps Haddon's success can be measured in those moments where he obviously plays both cards at once. 'This will not be a funny book', Christopher asserts. 'I cannot tell jokes because I do not understand them'.[54] Yet the book is alive with endless examples of humour, the kind of humour that comes precisely because of Christopher's oblique take on the world he inhabits. For many, there is nothing funny about autism, but anyone who has an association with the condition knows this is not true, and to deny a relationship between autism and humour is to deny it a basic humanity. Equally, in ordering his story, Christopher (and therefore Haddon) chooses to label his chapters with prime numbers (2, 3, 5, 7, 11 …) and not the usual cardinal progression (1, 2, 3, 4, 5 …). Prime numbers are unique yet ubiquitous. They are, suggestively, an *apt* metaphor for autism – individual and special, yet everywhere. As Christopher himself says of them: 'Prime numbers are what is left when you have taken all the patterns away. I think prime numbers are like life. They are very logical but you could never work out the rules, even if you spent all your time thinking about them.'[55]

What *The Curious Incident of the Dog in the Night-Time* includes, and what is so often missing from accounts of autism, is an idea of pleasure. Nearly all the stories that circulate about the condition are of difficulties, of screams and rage, of despair. It is frequently referred to, especially in the public media, as tragic, a terrible and cruel absence of so much that makes being human the most familiar wonder we know. The idea that anything associated with this could in any way contain pleasure seems too perverse, too contradictory. Yet in many ways autism centres on an idea of pleasure. The pleasure of the straight line of toys, of the endlessly repeated video, of that bit of wallpaper – all these are common to those who have associations with autism. And it is vital to stress that this pleasure should not necessarily be seen in terms of a negative habit, a fixation that keeps the pain of the rest of the world at bay, a prop. While the difficulties that can come with the condition are not to be denied, often there are manifestations of pure and simple pleasure, something loved for itself. Mr Jeavons, Christopher's school psychologist, believes that Christopher likes maths 'because it was safe' and because 'there was always a straightforward answer at the end', an idea that presupposes the subject as a kind of support. But, as Christopher asserts, 'Mr Jeavons was wrong ... and numbers are sometimes very complicated and not very straightforward at all', and it is exactly this complexity that is the basis of the attraction he feels towards the subject.[56] Christopher's 'likes' in the novel are pleasures; he likes *The Hound of the Baskervilles* and Sherlock Holmes because 'if I were a proper detective he is the kind of detective I would be. He is very intelligent and he solves the mystery.'[57] In this sense, Christopher's sense of pleasure is similar to that reported in autistic life writing. The kind of essentially personal activity Grandin describes when she uses her 'squeeze machine', her homemade device that applies physical pressure evenly over her body, is idiosyncratic and may appear odd to outsiders, but it is clearly a point about pleasure and preference.[58]

Subtle and intelligent though *The Curious Incident of the Dog in the Night-Time* is, it is perhaps not *the* great literary text of autistic presence. That honour properly belongs to Herman Melville's story 'Bartleby the Scrivener', first published in the November and December issues of *Putnam's Monthly Magazine* in 1853.[59] To make such an assertion, especially to choose a text from a period before autism was a diagnosable condition, might seem counterintuitive. As we saw with the discussion of Kanner, Asperger and the original formations of the medical concept of autism, there are many specific reasons to see the condition as one that is tied to a series of twentieth-century contexts from which its clinical delineation emerged. Yet noting the processes through which autism was named and acquired its current diagnostic formations does not suppress the need to attempt to locate the ways in which the condition was represented before the 1940s. For all that there is much about autism that is tied into the contemporary period, and even taking into account the talk about recent 'epidemics', it is not what Showalter terms a 'mimetic disorder', one that 'mimics culturally permissible expressions of distress'.[60] As a neurological condition, autism has been, in one form of another, an ever-present part of human history. Without a name, or bound up with a different name ('idiocy', 'retardation'), it has not been absent from any population. We should, therefore, not be surprised to find representations from before the twentieth century in which we can read a sense of autistic presence; and even if there are great complexities involved in untangling the workings of such representations, that does not mean we should not attempt to do so. Retrospective diagnosis is, as mentioned in the Introduction, a fraught process that is all too open to the abuse of the lazy claim, but it can also be a radical critical intervention that is enlightening in extending the parameters of how we understand and read disability.

Melville's story is acknowledged as one of the classic pieces of short fiction in the American canon, discussed and analysed from multiple critical viewpoints from the mid-twentieth century onwards (it was well beyond Melville's death in 1891 that the full value of his writing began to be appreciated). The tale itself is narrated by an unambitious lawyer, a figure who describes himself as 'an eminently *safe* man' who 'has been filled with a profound conviction that the easiest way of life is the best' (p. 14). With the expansion of his work, he takes on an extra copyist to help with the production of legal documents. The copyist is Bartleby, a man with no known origins, but one who settles down well to his job. However, over time, Bartleby begins to withdraw from the workings of the office. He initially refuses to sit with the lawyer and go over documents, and subsequently refuses to do any copying at all. He then stops work altogether and refuses to leave the office. Faced with the embarrassment of this increasingly still and silent figure in his office (Bartleby comes to move less and less as the story progresses), especially in front of his peers, the lawyer actually moves office to 'rid himself' of Bartleby. But Bartleby remains in the old office until he is forcibly removed, arrested as a vagrant, and taken to the Halls of Justice, where he dies after refusing any food.

I want to claim that 'Bartleby the Scrivener' presents a radical narrative of autistic presence, and that it does so some ninety years before the condition began to be recognized within the terms of clinical medicine (at the time of the story's composition, the attitude towards disability in the US involved both exclusion and education, with the creation of numerous institutions which in fact served to harbour the poor as much as care for the impaired).[61] There are two aspects to this claim. The first is that the representation of Bartleby is recognizably that of an autistic individual and that the text offers a clear account of autistic behaviour. The narrator's descriptions of Bartleby time and again echo the description of impairments – of communication, imagination and socialization – that would come to be central to twentieth-century outlines of autism. The second element to the claim is what we might call the critical consequences that come with the admission of the fact of a narrative autistic presence, namely the manner in which Bartleby's subject position then determines the various analytical interpretations that can be mobilized in discussions of the story as a whole.

Firstly, the details of Bartleby's fictional autism. At the very beginning of the story we are told: 'Bartleby was one of those beings of
whom nothing is ascertainable, except from original sources' (p. 13).
He is, as it were, a literal version of himself, and the text of his presence fails to extend beyond those points of contact he makes with the
narrator: 'What my own astonished eyes saw of Bartleby, *that* is all
I know of him' (p. 13). The corporeality of this presence – Bartleby
never seems to go anywhere – means that he is incapable of being
discussed by analogy or metaphor – '*he was always there*' (p. 26) the
narrator says in an uncanny and almost precise prefiguration of the
phrases Kanner and Asperger would use nearly a century later when
describing their patients. As a scrivener, he is, of course, a copyist, a
role supposedly devoid of any necessary imagination, but rather one
rooted in mimicry. On his arrival at the narrator's office he is described
as 'a motionless young man' (p. 19). He possesses a 'great stillness'
and an 'unalterableness of demeanour under all circumstances' (p. 26)
that signify a particular physical, perhaps sensory, engagement with
his environment; he has an 'austere reserve about him' (p. 28) and,
when working, 'sat in his hermitage, oblivious to everything but his
own peculiar business there' (p. 23). In conversation, his words and
manner are marked by difference. His tone is 'flute-like' (p. 22) and,
when called into the lawyer's office to explain his actions, he does
not make eye contact (a common autistic behaviour), but rather
'kept his glance fixed upon my bust of Cicero, which as I then sat,
was directly behind me, some six inches above my head' (p. 30). His
conversation is literal – when the narrator finds him still in the office
after the firm has vacated the premises (the lawyer describes Bartleby
'silently sitting upon the banister at the landing') and asks him what
he is doing there, he receives the reply: 'Sitting upon the banister'
(p. 40). Bartleby works 'mechanically' (p. 20) and obsessively without
a break, devoted to the detail of his copying. He has no appetite, no
friends or family, cannot bear any change in his routine and, it seems,
possesses no social communication or interaction skills whatsoever.
He seems 'absolutely alone in the universe' (p. 32), an 'intolerable
incubus' (p. 38) who never leaves the office (even when the office
leaves him), and both in the office and the Halls of Justice sits or
stands passively facing a high wall. By the end of the story, in the
yard of the Halls of Justice he is 'strangely huddled at the base of the
wall, his knees drawn up, and lying on his side, his head touching the
cold stones' (p. 44), withdrawn from all human interaction. Finally,
in a fascinating example of a textual excess, with a nod to the idea
of the savant skills so associated with autism, the prison grub-man,

Mr Cutlets, introduces himself to Bartleby as 'your sarvant, sir, your sarvant' (p. 44).

This is not a realistic depiction of a person with autism, of course, and even as I cite these details I do not propose that they form some kind of diagnostic fact sheet against which Bartleby's autism might be measured. But these observations *are* part of a compelling fiction, with carefully constructed characteristics that mark Bartleby as a figure of significant difference, especially in terms of social behaviour. And it is arguably a point of observation, more than one of critical interpretation, that his characteristics map onto a general template of autistic subjectivity. Bartleby undoubtedly performs what we today can recognize as an autistic presence.

Bartleby's key action in the story is to assert his preference. When first asked to come into the narrator's office to help examine a document, 'in a singularly mild, firm voice' he replies simply: 'I would prefer not to' (p. 20). It is a phrase he repeats, with slight changes, some twenty-two times throughout the story, his final act of preference being to decline an offer of food at the Halls of Justice (p. 44), after which he seemingly wastes away to his death. Bartleby's statement is an irruptive force, especially because it is an assertion of the *positive*. His preference is not a response that should be read as a defence mechanism, and Bartleby himself draws a subtle distinction between '*prefer* not' and '*will* not' (and never suggests that he 'cannot') when responding to the lawyer (p. 25). At different times, the narrator's response to this act of preference is to be 'stunned' (p. 20), 'turned into a pillar of salt' (p. 21), 'ignominiously repulsed' (p. 25), 'mortified' (p. 30) and thrown into 'a state of nervous resentment' (p. 36). In trying to deal with Bartleby's presence, the lawyer moves through a range of emotions, from pity and sympathy to revulsion and rage. He convinces himself that the problem of Bartleby is one of solitude: 'His poverty is great; but his solitude, how horrible!' (p. 27) and, later, that 'his body did not pain him; it was his soul that suffered, and his soul I could not reach' (p. 29), or that 'he had now become a millstone to me, not only useless as a necklace, but afflictive to bear' (p. 32). Bartleby's singularity produces a multitude of differing responses from the narrator, whose readings and attempted explanations of his copyist's presence betray his anxiety and unsettlement.

However, as I intimated earlier, the textual evidence is only half of the reason we might think of this story as a radical narrative of autistic presence. The story's ultimate sense of a negotiation between majority and autistic perspectives comes less from a recognition of the details of Bartleby's presence, striking though they are, and more from

the explanatory narratives that are offered as possible reasons for his
behaviour.[62] In his confused attempts to explain Bartleby's behaviour,
the narrator works through different categories of potential norms in
order to establish a meaning for his employee's actions. When, in her
study of representations of physical disabilities in American culture and
literature, *Extraordinary Bodies*, Rosemarie Garland-Thomson defines
the term 'normate' to refer to what she terms 'the veiled subject position of cultural self, the figure outlined by the array of deviant others
whose marked bodies shore up the normate's boundaries', we can see
that the lawyer's various reactions to Bartleby form exactly such an
idea of self in opposition to his scrivener's seeming 'deviancy'.[63] It is,
in the end, the *lawyer's* presence that threatens to become destabilized
by the consequences of Bartleby's preference, and in all the bluster
of his various expressions – from his seeming sympathy and concern
to his rage and lack of comprehension – he necessarily has to build
a sense of a norm, configured in terms of both his own person and
(crucially) his business, that can oppose the threat Bartleby appears
to pose. There is little doubt that this idea of a unified sense of self is
vital to the story. Whatever the reading of Bartleby and *his* presence, it
is striking that the lawyer's two other copyists – Turkey and Nippers –
display characteristics, what the narrator terms 'self-indulgent habits'
(p. 18), that suggest that the two form some kind of schizoid sense of
a single person. Turkey is 'the civilest, nay the blandest and most rever-
ential of men in the morning, yet in the afternoon he was disposed,
upon provocation, to be slightly rash with his tongue, in fact insolent'
(pp. 15–16), while for his part Nippers is full of an 'irritability and
constant nervousness' (p. 18), but only in the morning. As the lawyer
remarks: 'Their fits relieved each other like guards. When Nippers' was
on, Turkey's was off; and *vice versa*' (p. 18). Such a situation is deemed
'a good natural arrangement under the circumstances' (p. 18). The
lawyer has, as it were, one functioning employee between the two, so
the business of the office is not disturbed. Bartleby's autistic constancy
and repetition, on the other hand, are genuine threats to the necessary
norms of both the lawyer and his work.

In the broader context of reading the story, however, we can see
that the many interpretive critical narratives that discuss the story
offer any number of potentially persuasive and cogently argued, but
nevertheless *normate*, accounts of the story's meaning. The genius
of the story is what is done with the various spaces, physical and
textual, that the presence of Bartleby opens up. As Melville scholars
have noted for decades, and as Robert S. Levine comments in his
introduction to *The Cambridge Companion to Herman Melville*, his best

fiction assumes 'a metacritical role of guiding and challenging readers' responses to his works by foregrounding issues of interpretation'.[64] In overt narrative terms, 'Bartleby' the story leaves the space of autistic presence undisclosed and open, and invites interpretations that might make sense of it.[65] So, among the many critical readings of the story there are narratives of: legal codification (working in a law office on issues of legal tenancy, amongst others, Bartleby is arrested and taken to prison for vagrancy); economic codification (Bartleby is bad for business because he cannot be removed from the premises), which also offers a wider critique of capitalism (the subtitle of the story is 'A Story of Wall Street', and reflects the walled street that Bartleby gazes upon); religious codification (the narrator notes that possibly 'Bartleby was billeted upon me for some mysterious purpose of an all-wise Providence', p. 37); humanitarian concern ('Poor fellow, poor fellow! Thought I, he don't mean any thing; and besides, he has seen hard times, and ought to be indulged', p. 36); and finally, in the epilogue, philosophical speculation ('Ah Bartleby! Ah humanity!', p. 45).

Criticism of Melville's story has followed these various routes, from Marxist interpretations through to biographical readings, reader response theories, psychoanalytical studies and assertions of parallels with religion or philosophy. To take just a few of the many examples, for Wyn Kelly in the 1996 study *Melville's City*, 'Bartleby' 'seems a straightforward account of the class struggle', in which the key interpretive category is the complex nature of housing laws that the story presents, and the ways in which Bartleby's claim to possession unsettles the subject position of the lawyer/narrator.[66] For Cindy Weinstein, Bartleby's preference is a point about labour, both that in the law office and the labour of writing itself, and reception. Bartleby's refusal to work asserts his right to keep the 'originality that cannot be copied', and the author's complex narrative strategies 'reflect at once Melville's decision not to capitulate to his critics and to find for himself a narrative position which protects him from personal violation'.[67]

It is probably Melville's complex engagement with an Emersonian tradition that works best in looking for a contemporary nineteenth-century philosophy through which to read the story, and for all of Melville's well documented antipathies to Ralph Waldo Emerson's thinking, there is no doubt that it is productive to read 'Bartleby' within the terms of a conversation with, and indeed a possible revision of, Emerson's ideas. In texts such as the 1841 essay 'Self-Reliance' and the later *Society and Solitude* (1870), Emerson outlined the ways in which society conspires to frustrate the subject's attempt to express his individuality. In 'Self-Reliance' he notes:

> Society everywhere is in conspiracy against the manhood of every one
> of its members. Society is a joint-stock company in which the members
> agree for the better securing of his bread to each share-holder, to sur-
> render the liberty and culture of the eater. The virtue in most request is
> conformity. Self-reliance is its aversion.[68]

In relation to a consideration of 'Bartleby', Emerson's account of the
selfhood necessary for individual fulfilment bears an uncanny resem-
blance to the subject position the scrivener comes to occupy:

> There is a time in every man's education when he arrives at the con-
> viction that envy is ignorance; that imitation is suicide; that he must
> take himself for better, or worse, as his portion; that though the wide
> universe is full of good, no kernel of nourishing corn can come to him
> but through his toil bestowed on that plot of ground which is given to
> him to till.[69]

Intriguingly, as a model for agency, such sentiments as these outline
a potential subject position for neurobehavioural difference as much
as the possibly more obvious majority, non-disabled, context, but in
thinking about Melville's engagement, and indeed contestation, with
Emerson, the majority of critics invoke the paradigm of a specific
concept of individual liberalism. For many, then, the story becomes
either an account of subjectivity framed by a detailed nineteenth-
century American context, or an outline of what Linda Constanza
Cahir calls 'Melville's prototypic Mysterious Stranger'. Cahir goes
on to note: 'For Melville, the mystery of Bartleby – the mystery of
the essential nature of a particular person – is an eternal, implacable
ambiguity, and our existential alienation from one another is a reality
whose cause we can never fully apprehend or overturn'.[70] Here, in the
grandest traditions of classic literature, the key explanatory category
is a universal humanism.

The Emersonian dimension to the story is entirely logical and
appropriate, but, in keeping with Melville's critique of what he took
to be Emerson's over-optimistic philosophy, it is possible to turn
the idea of 'Bartleby' as a radical narrative of autistic presence back
on to Emerson, and to see in Emerson's own language a description of the objectification and discrimination of the impaired by the
social majority. When, in 'Self-Reliance', Emerson observes 'for non-
conformity the world whips you with its displeasure. And therefore
a man must know how to estimate a sour face. The bystanders look
askance on him in the public street or in the friend's parlor',[71] the
language is exactly that which parallels the prejudiced gaze experienced
on a daily basis by those with disabilities. And, as Garland-Thomson
has noted, Emerson's essays repeatedly return to figures of disability

in order to provide a contrast with his asserted model of the working, self-governing self. Though she concentrates on physical impairments and especially on an idea of the body as a vehicle for the expression of American ideals, Garland-Thomson's observations work in terms of the cognitive and behavioural differences embodied within Bartleby. As she says of Emerson's thesis of liberalism individualism:

> Just as the dominant culture's ideal self requires the ideological figures of the woman to confirm its masculinity and of the black to assure its whiteness, so Emerson's atomized self demands an oppositional twin to secure its able-bodiedness. The freak, the cripple, the invalid, the disabled – like the quadroon and the homosexual – are representational, taxonomical products that naturalize a norm comprised of accepted bodily traits and behaviors registering social power and status…. With the body's threat of betrayal thus compartmentalized, the mythical American self can unfold, unobstructed and unrestrained, according to its own manifest destiny.[72]

The lawyer's sense of self is most definitely not 'mythical', and it is here that we can possibly see how Bartleby's neurobehavioural difference carries Melville's critique of Emerson's ideas. The lawyer's vanity and self-serving narration mock any idea of a heroic individuality, and Bartleby's disabled difference here works to point to exactly the shortcomings in the nineteenth-century thesis of American progress. In the story, Bartleby's autism threatens to unravel the secure, individualized sense of 'destiny'. He is a deeply radical figure.

Seen in this way, we can also claim that Bartleby's autistic presence works to provide an alternative to all the various majority culture's critical explanatory narratives. The story's presentation of this presence works to turn ideas of Melvillean interpretation back on themselves, as the various possible explanations of Bartleby's actions become contextualized as accounts based in mistaken, non-disabled theses when seen in the light of a logic of autistic presence. It is not so much that these explanatory narratives are red herrings, but rather that their varying uses are themselves contained by what I would suggest is the overriding force of the story's central hermeneutic location (as opposed to its narrative location) *within* the parameters of autistic presence. While it is very much the case that the majority of disabled characters in literary texts – Ahab in *Moby Dick*, Tiny Tim in *A Christmas Carol*, to take two other nineteenth-century examples – are given meaning from ideological positions outside their narrative sources, Bartleby's impairment remains at a crucial level unavailable to both the lawyer and the reader. He is incorrectly read in the story itself, and a challenge to the reading process in terms of its reception.

So, the very sense of the story's meaning is bound up with an idea of the autistic difference it presents. Of course, it can be claimed that the fiction's metacritical openness means that a reading of Bartleby as having autism is simply *one* of the possible interpretational versions of the tale, but the claim that a disabled difference animates the workings of the story as a *foundational* category is, I think, sustainable. Bartleby's autism *orders* Melville's tale and it can, and does, outflank and contextualize other readings of the scrivener's presence. In an interesting article that centres on the idea of Bartleby as a spectre or apparition (it is noticeable that the lawyer says at the start of the story that Bartleby '*appeared* to me' [my emphasis]), Naomi C. Reed notes that a reading of the copyist in this way reminds us 'of what current critics of the story seem to have forgotten: that Bartleby is strange', and that many such critics 'sacrifice Bartleby's strangeness by making him into a representative'.[73] Reed's article puts forward a new Marxist reading of how Bartleby disrupts commodities, but her understanding of his essential *difference* has parallels with a reading of his autistic presence, especially in the ways in which it emphasizes an idea of critical 'forgetting'. And, building on Reed's second observation here, I would stress that to see Bartleby as having autism is not to stress he is *representative* of the condition – he is too non-realistic for that – but that the idea of difference he embodies travels throughout the story, disrupting as it goes. In addition, and here one might take exception to Reed's thesis, seeing Bartleby as having a neurobehavioural condition stresses his humanity (a loaded word that is the last of the story itself) in a way that her account of him as an apparition does not. It is all too easy to see Bartleby as a figure 'who scarcely qualifies as a human being', as Andre Furlani does in a 1997 article on the story.[74] What such a criticism ignores, because it is blind to the nature of its presence, is that a disabled difference might be a different kind of humanity.

The narrator's conjecture, in the story's epilogue, about the despair Bartleby 'must' encounter in the Dead Letter Office, where he hears Bartleby had previously worked, is perhaps the last great narrative-critical act of the tale, where the lawyer (now not having the physical presence of Bartleby to hand) creates a meaning that allows for the philosophical speculation at the end:

> Yet here I hardly know whether I should divulge one little item of rumor, which came to my ear a few months after the scrivener's decease. Upon what basis it rested, I could never ascertain; and hence, how true it is I cannot now tell. But inasmuch as this vague report has not been without a certain strange suggestive interest to me, however said, it may prove the same with some others; and so I will briefly mention it. The report

was this: that Bartleby had been a subordinate clerk in the Dead Letter Office in Washington, from which he had been suddenly removed by a change in the administration. When I think over this rumor, I cannot adequately express the emotions which seize me. Dead letters! does it not sound like dead men? Conceive a man by nature and misfortune prone to a pallid hopelessness, can any business seem more fitted to heighten it than that of continually handling these dead letters, and assorting them for the flames?... Ah Bartleby! Ah humanity! (p. 45)

So, despite the continual presence of Bartleby in the lawyer's office, his corporeality, habits and language, it becomes far easier for the lawyer to settle upon a 'rumor', a 'vague report', of Bartleby having worked at the Dead Letter Office, from which to construct an overarching narrative of appropriate humanitarian concern, which allows him to close his version of Bartleby's story. But the story itself, of course, travels further than its narrator. The lawyer remains unaware of the nature of the presence he has encountered, for all his various attempts at explanation.

The fact that Bartleby dies at the end of the story does not necessarily suggest that autistic presence cannot be contained in the world, but can only waste away. Certainly, this is a valid reading of the story's conclusion. But this is, at all times, a radical narrative. Set against the possibility that the story is a narrative of exclusion, in which the impaired are denied a place in an evolving codified and capitalist society, is the clear fact that this is a tale about agency and will. It is surely no coincidence that, in a casual aside describing his 'leisure intervals', the lawyer informs the reader that he has been reading Jonathan Edwards' 1754 *Freedom of the Will* and Joseph Priestley's 1777 *Doctrine of Philosophical Necessity*, both texts which argue that the will is *not* free (p. 37). The narrator, so wrong about so many things in the story, is here reading the wrong texts about will and agency, a fact that is deeply ironic given his proximity to Bartleby throughout the story. Bartleby turns his back on the world, a world that clearly does not accord with his preferences, but he does so in terms he has dictated, his life – and arguably even death – a marker of a self-declared presence. For all the metacritical status of the story, and all the provisionality of any reading of 'Bartleby', it is perfectly justifiable to prefer this reading of the conclusion.

## IV

Bartleby works as a vital and radical marker of autistic presence because, like the condition itself and like the children examined by Kanner and Asperger, as well as the various proponents of autistic agency and difference who write about their lives, he *won't go away*. In the manner in which Bartleby as a character who articulates a positive preference combines with the narrative's own refusal to offer an outside definition of the difference of that presence, Melville's story recounts a working representation of autism's possibilities. The individual who won't go away is the condition that needs to be understood, an observation that links the nineteenth century to the contemporary, even as we acknowledge the story's pre-dating of the medical codification of autism. Bartleby is provocative. I like to think of him as being aligned with disability rights activists like Amanda Baggs, who, for all that they might inspire confrontation and even anger, are determined to present their lives on their own terms as they understand them. They assert both their preferences and their presence, knowing that they belong to a minority that will almost certainly be misunderstood.

The truth is, of course, that such assertions are themselves in a minority. It was important to start this study with accounts of positive presence because by far the majority of representations of the condition work in very different ways. Much of what follows in the chapters to come will be seeking to unpack and understand *mis*representations, even if the narratives in question mean well. It was important especially to listen to the voices of those with autism, like Grandin and Williams, because the majority of commentaries on the condition presume that those who are autistic are *not* listening, or reading, or watching. The disabled are talked *about* a lot but rarely conversed *with*. With autism, it is often the assumption that those with the condition are incapable of such conversations and communications. This is, of course, simply not true; even severely impaired, non-verbal, autistic individuals communicate. What these individuals say must be the first source of any understanding of the ways in which the condition functions in the world. Neurology and psychiatry have much to say about the specific formations of autism, its origins and manifestations, but it is in listening to those who live with and in the condition that the outlines of what it means to *be* autistic are most manifest. In discussing all the other ways in which the condition is portrayed, it will be good to bear this in mind.

## Notes

1  See http://www.autism-watch.org/general/dsm.shtml. Accessed 1 July 2007. See also the print version, *Diagnostic and Statistical Manual of Mental Disorders*, fourth edition (*DSM–IV*) (Washington, DC: American Psychiatric Association, 1994).
2  Douglas Biklen, *Autism and the Myth of the Person Alone* (New York: New York University Press, 2005), p. 36.

3  See http://www.opednews.com/articles/opedne_vin_lopr_070629_autism_and_9_11_3a_the.htm and http://www.belfasttelegraph.co.uk/news/opinion/article 2721215.ece. Accessed 1 July 2007.

4  Niall Ferguson, 'America has got Asperger's syndrome', *Daily Telegraph*, 25 May 2004. Available online at http://www.telegraph.co.uk/opinion/main.jhtml?xml=/opinion/2004/05/25/do2502.xml. Accessed 8 July 2004.

5  In its reporting of the killing by Cho of thirty-two people on 16 April 2007, the *Daily Mirror*, on 20 April, reported that Cho was 'diagnosed with autism as an eight-year old', an assertion seemingly taken from a family member and which has no material evidence to substantiate it.

6  Elaine Showalter, *Hystories: Hysterical Epidemics and Modern Culture* (New York: Columbia University Press, 1997), pp. 3–13.

7  Ian Hacking, *The Social Construction of What?* (Cambridge, MA: Harvard University Press, 1999), p. 118.

8  Laura Schreibman, *The Science and Fiction of Autism* (Cambridge, MA: Harvard University Press, 2005), p. 54. Bleuler's initial account of his patients can be found in 'Die prognose der Dementia Praecox (Schizophreniegruppe)', *Allgemeine Zeitschrift fur Psychiatrie und Psychisch-Gerichtliche Medizin*, no. 65 (1908), pp. 436–64.

9  Leo Kanner, 'Autistic disturbances of affective contact', *Nervous Child*, no. 2 (1943), p. 242 and p. 245 – italics in original. The article is reprinted in A. M. Donnellan (ed.), *Classic Readings in Autism* (New York: Teachers College, Columbia University, 1985).

10  Kanner, 'Autistic disturbances of affective contact', p. 250.

11  Biklen, *Autism and the Myth of the Person Alone*, p. 34.

12  Majia Holmer Nadesan, *Constructing Autism: Unravelling the 'Truth' and Understanding the Social* (New York: Routledge, 2005), pp. 29–53.

13  Respectively, autistic spectrum disorder, obsessive-compulsive disorder, attention deficit hyperactivity disorder, attention deficit disorder, pervasive developmental disorder.

14  For the ways in which some of these terms became the staple terminology of eugenics movements, see Sharon L. Snyder and David T. Mitchell, *Cultural Locations of Disability* (Chicago, IL: University of Chicago Press, 2006), p. 19.

15  Kanner, 'Autistic disturbances of affective contact', p. 247.

16  Hans Asperger, '"Autistic psychopathy" in childhood', in Uta Frith (ed. and trans.), *Autism and Asperger Syndrome* (Cambridge: Cambridge University Press, 1991), p. 38.

17  Biklen, *Autism and the Myth of the Person Alone*, p. 46.

18  A. M. Baggs, 'In My Language', http://www.youtube.com/watch?v=JnylM1hI2jc. Accessed 31 May 2007.

19  See http://ballastexistenz.autistics.org/?page_id=2 for Baggs' own description of her decision to use this term. Accessed 4 June 2007. See also http://www.gettingthetruthout.org. Accessed 5 December 2005.

20  Temple Grandin, *Thinking in Pictures, And Other Reports from My Life with Autism*, second edition (London: Bloomsbury, 2006); Temple Grandin and Margaret M. Scariano, *Emergence: Labeled Autistic – A True Story*, second edition (New York: Warner Books, 2005).

21  Grandin, *Thinking in Pictures*, p. 31.

22  Grandin, *Thinking in Pictures*, p. 32.

23  Ralph James Savarese, *Reasonable People: A Memoir of Autism & Adoption* (New York: Other Press, 2007), pp. 199–200.

24  Grandin, *Thinking in Pictures*, p. 50.

25 Grandin, *Thinking in Pictures*, p. 167.
26 See 'Einstein's second cousin' in *Thinking in Pictures*, pp. 204–21. For the quote, see p. 122.
27 Grandin, *Thinking in Pictures*, p. 210.
28 Grandin, *Thinking in Pictures*, p. 217.
29 Grandin, *Thinking in Pictures*, p. 53.
30 Temple Grandin and Kate Duffy, *Developing Talents: Careers for Individuals with Asperger Syndrome and High-Functioning Autism* (Shawnee Mission, KS: Autism Asperger Publishing Company, 2004).
31 Grandin, *Thinking in Pictures*, p. 43.
32 David T. Mitchell and Sharon L. Snyder, 'Introduction: disability and the double bind of representation', in David T. Mitchell and Sharon L. Snyder (eds), *The Body and Physical Difference: Discourses of Disability* (Ann Arbor, MI: University of Michigan Press, 1997), p. 10.
33 Grandin, *Thinking in Pictures*, p. 50.
34 Donna Williams, *Nobody Nowhere: The Extraordinary Autobiography of an Autistic* (New York: Times Books, 1992), 'Author's note' and p. 54.
35 Williams, *Nobody Nowhere*. The untitled poem follows the book's title page and dedication.
36 Williams, *Nobody Nowhere*, pp. 101–2.
37 See Donna Williams, *Autism – An Inside-Out Approach* (London: Jessica Kingsley, 1996), pp. 1–6.
38 Biklen, *Autism and the Myth of the Person Alone*, p. 51.
39 Williams, *Nobody Nowhere*, p. 114.
40 Donna Williams, *Somebody Somewhere: Breaking Free from the World of Autism* (New York: Times Books, 1994), pp. 11–12.
41 Williams, *Somebody Somewhere*, p. 13.
42 Donna Williams, *Like Color to the Blind* (New York: Times Books, 1996).
43 'Putting autism on trial: an interview with Amanda Baggs by autistic author Donna Williams', *American Chronicle*, 5 July 2007, http://www.americanchronicle. com/articles/viewArticle.asp?articleID=31329. Accessed 9 July 2007.
44 I am grateful to Irene Rose for this information. See the appendix to her paper 'Autistic autobiography – introducing the field' (October 2005), http://www. case.edu/affil/sce/Texts_2005/Autism%20and%20Representation%20Rose. htm. Accessed 7 September 2006.
45 Williams, *Nobody Nowhere*, p. 115.
46 Daniel Tammet, *Born on a Blue Day: A Memoir of Asperger's and an Extraordinary Mind* (London: Hodder & Stoughton, 2006).
47 Kamran Nazeer, *Send in the Idiots: Stories from the Other Side of Autism* (London: Bloomsbury, 2006).
48 David Lodge, *Thinks* (London: Penguin, 2002), p. 134.
49 Vikas Swarup, *Q&A* (London: Doubleday, 2005), p. 237.
50 Swarup, *Q&A*, p. 280.
51 Mark Haddon, *The Curious Incident of the Dog in the Night-Time* (London: Jonathan Cape, 2003), p. 20.
52 Haddon, *The Curious Incident of the Dog in the Night-Time*, p. 174.
53 Haddon, *The Curious Incident of the Dog in the Night-Time*, p. 96.
54 Haddon, *The Curious Incident of the Dog in the Night-Time*, p. 10.
55 Haddon, *The Curious Incident of the Dog in the Night-Time*, p. 15.
56 Haddon, *The Curious Incident of the Dog in the Night-Time*, p. 78 and p. 82. The comments come either side of Christopher's explanation of 'The Monty Hall Problem', a notoriously deceptive mathematical problem.

57 Haddon, *The Curious Incident of the Dog in the Night-Time*, p. 92. The connection Uta Frith makes between Sherlock Holmes and autism is clearly one Haddon is aware of. See Uta Frith, *Autism: Explaining the Enigma* (Oxford: Basil Blackwell, 1989), pp. 43–4.

58 See the chapter entitled 'The squeeze machine: sensory problems in autism', in Grandin, *Thinking in Pictures*, pp. 58–83.

59 All references here are to Harrison Hayford *et al.* (eds), *The Writings of Herman Melville, Vol. 9: The Piazza Tales and Other Prose Pieces, 1839–1860* (Evanston, IL: Northwestern University Press/Newberry Library, 1987). Subsequent references are in parentheses in the text.

60 Showalter, *Hystories*, p. 15.

61 Snyder and Mitchell, *Cultural Locations of Disability*, chapter 1.

62 It is this point that differentiates my discussion here from the one critical article that does link Bartleby to autism, William P. Sullivan's 'Bartleby and infantile autism: a naturalistic explanation', published in the *Bulletin of the West Virginia Association of College English Teachers*, no. 3 (1976), pp. 170–87. Available online at http://web.ku.edu/~zeke/bartleby/sullivan.html. Accessed 3 January 2006. Sullivan notes that Bartleby displays characteristics consistent with those associated with autistic impairment and sees him as the manifestation of 'infantile autism in the adult phase … a high-functioning autistic adult'. Reading the character through the diagnostic descriptors for autism, Sullivan sees the story as one of 'pathos' and 'tragedy too, in the resonance of what might have been'. But beyond the linking of autistic behaviour with Bartleby's character (the article notes that 'It is time to merge these parallels – fascinating story and fascinating syndrome'), Sullivan does little with the implication/assertion that Bartleby might be autistic; indeed, as his title suggests, he sees Bartleby's autism as a naturalistic/realistic observation, whereas I feel it functions as a more radical point about interpretation, self and difference. Noticeably, Melville scholarship did not follow up on Sullivan's work to any degree.

63 Rosemarie Garland-Thomson, *Extraordinary Bodies: Figuring Physical Disability in American Culture and Literature* (New York: Columbia University Press, 1997), p. 8.

64 Robert S. Levine, 'Introduction', in Robert S. Levine (ed.), *The Cambridge Companion to Herman Melville* (Cambridge: Cambridge University Press, 1998), p. 3.

65 There are parallels here with Ato Quayson's reflections on the idea of disability as a hermeneutical impasse. See his *Aesthetic Nervousness: Disability and the Crisis of Representation* (New York: Columbia University Press, 2007), pp. 49–50.

66 Wyn Kelly, *Melville's City: Literary and Urban Form in Nineteenth-Century New York* (Cambridge: Cambridge University Press, 1996), pp. 201–2.

67 Cindy Weinstein, 'Melville, labor, and the discourses of reception', in Robert S. Levine (ed.), *The Cambridge Companion to Herman Melville* (Cambridge: Cambridge University Press, 1998), p. 215 and p. 216.

68 Ralph Waldo Emerson, 'Self-Reliance', in Nina Baym *et al.* (eds.), *The Norton Anthology of American Literature*, third edition (New York: Norton, 1979), vol. 1, p. 958.

69 Emerson, 'Self-Reliance', p. 956.

70 Linda Constanza Cahir, *Solitude and Society in the Works of Herman Melville and Edith Wharton* (Westport, CN: Greenwood Press, 1999), p. 58 and p. 60.

71 Emerson, 'Self-Reliance', p. 960.

72 Garland-Thomson, *Extraordinary Bodies*, p. 44.

73  Naomi C. Reed, 'The specter of Wall Street: "Bartleby the Scrivener" and the language of commodities', *American Literature*, vol. 76, no. 2 (June 2004), p. 247 and p. 265.
74  Andre Furlani, 'Bartleby the Socratic', *Studies in Short Fiction* (summer 1997). Available online at http://findarticles.com/p/articles/mi_m2455/is_3_34/ai_ 59211541. Accessed 24 July 2007.

# CHAPTER 2

# Idiots and savants

I

If autism is the neurological condition of fascination of the moment, then savantism is undoubtedly the element of autism that appears *most* fascinating. Indeed, when seen through the contemporary lens of popular representation, autism and savantism appear to have become almost synonymous, to the point where it could be asked whether it is possible to be a savant *without* also having autism, or equally whether it might be supposed that all those who are autistic possess savant abilities. These questions are more cultural than neurological, and they point to the complexities surrounding the current understanding and portrayal of autism. To untangle them requires thinking and reading practices that can work through a history of medical portrayal and that are attentive to the workings of cultural narrative.

Savant skills excite in the ways in which they represent seemingly impossible capabilities and talents; they are exceptional and 'beyond' that which is considered normal human performance. In the popular imagination, savantism is usually associated with mathematical or memory skills – the ability to name what day any particular date fell in any given year, or to calculate the cube root of a large number, or to play a piece of music after hearing it only once – and the recent past has been full of documentaries and other media accounts of those individuals capable of performing such feats, people presented as objects of a curious interest. Interest in savant ability is strangely double. On one level it involves conversations about the physical make-up of the brain – the relationship between the left and right hemispheres, or the sources of processing abilities – while on another it is an example of a fascination with a form of sleight-of-hand magic, a 'How is that done?' response to something amazing. It is both seriously scientific and frivolously entertaining at the same time.

But, in addition, savantism is seen to come at a price. The degree of awe savant talents produce is matched by the idea that these skills act to compensate for the disability with which they are associated. Hence the common attachment of the word 'idiot' to 'savant', to designate this double aspect of ability and impairment. The term 'idiot savant' itself dates from 1887, when John Langdon Down, discussing his own patients in his book *Mental Afflictions of Childhood and Youth*, used it to describe those individuals given to prodigious feats of memorization. Though the phrase has now arguably become outdated, it nevertheless retains a certain popular usage, still turning up in magazine articles and on television. Looking back less than twenty years, we can see that the term had a clear academic use as well. Michael J. A. Howe's 1989 study *Fragments of Genius* has, as its subtitle, *The Strange Feats of Idiots Savants*, and in his introduction Howe not only explains the processes by which he came to use his chosen terms, but also gives an indication of the place autism occupied in relation to ideas of the savant at the time of his writing:

> 'Idiot savant' is the term that has most frequently been used to designate mentally handicapped individuals who are capable of outstanding achievements at particular tasks, but scientists reporting on these people have also introduced a number of alternative labels. These include 'talented imbecile', 'parament', 'talented ament', 'retarded savant', 'schizophrenic savant', and 'autistic savant'. Some authors have used lengthier descriptive terms, such as 'children with circumscribed interest patterns'. Others write of the 'savant syndrome'…. Whatever the chosen forms of words, it is important to be clear that whilst having some kind of descriptive terminology is undoubtedly useful for broadly classifying people, any suggestion that the chosen term can also serve to explain their attributes should be resisted. It would be unwise, for instance, to make any explanatory inferences when terms such as 'autistic savant' or 'schizophrenic savant' are encountered. They are useful descriptive labels but really no more than that.[1]

Howe's book feels as if it comes from a different era. Phrases such as 'retarded', 'limitations', 'feeble-minded' and 'backward' litter his prose, and his case study and inquisitive method conveys the clear feeling that the subjects of which he speaks are human curiosities, only just falling short of being freak-show exhibits:

> One of the weirdest reported cases was that of a man who, although profoundly retarded to the extent that he could not even dress himself

or speak a single word, had the curious ability to spin corrugated metal dustpans and other objects on the index fingers of either of his hands.[2]

The sentiments of his observations seem clear enough, but beyond such objectification it is intriguing to see, here in the recent past, the extent to which autism and savantism were separated. As the above quote on categories demonstrates, autism takes its place in Howe's scheme alongside other terms and phrases as potential descriptive labels for savant behaviour. Schizophrenia aside, we might note how a number of these – 'circumscribed interest patterns', for example – would now fall under the umbrella of autism itself. Inadvertently, Howe's study points to the extent to which the category of autism has expanded in the contemporary era.

But if the words 'autism' and 'savant' have come to align themselves with one another, the extra word 'idiot' still hovers in the background, leaving traces, as in a palimpsest, of its presence and meaning. Donald Treffert, one of the medical consultants who worked on the 1988 film *Rain Man*, published his book *Extraordinary People: Understanding 'Idiot Savants'* in 1989. Uta Frith, a far more sensitive researcher than Howe and a figure more foundationally important to the study of autism than Treffert, both uses and italicizes the words – *idiot savant* – in her groundbreaking 1989 study *Autism: Explaining the Enigma*, though by the 2003 second edition of the work the phrase has turned into the more straightforward 'savant'.[3] It is well and good that such changes are made, of course, but, as we shall see, in popular representations of autism the idea of the idiot and simpleton remain in certain forms, and certainly the notion of compensation, the ability/disability split, is strongly featured in texts that portray savants.

Mapping idiocy and autism together is, however, no easy task. It is impossible to be properly attentive to all the historical contexts in which autism has been represented because of the difficulties in identifying the representations of the condition. The cultural archives of the portrayals of idiocy, like those of 'the fool' in previous centuries, offer only hints and glimpses, which makes informed analysis particularly difficult. Equally, though autism has developed specific diagnostic criteria only relatively recently, the same cannot be said to be true of 'idiocy' at any point during the term's usage. There is no such medical condition and while any reading of its various modern formations will underline a common idea of neurobehavioural expressions, it is difficult to be more specific about its forms. As Martin Halliwell has demonstrated in his cultural history of idiocy, its representative nature is unfixed, with the idiot figure in literature or film frequently being 'a symbolic repository for that which defies categorization'.[4] However, as noted at the beginning of the last chapter, in its very contemporary representations autism is increasingly becoming a term used with imprecision, and – again with the ghost of the 'idiot savant' as a guide – it is possible to think of the two terms as different but comparable in a scheme of loose semantic deployment. There are grounds for such a linkage, in particular when thinking of the imprecision with which the savant figure is used and discussed. But more important than this is to see the ways in which the idiot figure, derided and sentimentalized, the subject of both fascination and contempt, has transformed into the savant, the human calculator or 'living Google', the figure with the extraordinary mind.

The 'living Google' epithet was applied to Kim Peek – the man on whom Dustin Hoffman's character of Raymond Babbitt in *Rain Man* was based – in a television documentary screened in the UK in February 2006.[5] Peek is a celebrity in autism circles, a figure to match Temple Grandin or Donna Williams, and the subject of numerous feature articles and documentaries. Peek's own father describes him as a '*mega*savant', and his mathematical and memorization abilities indeed are considerable.[6] He is arguably the fastest reader in the world, capable of reading each of the two pages of an open book with a different eye at once, and of memorizing nearly all of the content of the books he has read. The parallel made between Peek and Google is, of course, a peculiarly contemporary one, an analogy that might seem obvious today but is clearly conditioned by the increasingly common idea that autism can be understood through comparisons with technology, and particularly computing. But what kinds of link might have been made in relation to a figure such as Peek in an era before such communications technology existed? Might someone with his memorization skills have become one of the gifted individuals touring the cities of Europe and impressing audiences with the ability to master several languages, or perform virtuoso music recitals? Or would he have been defined by the parameters of idiocy? Quite possibly both might have been the case. Jebediah Buxton, an eighteenth-century British labourer, was known for his prodigious memory skills and calculation ability; Gottfried Mind was a 'cretinous imbecile' whose talent in drawing earned him a reputation across Europe in the late eighteenth century; in the mid-nineteenth-century US, 'blind Tom' was a famed musical savant, non-verbal and defined either as an 'imbecile' or 'idiot', who played for a President in the White House and was the subject of a case study by French physician Edouard Séguin, one of the most noted writers on idiocy of the time and author of the 1866 *Idiocy and Its Treatment by the Physiological Method*.[7]

As the nineteenth century progressed, the term 'idiot' became more precisely defined, moving away from the larger category of madness. In her account of the representations of idiocy in nineteenth-century fiction, Hilary Dickinson observes that before the 1800s the idea of 'the idiot' was fundamentally abstract and that during the first half of the century the term was heavily associated with both madness and a general idea of eccentricity; in contrast, the narrative of the late Victorian period saw 'intellectual impairment as a distinct condition, having a similarity to medical notions of idiocy and its aetiology'.[8] If this kind of medical specialization suggests the ways in which the specific role of the child psychiatrist could emerge in the twentieth century, to lead to a figure such as Leo Kanner, then the history of representation Dickinson charts alerts us to how an idea of impairment slowly developed out of the overlapping ideas of body, mind and soul that circulated around cognitive disability in the nineteenth century.

Halliwell quotes Frederic Bateman, a Fellow of the Royal College of Physicians, in his 1897 account of idiocy:

> An idiot is a human being who possesses the tripartite nature of man – body, soul and spirit – ... but who is the subject of an infirmity consisting, anatomically, of a defective organization and want of development of the brain, resulting in an inability, more or less complete, for the exercise of the intellectual, moral and sensitive faculties. There are various shades and degrees of this want of development, from those whose mental and bodily deficiencies differ but slightly from the lowest of the so-called sound-minded, to those individuals who simply vegetate and whose deficiencies are so decided as to isolate them, as it were, from the rest of nature.[9]

In looking to identify autism as being possibly manifested within the wider category of idiocy, it is the last observation that is of most interest here. The idea of isolation, the separation 'from the rest of nature' because of severe 'deficiencies', fits the broad patterning of impairments that come with autism as well as of a number of other conditions. Crucially, of course, this manifestation comes at the lowest possible end of Bateman's 'various shades and degrees of this want of development'; it is an extreme form of idiocy that produces the inability to exercise the key 'faculties' seen to constitute the essential 'nature of man'. If this is, indeed, where we might find autism, it is in the presumed low-functioning, vegetative status of the *most* impaired.

What all writers on idiocy agree upon is that categorizations such as these can be understood only within the context of the discourses present at the time they are used. So to try to read the figure of autistic presence in, say, the eighteenth or nineteenth century requires not only some indicators of a representation of the condition, but the subsequent placement of such a recognition within the parameters of a fundamentally cultural category as they are outlined at the time of the text's production. As indicated in the discussion of Melville's 'Bartleby the Scrivener' in the previous chapter (though Bartleby himself is far from being any kind of conventional 'idiot' figure), I do sense this is a possible, if fraught, process. Even if we recognize what we feel to be only a trace of autism through such reading processes, we go some real way to establishing a tradition of representation that acts as a base for the fascination with the condition that characterizes the contemporary moment.

II

*B*arnaby Rudge was Charles Dickens' fifth novel, published in 1841, the start of a decade when, as Dickinson notes, 'medical opinion in Britain, responding to developments in Switzerland and France, came to view idiocy as improvable by means of education'.[10] The novel's narrative deals with the anti-popery Gordon riots of the 1780s, with those conflicts usually read as presenting Dickens' thinly veiled fears over the rise of the Chartist movement in the 1830s. Patrick McDonagh, in his reading of 'idiocy' in the novel, also notes its concentration on 'the proper and just exercise of authority, specifically paternal authority' in its outlining of anxiety.[11] Barnaby himself is a somewhat strange eponymous character – as McDonagh notes, he is absent for a large section of the middle part of the novel, namely chapters 26 to 45[12] – but he is recognizably a figure who works in metaphorical terms to convey much of the novel's social and political commentary.

Dickens' narrative itself terms Barnaby an 'idiot' soon after his first appearance, in the third chapter of the novel.[13] The first full description of the character is worth quoting in some detail, however:

> He was about three-and-twenty years old, and though rather spare, of a fair height and strong make. His hair, of which he had a great profusion, was red, and hanging in disorder about his face and shoulders, gave to his restless looks an expression quite unearthly – enhanced by the paleness of his complexion, and the glassy lustre of his large protruding eyes. Startling as his aspect was, the features were good, and there was something even plaintive in his wan and haggard aspect. But the absence of the soul is far more terrible in a living man than in a dead one; and in this unfortunate being its noblest powers were wanting.
> 
> His dress was of green, clumsily trimmed here and there – apparently by his own hands – with gaudy lace; brightest where the cloth was most

worn or soiled, and poorest where it was at its best. A pair of tawdry ruffles dangled at his wrists, while his throat was nearly bare. He had ornamented his hat with a cluster of peacock's feathers, but they were limp and broken, and now trailed negligently down his back. Girded to his side was the steel hilt of an old sword without blade or scabbard; and some parti-coloured ends of ribands and poor lass toys completed the ornamental portion of his attire. The fluttered and confused disposition of all the motley scraps that formed his dress, bespoke, in a scarcely less degree than his eager and unsettled manner, the disorder of his mind, and by a grotesque contrast set off and heightened the more impressive wildness of his face. (p. 35)

This is, within the context of nineteenth-century descriptions of the idiot figure, a relatively standard description. As McDonagh notes, 'Dickens places Barnaby firmly within the tradition of literary representations of the wild "idiot", drawing on the traditional fool's motley'.[14] Barnaby's interior state is reflected by the wild nature of his appearance and dress, which communicate not only the 'disorder' of the mind but his lack of a soul as well. There is nothing specific to this outline that might invite any speculation as to whether Barnaby can be deemed autistic, although there seem generic parallels with the late-eighteenth-century case of Victor, the 'Wild Boy of Aveyron', a figure Uta Frith has discussed in terms of possible autism.[15] Yet there are, in and around this first description, a number of instances of Barnaby's behaviour, and a number of critical conclusions that might be drawn from these, that bring an idea of autism into this particular representative frame.

Firstly, Barnaby's initial action, even before he appears to other characters in the novel, is one of repetition. Gabriel Varden, the locksmith and exemplar of honest citizenry who is at the heart of the narrative, overhears 'a loud cry at no great distance ahead' when on the road to London (p. 33). The cry is 'repeated – not once or twice or thrice, but many times' (p. 34). As Varden approaches the scene, to find Barnaby crouched over the body of Edward Chester, who has been the victim of a robbery, the locksmith recognizes Barnaby, and asks in turn whether Barnaby knows who he is. Barnaby's response is to nod:

He nodded – not once or twice, but a score of times, and that with a fantastic exaggeration which would have kept his head in motion for an hour, but that the locksmith held up his finger, and fixing his eyes sternly upon him caused him to desist. (p. 34)

This first manifestation of Barnaby's repetition might make us think of Bartleby's own predisposition to repeat, and of the potential pleasure or preference in such an act, but it also crucially mirrors central structures of the novel's thematic method. As John Bowen writes in his introduction to the 2003 Penguin edition of *Barnaby Rudge*, the idea of repetition is integral to the novel's portrayal of history in particular: 'For in this novel, history is a repetitive and strangely doubled business. Instead of safely progressing, here things repeat and repeat. Characters, names, events, all return or are in danger of returning.'[16] For Bowen, the novel repeats endlessly, leading even to 'many differing competing times and temporalities imposed on top of each other in the book', from 'Varden's secular and progressive time' to Barnaby's 'haunted and repetitive life outside time'.[17] As with Herman Melville's story, here the very performance of cognitive impairment is linked structurally to the fiction's symbolic economy. It may not be as overt as the novel's concentration on its central historical and social themes, but the link is there nonetheless, pulling Barnaby away from just being a simplistic 'idiot' figure.

The initial depictions of Barnaby seek to separate him from the other characters in differing ways. His supposed 'absence of soul' and a seeming 'wildness and vacancy' (p. 50) set him apart from characters who espouse a moral or rational purpose, and there seems an initial connection with Hugh, the ostler at the Maypole pub, who – like Barnaby – is often described within the text in bestial terms.[18] Barnaby's idiot 'innocence' in fact saves him from the criminality that is seen to be inherent in Hugh, however, which hints at the ways in which he might be 'educated' in the future. But the depiction of Barnaby's difference is crucial here. It speaks not only of the kind of isolation noted earlier in connection with the Bateman quote, but alludes to impairments that we might see as being recognizably autistic. As Gabriel Varden and Edward Chester sit and discuss Barnaby, with the subject of their conversation sitting but a few yards from them, Barnaby, 'smiling vacantly', is 'making puzzles on his fingers with a skein of string'. Though he is absorbed in the details of the patterns he is making, Barnaby is – according to Varden – still in all probability taking note of their conversation: 'Speak low if you please', Varden says, 'Barnaby means no harm, but I have watched him oftener than you, and I know, little as you would think it, that he's listening now'. The narrative voice then notes that 'it required a strong confidence in the locksmith's veracity to lead any one to this belief, for every sense and faculty that Barnaby possessed, seemed to be fixed upon his game, to the exclusion of all other things' (p. 58). Barnaby's fixed attention, and his seeming ability to engage, at a sensory level, from the periphery of events, displays a relationship with his environment recognizable from accounts of autistic subjectivity. Kanner might have noted in such behaviour 'disturbances of affective contact' (see chapter 1) or an obsessiveness in Barnaby's relationship with objects. The novel is full of Barnaby's sensory reactions to his surroundings – 'don't let me see it – smell it – hear the word. Don't speak the word – don't!' (p. 37), he cries when troubled by the 'bloody' body of Edward Chester, a reaction that combines responses associated with both sight and language. And, as Bowen notes, this kind of sensory difference is, as with the repetition mentioned earlier, something we can see as being built into the book as a whole: 'The novel constantly emphasizes the impossibility of relying on one's senses to understand the world'.[19] In this formulation, Barnaby's sensory experience of the world around him is curiously foundational, not eccentric and idiosyncratic.

Crucially, Barnaby's fragmented sensory responses, his own jigsaw puzzle comprehension as it were, are also evidenced at a pivotal moment in the novel's presentation of the political insurrection central to its overall effect. Despite the efforts of his mother to prevent it, Barnaby becomes part of George Gordon's 'mob' that marches upon Westminster. His participation in the march is precipitated by his being handed a flag – 'the gayest silken streamer in this valiant army' (p. 403) – which comes to consume his total attention as the protest progresses:

> Forgetful of all other things in the ecstacy [*sic*] of the moment, his face flushed and his eyes sparkling with delight, heedless of the weight of the great banner he carried, and mindful only of its flashing in the sun and rustling in the summer breeze, on he went, proud, happy, elated past all telling. (pp. 404–5)

Indeed, Barnaby's attention is so taken by the flag he carries that he shuts out all other sensory stimulants. The gruff hangman with whom Barnaby walks refuses to understand when his comments addressed to Barnaby receive no reply. He 'nudg[ed] Barnaby roughly with his elbow. "What are you staring at? What don't you speak?"' But, as the narrative says, 'Barnaby had been gazing at his flag, and looked vacantly [at] his questioner' (p. 405).

The importance of this moment is that Barnaby's part in the riots makes clear Dickens' overall attitude towards the novel's ideas of leadership, authority and the potential of the disabled. Because of the 'disorder' of his mind, Barnaby does not understand the political or moral consequences of his being part of Gordon's protests. He fails to see the true purpose of the crowd, rather experiencing it as a set of sensory activities that provide their own logic and produce his focus upon the flag he carries. Here he is truly the novel's 'poor idiot', a figure who, as McDonagh puts it, 'provides Dickens with a valuable and nuanced cipher – or a prosthetic – for an unruly crowd deficient in proper leader-ship'.[20] Barnaby's participation in the protest will lead to his arrest and the possibility of his being hanged, before Varden saves him from the gallows. As such, in the last third of the novel he carries the full weight of Dickens' melodramatic ruminations on 'proper' conduct and individual, as well as social, behaviour. Intriguingly, as the novel closes and Barnaby comes to realize the nature of 'the shock he had sustained' (p. 687), the narrative voice informs us that 'although he could never separate his condemnation and escape from the idea of a terrific dream, he became, in other respects, more rational' (p. 687). Within the parameters of an idea of the educable 'idiot', Barnaby learns from his experiences and, crucially, he learns in terms of a clear rationality.

In his article 'Idiots', written for *Household Words* and published in June 1853, Dickens made explicit what was implicit in his novel over ten years before:

> Study of the subject has now demonstrated that the cultivation of such senses and instincts as the idiot is seen to possess, will, besides fre-quently developing others that are latent within him but obscured, so brighten those glimmering lights, as immensely to improve his condi-tion, both with reference to himself and to society.[21]

As a consequence of his participation in the riots, Barnaby receives the opportunity to become 'improved'.

So, in many ways the novel closes with Barnaby's disabled status being overwritten. He becomes the figure on whom conclusions sur-rounding anti-authoritarian activities, or personal moral conduct, or the proper notion of gendered social relations, can be drawn. In this sense he is a typical representative of the nineteenth-century prosthetic disabled character. But the textual excess of Barnaby's focus on his flag remains, as do his repetition and his wider sensory experiences of events, and all these echo through the text in multiple ways. It is perfectly possible, for all the melodramatic conventions central to *Barnaby Rudge*'s method, nevertheless to pick out a narrative of difference, in this case one recog-nizably associated with an autistic presence.[22] Barnaby's fragmented sensory experience of the world is buried beneath endless layers of fictionalizing devices and practices. It is, perhaps, barely readable. But it *is* there, and the faint traces it offers (traces that are, of course, to be expected when we remember that disability is nearly always presented in such ways) provide enough to allow for an exploratory connection to be made with the ideas of autism that take form over a century after Dickens wrote. After all, whatever we might make of the fact, Barnaby does wave his flag on his own terms.

## III

I do not want to suggest that *Barnaby Rudge* equals 'Bartleby the Scrivener' in the complexity of its representation of autism. Melville's story is astonishing and unique in the ways in which the logic of its portrayal of impairment seems able to anticipate and accommodate any critical reading of its effects. Dickens' novel does not approach such a position. Rather, we might see *Barnaby Rudge* as being far more typical in its alignment of disability with the conventions of fictional sentiment or melodrama, and the mobilization of ideas about society and culture. It is, however, precisely such typicality that provides the orthodox connections (as opposed to a more radical lineage) between portrayals of autism across the modern and contemporary periods. The forms by which Barnaby's character is connected to ideas of the personal or public good, or the ways in which he is made to work to metaphorize cultural states, repeat themselves time and again across texts in which we specifically see an 'autistic idiot' being presented.

In this way, we can look from Joseph Conrad to Anita Desai, or from Virginia Woolf to Keri Hulme, with numerous instances in between, for examples where specific notions of 'autistic idiocy' are mobilized. These are not, of course, all of the same degree. Cultural texts dip into disability as often as they see fit, selecting aspects of this condition or that as narratives are seen to require them. It is really only from the late 1980s onwards that we can point to the employment of characters chosen precisely because they *are* autistic, with a working knowledge of the condition built into the representation. Up to that point there are traces, suggestions and versions, but, even as we note these as misrepresentations, we need to understand them not as somehow incomplete (and therefore invalid) portrayals of *real* figures with autism, but rather as the logical outcome of a textual practice that sees autistic/cognitive impairment as a reservoir of potential story lines, and uses elements of the condition accordingly.

Twice in Joseph Conrad's writing – in the story 'The Idiots', written in 1896 and published in the collection *Tales of Unrest* in 1898, and in the 1907 novel *The Secret Agent* – there are representations of figures with noticeably autistic tendencies.[23] 'The Idiots' is an early, unsubtle story, derivative in its adoption of plot lines taken from Guy de Maupassant's fictions of French peasantry. It portrays the destruction of a family that cannot come to terms with the presence of 'idiot' children. An unnamed narrator describes how Jean-Pierre and Susan Bacadou, a Breton peasant couple, have four children, each severely impaired with an 'imperfect thing that lived within them'.[24] As the narrator recounts:

> I saw them many times in my wandering about the country. They lived
> on that road, drifting along its length here and there, according to the
> inexplicable impulses of their monstrous darkness. They were an offence
> to the sunshine, a reproach to empty heaven, a blight on the concen-
> trated and purposeful vigour of the wild landscape. (p. 83)

Portrayed as such, the children are more spectres than people, but the
details that are given of their behaviour are recognizably autistic. The
first child the narrator sees 'looked at us over his shoulder when we
brushed past him. The glance was unseeing and staring, a fascinated
glance' (p. 82). Following the birth of the third child, the narrator
comments:

> That child, like the other two, never smiled, never stretched its hands
> to her [Susan], never spoke, never had a glance of recognition for her in
> its big black eyes which could only stare fixedly at any glitter, but failed
> hopelessly to follow the brilliance of a sun-ray slipping slowly along the
> floor. (p. 92)

These comments are almost like a case study (albeit in pejorative
terms) in the precision of their observation of autism in the very
young, recording impairments in communication and interaction, as
well as the sensory difference that accounts for the fixed stare on
the 'glitter' – itself an intriguing parallel with Barnaby's flag and his
intense focus.

  After this birth of the third child, and as Jean-Pierre and Susan's
marriage becomes increasingly pressurized by the problems of caring
for disabled children, the narrative nods towards the impairments
of the children being genetic: 'There were three of them. Three! All
alike! Why? Such things do not happen to everybody – to nobody he
ever heard of. One yes – it might pass. But three! All three' (p. 96).
When the fourth child is equally impaired, the strain upon the parents
becomes impossible to bear. Jean-Pierre, increasingly drunk, threatens
Susan with violence (and, it is implied, rape) and in self-defence she
murders him before confessing to her mother and then running to the
coast, where she falls to her death.

  'The Idiots' is in many ways a typical disability story. The four
children are barely in the narrative at all; they are simply figures by
the roadside, presences in the margins of the story that has its central
concerns elsewhere. But they animate all that happens – the central
relationship between Jean-Pierre and Susan becomes dominated by
their off-page presence, the 'cause' of the tragedy of the two deaths
at the end. Reflections on his children come to dictate Jean-Pierre's
thinking; indeed, the genetic dimension to the children's disability

(and it is implied that Susan's father had some form of impairment as well) fits with the fiction's more overt theme of inheritance, as Jean-Pierre realizes that none of his children will be able to take over the running of the farm and fears it will pass to distant relatives. The real inheritance, of course, is idiocy and madness (the story makes no real distinction between the two), of which the children are seen to be brooding, spectral examples.

Madness and idiocy spread out from the children in the text, as some sort of force that consumes others. It is implied that the madness into which Jean-Pierre descends, and that of Susan, who is described as a 'miserable madwoman' (p. 108) after she has killed her husband, is connected to the children. Autism here is a force that unravels lives, simply by being what it is. But there are also, as with *Barnaby Rudge*, small moments of textual excess in which it seems as if the narrative itself becomes contaminated by the condition. When Susan comes to confess the murder to her mother, her words are 'incomprehensible' (p. 106) and a workman in the bar where this scene takes place sits 'with a lost gaze, humming a bar of some song, which he repeated endlessly' (p. 104). Probably most strikingly, the story descends into melodrama, that most common genre used to contain disabled presence, as Susan's flight across the cliffs before her death adds a Gothic tinge to what has gone before. Specifically, 'The Idiots' is a melodrama which deals with the break-up of the family unit because of the difficulty of raising disabled children. As such, it reads as a prescient text that anticipates much similar writing on autism in the contemporary period, where issues of the family take centre stage.[25]

Family is equally central to *The Secret Agent*, another story in which a wife stabs and kills a husband because of an impaired family member, but Conrad's later work is much more sophisticated in its plotting of the resonances of disability. The character with autism is Stevie, the brother of Winnie, who, along with her husband, Adolph Verloc, is one of the central characters of the text. Stevie is a boy described as being 'delicate, and in a frail way, good-looking, too, except for that vacant droop of his lower lip'.[26] He is, in the terms of a tradition emerging out of nineteenth-century representation, a recognizable 'idiot', but we might note a number of key characteristics and behaviours. Stevie is frequently seen to be over-literal, disturbed by conversations he hears – Winnie notes at one point that he 'was out of his mind with something he overheard about eating people's flesh and drinking blood' (p. 56) when the 'cannibalistic' nature of the economy is being discussed by political agitators in the Verlocs' home – and easily upset if an event or comment has multiple meanings. He communicates in terms

and phrases rather than sentences, and his language is often 'robbed …
of the power of connected speech' (p. 132) when he is agitated. At one
point in the text he is described as 'capering all over the place down-
stairs' (p. 54) when he should be in his bed. At the same time, Stevie is
often portrayed as being quiet and focused, or 'staring vacantly', when
calm (p. 41). Outdoors, he easily becomes lost if his preferred routes or
modes of travel are disturbed. Most noteworthy is his repetitive drawing, produced while he sits at the table in the Verlocs' house:

> Mr Verloc, getting off the sofa with ponderous reluctance, opened the
> door leading into the kitchen to get more air, and thus disclosed the inno-
> cent Stevie, seated very good and quite at a deal table, drawing circles,
> circles; innumerable circles, concentric, eccentric; a coruscating whirl of
> circles that by their tangled multitude of repeated curves, uniformity of
> form, and confusion of intersecting lines suggested a rendering of cosmic
> chaos, the symbolism of a mad art attempting the inconceivable. The
> artist never turned his head; and in all his soul's application to the task
> his back quivered, his thin neck, sunk into a deep hollow at the base of
> his skull, seemed ready to snap. (pp. 45–6)

We might read Stevie's circles in terms of the pleasure he encounters while producing them, the repetition of the geometric form being
itself the very point of the drawing. Such an action is entirely consistent with the logic of autism. But this is also precisely the moment
where, as the narrative indicates, the circles cannot be left alone.
They become metaphor, the 'rendering of cosmic chaos', the evidence
of 'mad art', and they indicate the manner in which Stevie will be
treated in the fiction as a whole. For, as in the other examples we have
seen so far, it is the idea of the idiot's innocence that most appeals to
Conrad. Stevie dies when a bomb he is unwittingly carrying explodes;
he is 'blown to fragments in a state of innocence and in the conviction of being engaged in a humanitarian exercise' (p. 215). Set up by
Verloc to carry the bomb to the Greenwich Observatory in London,
he stumbles against a tree in Greenwich Park and is killed. His death
is not only the direct catalyst for Winnie to murder Verloc, but the
idea of his moral and humanitarian exceptionality, qualities associated
directly with the perceived 'limitations' caused by his impairment, is
set against the remainder of the novel's accounts of terrorist activity,
political nihilism and personal betrayal. Stevie, 'a moral creature …
at the mercy of his righteous passions' (p. 143), and one who cannot
bear to see pain inflicted on any living creature, becomes the moral
centre of a story that reflects multiple personal failings, and a narrative
catalyst for the novel's other central concerns. His death is cathartic for
his sister, Winnie, releasing her from the marriage 'contract' she has

with Verloc and making her a 'free woman' (p. 211), whereas before she was bound by necessity to her husband. Equally, in a story full of ideas of political anarchism, it is Stevie who, in some critical readings, emerges as the 'real' anarchist, the only figure truly beyond social norms and demands. As such, his 'innumerable circles' are a kind of 'pure' anarchy, meaningless and yet profound.[27]

As with 'The Idiots', then, and indeed as with *Barnaby Rudge*, the individual with autism in *The Secret Agent* is peripheral to the majority of the fiction but central to its meaning, a process that is standard in the prosthetic narrative. These fictions enact a fascination of their own with the impaired figure. It is not the contemplation of the make-up of the brain or the exceptional ability that we associate with autism in contemporary culture that fascinates here; rather, it is ideas of the soul, and of individual and public good, that dominate. But although these inflections are different, it is best to see them as versions of a similar impulse, and – as we shall see – a melodramatic urge is common in such forms. The desire to read what is conceived of as the empty space of autism, the invitation it appears to offer to fill in its blanks, is a constant throughout cultural representation. It is obvious that it will take differing forms in differing contexts, but the initial fascination stems from the same source: the combination of wonder and fear that is seen to be inherently produced by the disabled subject.

Such a combination proved to be a heady mix for writers seeking inspiration in the first decades of the twentieth century, especially in the shadow of Sigmund Freud and a subsequent increase of attention on the workings of the mind. Modernism's overlapping ideas of health, illness, madness, disability and difference – of which *The Secret Agent* is an early example – produced numerous examples of exceptional and extraordinary characters. In the specific terms of an idea of the 'autistic idiot', however, it is, rather, a non-fictional example which might hold centre stage. Virginia Woolf's half-sister Laura Stephen, born in 1870 and so some twelve years older than her famous sibling, was, judging by the evidence that we can piece together from contemporary memoirs and letters, almost certainly autistic. In her magisterial biography of Woolf, Hermione Lee outlines the stresses faced by the Stephen family in dealing with Laura before she was sent away to an institution, probably in the early 1890s, and comes to the conclusion that she possibly had a 'form of autism'.[28] Certainly, the accounts of speech impediments, repetitive communication and gestures, and emotional outbursts appear to fit such an observation. But Lee is at her most perceptive when she comments upon the implications of Laura's presence for Woolf's sense of her own mental health:

> Laura matters a great deal, though Virginia Woolf hardly ever referred to her, and she played no active or lasting part in the life of her half-sister. She matters because she was an abnormal daughter of Leslie Stephen who lived in the same house as Virginia, and was 'put away'. How we read her treatment by her family must influence our reading of Virginia's mental breakdowns and her treatment.[29]

As Lee notes, Woolf 'would have been appalled at being identified with Laura…. *She* is not an "idiot" or an "imbecile"; *she* is not put away; *she* is the daughter who learned to read and write. Laura's influence works through fearful opposition, not identification.'[30] For Woolf, her half-sister lived in some world beyond mere mental ill health, a world full of the truly terrifying. Woolf's famous observation from 1915 – upon meeting 'a long line of imbeciles' while out walking, she noted that 'everyone in that long line was a miserable shuffling idiotic creature…. They should certainly be killed' – fully declares the scale of her fear and revulsion.[31] It is impossible to say how Woolf's memory of growing up with Laura might have influenced her work and notions of mental stability, and even more difficult to know what Laura's own life was like, but here is another possible autistic presence that emerges from the margins to revise our sense of what we think we know. Certainly the phrase 'a room of one's own' might be seen to take on a different meaning when considering 'idiotic, imbecilic' Laura.[32]

The category of the 'idiot' figure is, of course, much wider than that dimension specified by its interactions with autism, and from Gustave Flaubert and Fyodor Dostoevsky to John Steinbeck and Harper Lee the idea of the idiot has displayed the creative engagement between the literary and medical opinions of the time.[33] Possibly the most remarkable idiot figure in twentieth-century literature is Benjy Compson, in William Faulkner's *The Sound and the Fury* (1929), whose idiocy forms part of Faulkner's extraordinary modernist experiment in the narration of time and events. Although there are seeming parallels between Benjy and orthodox autistic behaviour – most famously when he screams[34] as he is driven an unusual way around a monument and the predictable regularity of a journey he takes often is shattered – Faulkner based the character on Edwin Chandler, a local Mississippi man with Down's syndrome.[35] However, if such figures animate all manner of narrative possibilities, then we might note that those aspects specific to autism – ideas of impairment in social interaction and obsessive repetition in particular – give the fictions which contain them an individual inflection. If there is a public image of the 'idiot' as garrulous and expansive, the vocal village idiot or 'fool' for example, then the idea of being 'trapped within', withdrawn and silent is a more conventional stereotype of the person with autism. The difference can often mean very different narrative usage.

In, for example, Anita Desai's 1980 novel *Clear Light of Day*, part of the narrative deals with the Partition of India and Pakistan in 1947. Desai portrays the sense of stasis of life in 'old' Delhi following political and social change: 'That is the risk of coming to Old Delhi', says Bim, one of the central characters, who has remained in an old family home in the old part of Delhi when others, particularly her sister, Tara, have left, 'Old Delhi does not change. It only decays. My students tell me it is a great cemetery, every house a tomb.'[36] Living with Bim is her brother, Baba, an autistic adult (although the narrative never designates him as such) whose condition is used to establish the idea that Bim and her life are caught in time. Baba, who notionally has an office job, is actually restricted to his room, where he plays favourite records, associated with the period immediately before Partition, over and over again. On a visit to see her family, Tara goes into Baba's room:

> He was sitting on his bed, a strong cot spread with a cotton rug and an old sheet, that stood in the centre of the room under the slowly revolving electric fan. He was crouched low, listening raptly to the last of 'Don't Fence Me In' unwinding itself on the old HMV gramophone on a small bamboo table beside his bed. The records, not very many of them … were stacked on a shelf beneath the table in their tattered yellow sleeves. The string cot, the table, the HMV gramophone, a canvas chair and a wardrobe – nothing else…. Baba looked up at her.
> Tara stood staring, made speechless by his fine, serene face, the shapeliness of his long fingers, his hands that either moved lightly as if in a breeze or rested calmly at his sides. He was an angel, she told herself, catching her lip between her teeth – an angel descended to earth, unsoiled by any of it.[37]

But if such comments seem to suggest that Baba is the recognizable 'innocent idiot', they are soon undercut by the continuation of Tara's thoughts:

> But then why did he spend his days and years listening to this appalling noise? Her daughters could not live through a day without their record-player either; they, too, kept it heaped with records that slipped down onto the turntable in a regular sequence, keeping them supplied with an almost uninterrupted flow of music to which they worked and danced with equal ease. But, she wanted to explain to him, theirs was an ever-growing, ever-changing collection, their interest in it was lively, fresh, developing all the time. Also, she knew they would outgrow their need of it…. But Baba would never leave his behind, he would never move on.[38]

The description of Baba as an 'angel' is, in fact, a family myth, and it is Tara's thoughts on her own family that jolt her out of this impression.

Baba's impairment is real, but in this context Tara cannot help but associate him with the lack of change she sees around her.

Desai's novel uses music – and noticeably Indian music, and not the American music to which Baba listens – to move Bim and her family out of their torpor. At the narrative's close, Bim and Baba listen to a guru and his protégé sing classic raga songs, which represent not only a historical legacy but also the continuation of that tradition into the future. As the songs continue, and as Bim sees the possibilities inherent in that future, she turns to talk to her brother. In response, Baba 'gave a single nod. His face was grave, like an image carved in stone, listening.'[39] It is a short description, but the inference is that Baba is engaged with both his sister and the music, understanding its importance. The novel refuses to sentimentalize the situation – there is no suggestion that Baba is any less impaired – but the change that Desai wishes to communicate is here illustrated.

In *Clear Light of Day*, then, autism is still used in metaphorical terms, but arguably without the connection to morality and melodrama that defined the texts discussed earlier. The idea of Baba's idiocy does not completely overdetermine him, and though he is a peripheral figure in the novel, he can still be seen to emerge, at the fiction's end, as a character both recognizably human and, crucially, *included* in the transformation of his family. This kind of narrative treatment – the use of autistic tendencies without the depiction of a character who is purposefully autistic, and the framing of disability to suggest themes without the overt addition of sentimentality – can be found in a number of texts from previous decades. It is there in the portrayal of Simon, the mute central character of Keri Hulme's *the bone people* (1983), whose sensory engagement with the world and emotional outbursts when frustrated point to the deployment of ideas of autism even if Simon himself is not recognizably a figure with autism. It is there, too, in the silent Sonny of Pauline Melville's *The Ventriloquist's Tale* (1997), who 'explode[s] into a windmill of agitated, ungainly movement' when 'his passionately guarded enclosure' is disturbed by unwanted conversation. It is, as Ato Quayson has noted, arguably to be found in the central character of J. M. Coetzee's haunting *Life & Times of Michael K* (1983), a figure described as being 'like a stone.... A hard little stone, barely aware of its surroundings, enveloped in itself and its interior life'.[40] Interestingly, all of these examples (including Desai) use the suggestion of cognitive impairment as part of their outlining of the dynamics of postcolonial societies and cultures, exploring (to cite two specifics) the interaction between Māori and Pākehā within New Zealand in Hulme's novel, or the account of civil unrest in South Africa in Coetzee.[41] The link between disability and culture is central to many fictions, of course, but it is intriguing to speculate why the connection in a number of postcolonial texts lacks the overt sentimentality and moralizing that is found in other examples.

For the fact is that the 'autistic idiot' figure is still recognizable in its nineteenth-century forms in any number of popular texts. This is especially the case in visual media. In television drama, especially crime programmes, there is frequent variation on the central theme whereby an individual with autism may be the key witness to (say) a murder, but is represented as being unable to communicate relevant details to investigating authorities. In cinema, Halliwell has noted that 'with the wave of cinematic representations of mental and neurological conditions in the 1990s … the screen-life of idiocy has taken on a life of its own'.[42] Robert Zemeckis' 1994 film *Forrest Gump* is the exemplary text of such a wave. Loosely based on Winston Groom's 1986 novel (in which Forrest terms himself an 'idiot' and a 'halfwit') Zemeckis' film removes the overt references to idiocy found in Groom's novel and replaces the edgy difference of the book with a more recognizably sentimental, conservative narrative.[43] Arguably, there is a postmodern quality to a film like *Forrest Gump*, with its implied revisions of history and sense of the modern picaresque, but equally the argument can be made that, in such narratives, the disabled figure is again a cipher, an overwritten character providing a twist to the story line. For all that such portrayals might carry the scientific language of contemporary approaches to disability, and for all that the narrative forms involved might reflect contemporary ideas of storytelling, their heritage connects directly to previous centuries and the prosthetic use of the idiot figure.

So, even as we trace the route to the current obsession with the savant figure, there is no escaping the legacy of the idiot. Much as we might wish the pejorative word in the pairing of 'idiot savant' to have fully dropped away, leaving only an idea of exceptionality and ability, the truth is that the heritage of the idiot is too considerable for its erasure to be that straightforward. As we shall see, the savant is shadowed by the idiot, even if the distance between the two is increasing.

## IV

During Barry Levinson's 1988 film *Rain Man*, in the bathroom of a Texas motel Charlie Babbitt (Tom Cruise) asks of his brother Raymond (Dustin Hoffman), 'Why do you always have to act like an idiot?' The scene comes at a pivotal moment in the film, just before

Charlie realizes that his brother is the 'Rain Man' he remembers from when he was a small child, the figure who looked after and protected him. It is the last time in the movie that Charlie calls Raymond an idiot, though up to that point he has made a number of such references. 'Stop acting like an idiot', he tells Raymond in the first hotel the two stop at after Charlie has taken his brother from the institution where he has been living since leaving the Babbitt family home. 'Stop acting like a fucking retard', Charlie barks at Raymond in a roadside restaurant, as the couple order pancakes during a stop on their drive from Cincinnati to Los Angeles. 'This guy's a fucking fruitcake', Charlie says to himself when, after the pair view an accident on the interstate, Raymond insists on getting out of the car and walking by the side of the road. In his seemingly challenging behaviour, supposed lack of rational action and clear social impairments, Raymond, it appears, is very much the recognizable idiot.

Except that he is not. *Rain Man* is the foundational text for all the various contemporary representations of autism, the breakthrough story that gave the condition a public profile when before it was, to a large degree, confined to medical and educational specialists, and the families of those individuals who had autism. And in Raymond Babbitt, the public were exposed to a fictional character containing far more complexity than any representation of autism up to that point. Director Barry Levinson and story developer Barry Morrow used a series of consultants – including Donald Treffert and psychologist Bernard Rimland – with medical expertise on autism to provide the film with an attempt at authentic detail. Such scientific accreditation signalled a desire for a fidelity to the movie's subject matter and a clear intent to avoid the prosthetic use of the disabled figure. When Dr Bruner (Jerry Molen), the psychiatrist at Wallbrook, the institution where Raymond lives, outlines the details of autism to Charlie, he is in effect equally explaining the condition to an uninformed audience:

> There's a disability that impairs the sensory input and how it's processed…. Raymond has a problem communicating and learning. He can't even express himself or probably even understand his own emotions in a traditional way. There are dangers everywhere for Raymond. Routines, rituals – that's all he has to protect himself…. Any break from the routines and it's terrifying.

Such an explanatory scene, in which a clinical idea of autism is conveyed to the audience via a conversation with a leading character, becomes standard in many of the post *Rain Man* films which feature the condition. Ostensibly at least, the sentimental language of the idiot is replaced by the hard formulations of the scientific.

In fact, Bruner's first characterization of Raymond is an underlining of his savant status. 'He's an autistic savant', he says at the start of his explanation to Charlie, 'some people like him used to be called idiot savants. They have certain deficiencies, certain abilities'. To Charlie's comment that his brother is 'retarded', Bruner counters that he is 'autistic ... high-functioning'. Autism is introduced in *Rain Man* as being a condition twinned with savantism, a pairing that has had considerable consequences for the majority of representations of the condition in the years since the film was made. In the replacement of the autistic idiot with the autistic savant we can trace a clear move from an idea of disability to one of ability, but arguably the degree of misrepresentation and fascination remain. The paradigm through which the viewer of *Rain Man* watches Raymond might shift slightly on its axis, but that axis is still a foundational marker of disproportionate wonder.

Raymond's savant skills are associated with memorization and mathematics. He memorizes a phone book up to the letter G, and is able to tell a diner waitress her home phone number when he sees her name on a lapel badge. He has archive-like detail in his knowledge of baseball trivia and the detail of plane crashes, and it is in a second diner outside Las Vegas that his memorization of jukebox information leads Charlie to the idea that he will be able to count cards at the city's casinos. His initial mathematical skill – immediately correctly identifying the number of toothpicks spilled on to a floor – is reproduced when he 'performs' his talent for a small-town doctor, who asks him the answers to complicated mathematical questions. 'He's a genius', Charlie states, 'he should be working for NASA'; but, in a reinforcement of the deficiency/ability model outlined by Bruner, it then transpires that Raymond cannot perform such sums when they are applied to everyday objects, or guess what the monetary value of such everyday objects is: he assumes both a candy bar and a car cost 'one hundred dollars'.

Raymond's savant abilities are seen to be innate, but in the world of the filmic narrative they are also tied into the complexities of his character. His card counting when playing blackjack in Las Vegas is not some form of remote operation. Rather, it is linked to his developing relationship with his brother Charlie, who moves from a caricature of 1980s self-obsession to caring family member as the film progresses. Equally, aspects of his memorization and repetition skills – such as his regular iteration of the Abbott and Costello 'Who's on First?' sketch – work as a means of self-comfort when he is in positions of stress. Raymond repeats the sketch to himself whenever he finds himself in a new place or when his own space is in any way threatened, for example when Charlie and his girlfriend Susanna (Valeria Golino) first visit his room in Wallbrook.

All of the above displays a complexity of characterization, and yet the reception of the film demonstrates that by far the most overwhelming aspect of Raymond's character appears to be his savant abilities. It was this behavioural feature that captured the public imagination, leading to a number of individuals with autism appearing on television, or as the subject of magazine articles, where they performed mathematical and memorization acts for amazed audiences. Intriguingly and possibly somewhat disturbingly, this kind of reaction is similar to that presented by Fran Peek (father of Kim) in his account of the first meetings between his son and both Barry Morrow and Dustin Hoffman in the film's pre-production period. In *The Real Rain Man*, Peek notes that, at the very first meeting between Kim and Morrow, in 1984, the screenwriter's immediate focus was upon Kim Peek's savant skills. Morrow says to Fran, describing his initial conversation with Kim:

> I also told him my date of birth, and he gave me the day of the week I was born, the day of the week this year, and the day of the week and year I would turn 65 so I could think about retiring. We also discussed events of the Revolutionary War, the Civil War, World Wars I and II, Korea and Vietnam. No way could one person know that much. No way![44]

Similarly, the first meeting with Hoffman is described as being an almost endless series of questions 'about British monarchs, the Bible, baseball, horse racing, dates, times and places'. Hoffman, according to Fran Peek, 'just sat there in lingering disbelief, wanting to hear more'.[45]

This privileging of savantism requires explanation. In terms of Fran Peek's representation of his son's relationship with the processes of making *Rain Man*, it is understandable that a father should seek to stress his son's abilities rather than his difficulties, but it is nevertheless unnerving to read an account of the interaction between Kim and the filmmakers in which he is, first and foremost, seen as a form of human database.[46] In terms of the apprehension of the film as text, however, *Rain Man* is an example of the kind of 'excessive interpretation' and a version of the 'aesthetic nervousness' of which Ato Quayson writes. Quayson notes that 'in works where disability plays a prominent role, the reader's [and here we might substitute viewer's] perspective is also affected by the short-circuiting of the dominant protocols governing the text',[47] an act that, accordingly, invokes a renewed relationship between the aesthetic and ethical domains that Quayson sees as being vital for an understanding of the representation of disability. Certainly we can see how the narrative of *Rain Man* foregrounds questions of ethics. It places the question of Raymond's care centrally in the story, as well as working in terms of the kind of short-circuiting Quayson identifies – a disabled unsettling of the text.

But it is noticeable that one product of such short-circuiting is precisely this concentration on Raymond's savant ability, that is, the stressing of an element of the character instead of the whole. The clear ethical questions raised by the film, and the revision of the idea of 'normalcy' it offers, struggle to emerge from the notions of wonder it also promotes. To take one example, part of the film's exploration of the effects of impairment lies in the manner in which it juxtaposes the two brothers. Raymond has the diagnosed neurological condition, but the narrative suggests that it is Charlie who is clearly impaired, especially in terms of personal expression and social interaction. In the first third of the film – that is, from the opening scene featuring Charlie's business of importing cars to his removal of Raymond from Wallbrook – Charlie's language is characterized by constant repetition and a seeming inability to listen. As he sits waiting during the reading of his father's will in the office of the family's lawyer, the camera focuses in close on his fingers as they drum on the table. On hearing that he has been left next to nothing (a car and some rose bushes), Charlie, with barely controlled anger, states, 'I got the rose bushes. I definitely got the rose bushes. I *definitely* got the rose bushes', a commentary that clearly intentionally replicates Raymond's own sentence structure, particularly with the reliance on 'definitely', a key word in Raymond's vocabulary. Equally, while driving with Susanna in the scene in which he is phoned and told of his father's death, Charlie is strikingly non-communicative and emotionless. 'Listen', Susanna says after the scene starts with silence, 'I don't want to be demanding here, but do you think you could possibly say ten or twelve words before we get to the hotel?' When Charlie, unresponsive behind his sunglasses, claims there is nothing to talk about, she adds, 'I feel as though you're excluding me from what's going on'. On hearing of his father's death, Charlie shows no emotion whatsoever, even asking 'Is there anything else?' before ending the call.

The parallels here are meant to be obvious. Charlie's self-absorption, seen as the personification of a 1980s excess, is characterized by a range of behaviours that, in a different form, fall within the diagnostic criteria used to identify autism. As the narrative proceeds, it is precisely the interaction with Raymond's humanity that will be the catalyst for Charlie's 'overcoming' of his own impairments. When he rejects Bruner's cheque near the end of the film, a payment intended to make him drop his custody case, the audience can feel satisfied that he has learned an appropriate lesson in human worth. Yet this narrative exists alongside another in the film, namely that of Raymond's special abilities. *That* narrative has its conclusion in the Las Vegas casino scenes, where the exceptionality displayed by Raymond's skills in memorizing the cards crowns the representation of what appear to be superhuman abilities. It can be argued that the narratives coexist in an unproblematic fashion, with Raymond's savantism adding an element to his brother's appreciation of his abilities as opposed to his impairment, but the portrayal of sentimental savantism in Hollywood films following *Rain Man* suggests otherwise. Rather, it appears that the paradigm of representation that Levinson's film established is one where the emotional story becomes folded into the broader wonder generated by the savant skill. As we shall see in the discussion of the wider representation of autism in film in the next chapter, such a narrative became standard after 1988.

There is another key element in the relationship between autism and savantism that *Rain Man* exemplifies, however. Like *The Curious Incident of the Dog in the Night-Time*, its status as a foundational text means that it acts to *produce* an idea of autism, a process of conveying knowledge that allows the viewer (or reader) to feel that she or he has engaged in a significant learning moment. Audiences for both film and book emerged from their respective experiences with an additional sense of both the detail and the ethical issues of autism – they are both texts that make you feel that you know more about the condition. Both have this quasi-sociological dimension to the manner in which their representation of autism has been read. And it is here that the mapping of savantism onto autism in *Rain Man* – it is noticeable that, for all his skills in mathematics, Christopher in Mark Haddon's novel is not a savant – becomes most acute. As a hugely popular cultural product that highlighted a disability that was little known at the time of its release, *Rain Man* instituted the public sense of what autism was. Hoffman's performance became the accepted account of autistic behaviour and subjectivity, especially when it became know that he had undertaken such dedicated research in preparing for the role. And, because of the force of this particular portrayal, savantism and autism largely became synonymous, the love and marriage of cognitive impairment. All representation that followed *Rain Man* had Hoffman's embodiment of autism as their baseline, and the condition was established with savant skills at its centre.

V

In the wake of the success of *Rain Man*, the figure of the autistic savant became the emblem of the condition on which cultural interest came to focus. Such a focus has remained, even through the new explosion of interest in the very contemporary period. If, in the years immediately after 1988, there was a fascination with the idea of the human calculator – an amazement at the notion of the mind as a computer that abstracted the individuals concerned – then in more recent years there has been more interest in, and more care about, what autism means in terms of personality. But the wonder produced by the savant has remained more or less consistent, and *Rain Man* continues to serve as a guide. The film's centrality is such that, in 2003, Rich Shull, an American adult with autism, entitled the story of his own coming to terms with his condition *Autism, Pre Rain Man*. For Shull, the film is a 'curse' that placed limitations and boundaries on the public conception of autism, leaving 'old undiagnosed Autistics like me' to 'live in *Rain Man*'s shadow'.[48] For Shull, the shadow of Levinson's film closed down the parameters of how autism might be experienced and discussed. For the majority, however, it set up the template of expectation when it came to encountering autistic behaviour.

To take an extended example, on March 2004 Daniel Tammet, a twenty-five-year-old diagnosed with Asperger's, set a British and European record for the memorization and recitation of the number pi ($\pi$) – the ratio of a circle's circumference to its diameter – at the Museum of the History of Science in Oxford in the UK. In just over five hours, he recited the number, without error, to 22,514 places. Tammet's achievement became a media event, one consequence of which was the commissioning of a television documentary focusing on his life and abilities that screened in both the UK and the US. Entitled *Brainman* internationally, and *The Boy with the Incredible Brain* in the UK, the documentary not only included a series of scientific investigations into Tammet's abilities to visualize numbers through his synaesthesia, but it also sought to self-consciously recreate part of the central narrative of Levinson's film, taking Tammet to play blackjack in Las Vegas before a meeting with Kim Peek at the public library in Salt Lake City, Peek's home town. The *Rain Man* parallels, especially the trip to Las Vegas, are somewhat surreal. Tammet, who admits in his memoir *Born on a Blue Day* to having had 'mixed feelings about this proposed sequence' because 'the last thing I wanted to do was to trivialise my abilities or reinforce the erroneous stereotype that all autistic people were like the *Rain Man* character', was finally persuaded to undertake the journey because of both what he terms his own 'curiosity' and the fact that the programme needed 'some fun and visual sequences to cut between the more serious scientific ones'.[49]

Placing Tammet in the Las Vegas casino, as *Brainman* does, creates a peculiar chain of cause and effect in terms of a commentary on his abilities. In *Rain Man*, Raymond Babbitt uses his savant skills at number memorization to win a substantial sum of money, in scenes which are crucial to the workings of the film's narrative fiction. Tammet, like Raymond (and Kim Peek) a figure with no particular interest in playing cards, then attempts to recreate an achievement that was the product of imaginative storytelling in the first place. For Tammet, the event was 'light-hearted', but there can be no better indication of the film's foundational status with regard to the presentation of autism.[50] Interestingly, Tammet is not an especially successful player, losing the majority of his hands before winning on a statistically improbable gamble and making up his losses. In his memoir he notes that his 'feel for how the cards were playing' improved as the scene went on: 'I was making my decisions more quickly and feeling more comfortable at the table. I made a snap decision to play instinctively, going on how I was experiencing the flow of numbers in my head as a rolling visual landscape with peaks and troughs'. He makes no claim, however, that his winning hand was produced by anything other than 'instinct'.[51]

Tammet is an exemplary autistic figure for the contemporary moment. He is not only capable of visualizing numbers, but can also describe that process of visualization and articulate the patterns that form in his brain as he thinks mathematically. As a result, he can interact and cooperate with those scientists with whom he works, moving beyond being the model whereby case studies are the disabled raw data from which science draws its conclusions. It is possible with Tammet, in a way that was not with the children Kanner studied, for example, to feel that his personality and intellect are involved in the way he is discussed, and that he is a genuine participant in the experiments of which he is the focus. In the ways in which he is thus viewed by a majority audience, he can appear as both (still) a source of wonder and yet not as someone clearly being exploited. It is impossible to feel that Tammet is in any way 'retarded'. At the same time, however, it is striking that Tammet's own self-narrated journey to maturity is a process that has taken place in a number of public settings and in the context of being, to different degrees, on display. In *Born on a Blue Day*, he describes a childhood dominated by visual and tactile experiences of the world, and by the subsequent lack of comprehension of social interaction that is familiar from the writings of Donna Williams. Tammet was, in his own words, 'different' to all the other children he knew, in ways that, at the time, he could not 'express or comprehend'.[52] The confidence he has found as an adult has come, as his memoir recounts, from the utilization and recognition of his abilities. Yet, from his recitation of pi to his involvement with *Brainman*, interviews on the *Late Show with David Letterman* and CBS's *60 Minutes*, and the success of *Born on a Blue Day* (an international bestseller), Tammet has become the new public face of high-functioning savant autism, a combination of the use of appropriately ethical scientific enquiry and the display of 'wondrous' cognitive gifts. When, in the last section of *Brainman*, Tammet learns good conversational Icelandic (a language of which he had no prior knowledge) in a single week, it is on live television that his skills are tested. Tammet speaks fluently with two presenters for fifteen minutes, a feat that leads the tutor hired by the documentary filmmakers to aid his learning to describe him as 'not human!'[53]

To be cynical about the presentation of Tammet's exceptionality, and to see it as a peculiar manifestation of contemporary obsessions with autism, is not to pass judgement on Tammet himself. In *Born on a Blue Day*, he writes tellingly about the question of 'being a guinea pig for the scientists' and how he has reconciled himself to becoming the object of such enquiry. 'I have no problem with it', he notes of what has been a regular process of subjecting himself to assessment and testing, 'because I know that I am helping them to understand the human brain better, which is something that will benefit everyone'.[54] Yet Tammet's position under the gaze of television in particular, and his positive reaction to it,[55] inevitably raises the question of display and the phenomenon of an exposure to a public audience. Such positioning of the disabled as objects for consumption – as figures of wonder, disgust, pity, admiration or speculation – has, of course, been a constant for centuries. The UK screening of *The Boy with the Incredible Brain*, in May 2005, was as part of Channel 5's fifth 'Extraordinary People' series, a linking of life stories of those with disabilities that negotiates a spectrum between the visuals of the freak show and the heart-warming reassurances of the 'overcoming' narrative, both standard methods by which the difference of disability is culturally accommodated. In offering its audience what it deems celebratory accounts of humanity, 'Extraordinary People' also clearly engages in the tradition of figuring the human body (and manifestations of mind) as a visual spectacle, so Tammet's *Incredible Brain* takes its place alongside such titles as *The Boy with a New Head* and *The Woman with Half a Body*, both of which screened in 2007.[56]

In *Born on a Blue Day*, Tammet gives a fuller account of his own history, where the stability of a relationship with a partner is central to his sense of an adult self, a detail that has nothing to do with any notion of performance or spectacle. The memoir itself employs a trajectory of achievement, standard to such life narratives, that emphasizes both self-understanding and a successful engagement with the wider world that is threatening because of its difference. In its last chapters, however, as Tammet recounts the success of his television appearances and the development of the relationship with his partner, the tone of the book becomes interestingly reminiscent of Haddon's method of presenting Christopher's subjectivity in *The Curious Incident of the Dog in the Night-Time*. As Tammet gives the recipe for a sponge cake that demonstrates his love of cooking, or discusses his plans for the future, his sentence structure – the plain style, the almost childlike simplicity of the prose – mirrors Christopher's presentation of his life and achievements following his successful trip to London. When Christopher asserts 'I can do anything', at the close of Haddon's novel, he asserts his capabilities and achievements.[57] Tammet's memoir ends on a similar note, with an idea of the 'glimpse of heaven' that comes with getting close to the 'mystery of what it is to be human'.[58] Placing himself within such a mystery is central to eradicating the idea that autism is somehow more alien than human, part of a different 'world'. Yet, as with the *Rain Man* parallels, it is intriguing to see traces of Haddon's fiction in Tammet's life story. It is arguable that the general public interest that created the audience for Tammet's memoir came, in the first place, from the success of Haddon's novel. For all Tammet's achievements, it is the backdrop of fiction, and the expectations produced by such fiction, that appears as his immediate context.

Tammet's savantism – and therefore his autism – is, to a large degree, a phenomenon that his audience will understand. It is rendered comprehensible not simply because he has the ability to articulate much of its method, but also by its very make-up. His abilities in memorization and mathematical calculation are exactly those that a majority culture expects from an autistic savant. It is, however, ironic that the synaesthesia skills, the multi-sensory memory processes, which allow him to explain the ways he is able to perform such calculations are probably independent from his autism, the coexistence of the two conditions being an example of a personal neurological matrix. But, the achievements of his own life story notwithstanding, Tammet conforms to the fictional stereotype of the savant, although without the threat of any behavioural excesses that might create unease. His condition is, perhaps, autism as the audiences for his documentary and book would wish it to be – difficult and challenging but conquerable, yet also spectacular and beyond comprehension.

Autistic ability, however, comes in many forms, not all of which necessarily have such clean lines. What the 'savant' label denotes is not simply a sign of the neurological exceptional, a fact that might be the subject of scientific investigation, but also a sense of the more generally extraordinary, a cultural capacity for fascination. While Tammet's mathematical capabilities are typical of the most commonly understood notion of the savant, individuals with autism display noticeable talents in other spheres. Artist Stephen Wiltshire and musician Derek Paravicini (who were also the subjects of Channel 5's 'Extraordinary People' documentaries[59]) are high-profile savants whose memorization and interpretive skills differ from those of Tammet. They work in different areas, but the public reception of both echoes the sense of wonder that accompanies Tammet's achievements. Wiltshire, an artist with numerous publications to his name and the subject of a London retrospective in 2003, started to draw before he could talk, and the geometrical precision with which he renders cityscapes and buildings has for decades been one of the markers of autistic 'genius'.[60] Along with Temple Grandin, he is the subject of a chapter in Oliver Sacks' highly influential *An Anthropologist on Mars*.[61] Paravicini, who is blind and has autistic characteristics, gave his first major concert performance in London in 1989, when he was just nine years old. Self-taught without visual guides, his appreciation of music and the range of his techniques mean he spans a number of styles and genres, all while needing care and support for most aspects of his daily life.[62]

To judge the specific nature of the interest in figures such as Tammet, Wiltshire and Paravicini requires a delicate balancing act. All three have carved spaces in which they can express themselves and their talents. All are 'success' stories that emerge from a condition where failure is usually constituted as the norm. All have had substantial media exposure, have their own official websites through which they market their work, and travel internationally. These are substantial achievements for individuals with disabilities. At the same time, it is possible to draw conclusions about the nature of their specific identities as savants that do not negate such accomplishments. For all three, and for numerous other such figures so labelled, savantism performs a role in their social characterization. It acts as a mechanism by which the perceived excessiveness of autism can be contained. As a term, 'savant' is sufficiently open – indeed, its openness is integral to the word's working method – to allow for the difference of autism to be dissolved in the realm of the unknown in a manner that generates no fear or unease. Savants are safely understood in the ways in which their skills are, as yet, beyond understanding. They are also positive – especially in terms of creativity – examples of a condition habitually defined in terms of the negative.

And therein lies an interesting contradiction. The contemporary perception of autism centres on an idea of trauma – the 'epidemic' of new diagnoses that blights individual lives and families, the 'tragedy' of the child 'lost' to the condition. Yet, in a manner that has no statistical evidence to support it, the most common cultural representation of autism associates it with the idea of the savant, in other words, with ability and achievement. The two facts sit together uneasily, but it is clear that the second is a form of collective wish that the first were not true. If all those with autism could even possibly have savant skills, the argument runs, then the compensation for the disability, both for the individual concerned and for the society in which that individual lives, would be clear enough. It would be a tolerable equation, not perfect, but sufficient to keep that worst of fears, that the mind or body simply might not work, at bay.[63]

But what of autistic ability that is not so clearly able to be seen as a savant skill? What of capabilities that do not translate in a straightforward fashion into a non-disabled logic of what constitutes the condition, but rather keep a sense of disabled difference? Larry Bissonnette is, like Stephen Wiltshire, an artist, and also like Wiltshire he began drawing when a non-verbal child. But much of Bissonnette's learning took place when he was institutionalized, and in addition to his autism he has been, at different stages in his life, diagnosed as schizophrenic and clinically insane.[64] His presence, as constituted by his life story, his paintings and the writings that accompany them, disrupts the narrative by which a talented young child overcomes a disability through the utilization of a special skill. Bissonnette's abilities are clear and substantial. His paintings – mainly made with his hands, and mostly in acrylics on canvas and board – are often long rectangles in which urban or suburban landscapes or abstract horizontal patterns are juxtaposed with his own name and, on occasions, small Polaroid portraits, either of friends or of himself. Through such devices, Bissonnette is a clear presence in his own work, as the title of one 1997 piece – *Paints Get Really Loused Up By My Signature So Both Art and Letters Learn to Cohabitate* – emphasizes. His art is not connected in any way to savant memorization skills, but emerges with the difference inherent in his autistic subjectivity as a determining element in the very content of his painting. Bissonnette's comments on his own work, often typed using facilitated communication (on which see the Introduction), are in what Douglas Biklen calls 'an image-rich and distinctive writing style', one that can 'take considerable contemplation

Figure 1. *Untitled 5A*, by Larry Bissonnette, 2004 (19.5" × 47.5" mixed media on masonite, frame by artist).

to understand'.[65] A comment on one 1998 painting, *Bird Would Violate Airline Dapper Standards for Appearance But the Skies Sport Vivider Dayglo Colors When It Can Fly Freely and Uncensored by Mankind*, begins: 'Producing art is like making puppets on strings because massive edges of inspiration in creating graspable figures gets constricted by people's patterned control of sticks put on string'. Another comment, on the 1998 work *Placement of Photo Is Perfectly Aligned With Nothing*, reads 'Answers really to aesthetic value of work aren't written in magazines of specialty art but in already directed for getting most out of thinking of spiritually responsive autistic people'.[66]

As Bissonnette intimates here, his autism is central to his art. Speaking of the importance of touch at a conference on facilitated communication in May 1999, he noted, 'It lands basis for neurological collection of spatial awareness. Ladle of doing language meaningfully is lost in soup of disabled map of autism so I need potholder of touch to grab it'.[67] The 'soup of disabled map of autism', or what he calls in conversation with Biklen 'the island of autism', prompts a sensory response to working with material, and a need for visual expression, and these frame his works.[68] In many of his pieces, as with Figures 1 and 2, the parallel plane effect of the painting's content, its seeming reliance on a horizontal two dimensionality, combines with the artist's use of names and pictures to present Bissonnette, or his friends, looking back out at the viewer as he inscribes himself in the images he creates.

Placing 'Larry' – many of his comments on himself and his work refer to himself in the third person, a common autistic use of language – in his art in this way creates a centrality to his presence that negotiates a sense of his autistic self. It mediates between the difficulties of autism,

Figure 2. *Playful Larry Looks Out on Futuristic Land of Creativity & Identity Finding*, by Larry Bissonnette, 1996 (17.5" × 47.5" mixed media on masonite, frame by artist).

the challenges that Bissonnette feels his condition poses to his subjectivity, and a creative urge to produce meaning through visual images. As Bissonnette has said of his paintings, 'Tapping well of silence with painting permitted songs of hurt to be meted with creativity'.[69]

Bissonnette is not considered to be a savant, but even in making such a statement we can further understand the role that an idea of savantism performs in a cultural understanding of autism. Bissonnette's art explores with great subtleties a combined approach to being autistic, one that has roots in sensory perceptions, spatial awareness and an intellectual consideration of questions of ontology. It is a supreme example of autistic intelligence at work in a portrayal of disability. But it does not constitute the kind of traditional 'skill' that is seen to denote savantism, and it does not seek to section off its end product from the often convoluted factors inherent in the condition that produced it, unlike memorization and calculation skills. In a similar way, Bissonnette's work refuses the narrative that offers a transparent idea of autistic 'brilliance' for a majority audience, a narrative that savantism can and does provide. Instead, his art provides a particular form of human achievement, from a point on the neurobehavioural spectrum, which resists incorporation into standard explanatory accounts of what disabled difference is and how it works.

As with the life stories discussed in the last chapter, the particulars of Bissonnette's personal narrative complicate any straightforward account of autistic ability that we might read into his situation. His individual version of autism and his chosen working method represent a unique version of autistic expression. In the world of fiction, however, such particularities can be ignored, and the range of savant characters in recent writing show that a generic idea of the savant figure has increasingly become accepted as a common face of autism. In Barbara Gowdy's 1995 novel *Mister Sandman*, Joan Canary, an echolalic girl with autism, is a savant pianist whose difference allows her to explore tensions in her family. An autistic musical prodigy is also at the centre of Frank Conroy's *Body and Soul* (1993), in which Claude Rawlings, an alienated and poor young man in 1940s New York, gains entrance into the upper echelons of society through his talents. In Alessandro Baricco's *City* (2001), the central character, Gould, is a thirteen-year-old mathematical savant who creates an imaginary world free from human interaction other than with his governess. Likewise, a teenage mathematical savant is the central character of Gore Vidal's *The Smithsonian Institution* (1998), summoned to the Smithsonian in 1939 to help with the American war effort after a formula he has written in the margins of an algebra exam suggests the possibility of time travel. In Helen DeWitt's *The Last Samurai* (2000), Ludo is a child savant whose abilities with languages allow him to learn Greek, Hebrew, Arabic and Japanese, while Patricia Eakins' *The Marvelous Adventures of Pierre Baptiste* (1999) presents the fictional autobiography of the eponymous character, a slave savant, who ranges across the late eighteenth century. Niall Griffiths' *Runt* (2007) utilizes the idea of spiritual innocence in its portrayal, through the use of an internal monologue, of a teenage Welsh boy whose savant capabilities work in terms of the preservation of a folkloric memory. Elizabeth Moon's *Speed of Dark* (2002) twists the idea of savant ability with a near-future narrative in which medical intervention has eradicated autism but a group of adult savants, born before the scientific discovery, are kept employed by a faceless multinational company that uses their pattern-solving abilities in its research. Possibly most strange in its idea of savantism is James F. David's 1997 thriller *Fragments,* where a research scientist combines the minds of five savants in order to attempt the production of a 'super intellect'.

Presented in a list such as this, these various titles might seem to suggest an eclectic mix. In truth, however, there is great commonality in the novels and their portrayal of savant ability. All use the notion of an 'unknowable' savant skill to create what is fundamentally a flexible and open space in their fiction. Such a space allows for the fascination central to the majority view of autistic savantism, the unlocated cultural wondering that underpins a general sense of the condition; but in narrative terms this space also allows for a process of refraction by which key elements of the story are explored precisely through the openness with which the fictional autism is constituted. This is the classic prosthetic disability narrative at work, of course, but with specific configurations here caused by the disability in question. So, in many of the texts mentioned above, an idea of alienation, other-worldliness or personal difference allows for the discussion of personal or familial relations; a sense of technical 'brilliance' (especially in the narratives concerning music or mathematics) calls into question other forms of human capability or achievement; notions of innocence illustrate and inform representations of prejudice and power; and the events of history are held up for examination precisely because of the prism of difference a savant subjectivity is seen to provide. In effect, autism has become an effective narrative tool here. Defined by its association with the savant, and subsequently reduced to a set of generalized behavioural characteristics, the condition appears sufficiently permeable (and yet *known*) for it to be mobilized in the representation of any number of questions and themes that are, at heart, not about disability. Explorations of how families should work, how outsiders should be treated, or how history should be written are, of course, issues for disabled and non-disabled communities alike, but as such themes are played out in fictions that base themselves around savant characters, the disability becomes a vehicle through which an essentially non-disabled perspective is articulated. The savant has become sufficiently and suitably generic that any actual notion of a *material* disability vanishes in the fictional playing of the character, and so it is the insertion of this generic marker into what are thought of as 'wider' themes that becomes paramount. Autism is endlessly fascinating, these novels seem to say, but never more so than when we might quickly characterize it and use it to look at something else.

## VI

The reliance on fiction that the savant now generates helps to understand what is the closing of a curious circle. For all the scientific precision that savantism invites, the imaging of the brain to understand neurological processing and the countless tests that a figure like Tammet has undergone, the figure of the autistic savant occupies a cultural position that is not dissimilar to that of the idiot in the nineteenth century. While there might not be a seminal reaction that sees the savant as retarded, and although there are certainly efforts to understand this aspect of autism in terms of a complex personality, the diffuse methods by which the specifics of the condition now appear through the processes of representation do parallel the cultural understanding of idiocy in a number of ways. Savant autism, as characterized in our time, has the same absence of coherence that marked 'the idiot' figure of an earlier era. Both are vehicles by which questions of morality and sentimentality can be explored; both can be seen to be marginal, even when their protagonists might be central, because their usage nearly always points away from the specifics of the impairment concerned. The characterization of the savant might seem far more precise that the traditional motley (both real and imagined) of the idiot, but it is best to see this as simply the operation of the mechanics of the contemporary period, where expertise and specialisms provide what is, in this case, illusory cover.

All this might seem counterintuitive. As Rosemarie Garland-Thomson has written, 'in our time, rationality has replaced wonder. Rationality seeks to master; wonder seeks to inflame', but we should understand that, with regard to autism, the cultural mechanics by which rationality works in the contemporary period involve the selective use of wonder.[70] It has become impossible to disassociate the two. The more that neurologists appear in television documentaries discussing the make-up of the brain, the more audiences want to see evidence of card counting or 'impossible' mathematical feats in those same programmes. And in the world of fictional representation, the only limits placed on the portrayal of savant abilities are those provided by the imagination. The 'special' abilities contained with films such as the *X-Men* trilogy (2000–6), the ideas of 'mutantcy' in other comic book film adaptations such as *Hulk* (2003), *Elektra* (2005), the two *Fantastic Four* films (2005 and 2007) or the television series *Heroes* (2006–) can be seen to be extensions of this alignment of particular skill with an unarticulated difference. In this regard, autism can be seen to be strangely satisfying. In a time of rationality and scientific knowledge, it provides the space for wonder and awe, and no kind of autistic figure does this more than the savant. Allowing for autism to be 'incredible' in this way, of course, pushes the condition into the world of fantasy. It makes it easier to ignore the social dimensions, the apparently mundane questions of schooling or respite care or employment options for adults with autism. It keeps things at arm's length. There may be no more idiots, but there are still ways in which certain conversations can be avoided.

## Notes

1  Michael J. A. Howe, *Fragments of Genius: The Strange Feats of Idiots Savants* (London: Routledge, 1989), pp. 5–6.
2  Howe, *Fragments of Genius*, p. 10.
3  Donald Treffert, *Extraordinary People: Understanding 'Idiot Savants'* (New York: Harper & Row, 1989). Uta Frith, *Autism: Explaining the Enigma* (Oxford: Basil

Blackwell, 1989), pp. 84–5, and second edition (2003), pp. 146–50. In the second edition, the change from *'idiot savant'* to 'savant' is briefly discussed on p. 146, and then appears again only in the index, with a direction to 'savant'. But it is notable that Oliver Sacks still uses the term in his various writings that are collected together in his *An Anthropologist on Mars* (London: Picador, 1995).

4  Martin Halliwell, *Images of Idiocy: The Idiot Figure in Modern Fiction and Film* (Aldershot: Ashgate, 2004), p. 5.

5  *The Real Rain Man*, Channel 5, 27 February 2006.

6  Fran Peek, 'Preface', in *The Real Rain Man* (Salt Lake City, UT: Harkness Publishing, 1996), n.p. Interestingly, in that Preface Fran Peek asserts that Kim 'isn't autistic; on the contrary, now that he's come out among people he's very outgoing' (n.p.). This is a particularly personal view of Kim Peek by his father, who goes on to state that 'Some of Kim's behavioral characteristics are certainly similar to autistic behaviors, but autistic individuals generally are antisocial loners, don't like to be touched or cuddled, and usually show little compassion towards others' (p. 53). This is clearly a misrepresentation of the condition, and it would be hard to argue that Kim doesn't fit a number of the criteria by which autism diagnosis is achieved.

7  For more on these three figures, see Sacks, *An Anthropologist on Mars*, pp. 179–82.

8  Hilary Dickinson, 'Idiocy in nineteenth-century fiction compared with the medical perspectives of the time', *History of Psychiatry*, vol. 11, no. 3 (2000), p. 307. For an account of idiocy in the early modern period, see Jonathan Andrews, 'Begging the question of idiocy: the definition and socio-cultural meaning of idiocy in early modern Britain: Part 1', *History of Psychiatry*, vol. 9, no. 33 (1998), pp. 65–95.

9  Halliwell, *Images of Idiocy*, pp. 9–10.

10  Dickinson, 'Idiocy in nineteenth-century fiction', p. 292.

11  Patrick McDonagh, *'Barnaby Rudge*, "idiocy" and paternalism: assisting the "poor idiot"', *Disability & Society*, vol. 21, no. 5 (August 2006), p. 412.

12  McDonagh, *'Barnaby Rudge*, "idiocy" and paternalism', p. 142.

13  Charles Dickens, *Barnaby Rudge: A Tale of the Riots of 'Eighty* (1841; London: Penguin, 2003), p. 37. Subsequent references are in parentheses in the text.

14  McDonagh, *'Barnaby Rudge*, "idiocy" and paternalism', p. 413.

15  See Frith, *Autism* (2003 edition), pp. 35–43. The case of Victor prompted much of the speculation about the possibility of educating disabled children, leading directly to the 1840s context of potential 'instruction' that is central to Dickens' novel.

16  John Bowen, 'Introduction', *Barnaby Rudge: A Tale of the Riots of 'Eighty* (London: Penguin, 2003), p. xvi.

17  Bowen, 'Introduction', p. xvii.

18  For example, John Willet says of Hugh, 'He's more at ease among horses than men. I look upon him as an animal himself' (p. 98).

19  Bowen, 'Introduction', p. xxiii.

20  McDonagh, *'Barnaby Rudge*, "idiocy" and paternalism', p. 420.

21  Charles Dickens (with W. H. Wills), 'Idiots', in Harry Stone (ed.), *Charles Dickens' Uncollected Writings from* Household Works *1850–1859, Vol. II* (Bloomington, IN: Indiana University Press, 1968), p. 490. See also 'A curious dance round a curious tree', an account of an 'asylum for the insane', in the same volume, pp. 381–91. Both essays contain observations of patients we might genuinely recognize as individuals with autism, indeed, even with savant abilities. In 'Idiots', Dickens quotes one Dr Fodére, who had met 'with idiots gifted for

especial talents for copying designs, for finding rhymes and for performing music'. 'I have known others', he adds, 'put watches together and other pieces of mechanism; yet these individuals not only were unable to read books which treated of their arts, but were utterly incoherent when spoken to about them' (p. 492). In 'A curious dance round a curious tree', there is the description of 'a handsome young man deriving intense gratification from the motion of his fingers as he played with them in the air' (p. 387), a clear example of autistic 'stimming'.

22 Bowen notes the 'strong affinity' *Barnaby Rudge* has with melodrama and discusses the connection at length. Given the place of the melodramatic in contemporary literary and filmic representations of autism, this is an interesting link. See Bowen, 'Introduction', pp. xviii–xix.

23 This was noted in letters to the *Journal of Autism and Developmental Disorders* in the mid-1980s. See C. D. Webster, 'Conrad's "The Idiots": case examples of autism?', vol. 14, no. 3 (September 1984), pp. 346–7, and G. Patrick Farrell, 'Autism in literature', vol. 15, no. 4 (December 1985), pp. 441–2.

24 Joseph Conrad, *Tales of Unrest* (London: Eveleigh, Nash & Grayson, n.d. but 1898), p. 83. Subsequent references are in parentheses in the text.

25 In his letter to the *Journal of Autism and Developmental Disorders*, Webster notes that the story 'offers a powerful description of how the boys' [*sic*] parents reacted – disastrously as it turned out – to the strain and responsibility of raising children with severe communication disorders' (p. 347).

26 Joseph Conrad, *The Secret Agent* (1907; London: Penguin, 1994), p. 17. Subsequent references are in parentheses in the text.

27 Interestingly for the terms of this book, in his study *Cities of Affluence and Anger*, P. J. Kalliney talks of Conrad's anarchists being 'physically deformed by obesity or other maladies', and showing 'visible signs of physical and racial deterioration'. See P. J. Kalliney, *Cities of Affluence and Anger* (Charlottesville, VA: University of Virginia Press, 2006), p. 38.

28 Hermione Lee, *Virginia Woolf* (London: Chatto & Windus, 1996), p. 103.

29 Lee, *Virginia Woolf*, pp. 103–4.

30 Lee, *Virginia Woolf*, p. 104.

31 Quoted in Lee, *Virginia Woolf*, p. 104.

32 Virginia Woolf published her famous study *A Room of One's Own* in 1929.

33 Halliwell's study is the most comprehensive account of such a legacy. He notes, for example, Conrad's engagement in *The Secret Agent* with the ideas of Cesare Lombroso on idiocy and criminality. See Halliwell, *Images of Idiocy*, pp. 99–101. Halliwell also briefly discusses 'The Idiots' on p. 104.

34 'Bellow on bellow, his voice mounted, with scarce interval of breath. There was more than astonishment in it, it was horror; shock; agony eyeless, tongueless; just sound.' William Faulkner, *The Sound and The Fury* (1929; Harmondsworth: Penguin, 1964), p. 283.

35 See Michael Bérubé, *Life As We Know It: A Father, a Family and an Exceptional Child* (New York: Vintage, 1998), pp. xiv–xv, and Halliwell, *Images of Idiocy*, pp. 19–25.

36 Anita Desai, *Clear Light of Day* (Harmondsworth: Penguin, 1980), p. 5.

37 Desai, *Clear Light of Day*, p. 12.

38 Desai, *Clear Light of Day*, pp. 12–13.

39 Desai, *Clear Light of Day*, p. 182.

40 See Keri Hulme, *the bone people* (1983; London: Picador, 1986); Pauline Melville, *The Ventriloquist's Tale* (London: Bloomsbury, 1997), p. 74; and J. M. Coetzee, *Life & Times of Michael K* (1983; London: Vintage, 2004), p. 135. Pauline Melville

told me that a number of people had commented to her that Sonny appeared as a character with autism, but she had been completely unaware of this when writing the novel (personal interview, 11 May 2002). By all accounts, when he worked as a university lecturer in English in Cape Town, Coetzee would lecture on 'Bartleby the Scrivener' and suggest that Bartleby might be seen as an autistic character. Ato Quayson explores the connection between Michael K and autism in *Aesthetic Nervousness: Disability and the Crisis of Representation* (New York: Columbia University Press, 2007), pp. 147–73.

41 For an account of the relationship between disability and New Zealand culture in Hulme, see Clare Barker, 'From narrative prosthesis to disability counternarrative: reading the politics of difference in *Potiki* and *the bone people*', *Journal of New Zealand Literature*, vol. 24, no. 1 (2006), pp. 130–47.

42 Halliwell, *Images of Idiocy*, p. 215.

43 See Halliwell, *Images of Idiocy*, pp. 222–4. See also Winston Groom, *Forrest Gump* (Garden City, NY: Doubleday, 1986). Arguably, the literary Forrest does possess autistic traits. He is, for example, frequently rude or dismissive about others in a way that implies he does not understand how his words are received.

44 Peek, *The Real Rain Man*, pp. 28–9.

45 Peek, *The Real Rain Man*, p. 45 and p. 52.

46 Fran Peek's claim that Kim is not autistic has surely to be seen in this regard. In the way he presents the condition and term, Fran sees it as a clear negative that he does not wish to associate with his son's abilities. He notes that the character of Raymond in *Rain Man* is not a representation of Kim – 'Kim's authentic persona turned out to be too complex for the story to depict' – implying that the 'addition' of autism to Raymond's character (principally in terms of what he calls 'antisocial ways') produced a 'composite character'. Peek, *The Real Rain Man*, p. 63.

47 Quayson, *Aesthetic Nervousness*, p. 14 and p. 15.

48 Rich Shull, *Autism, Pre Rain Man* (New York: iUniverse, 2003), p. 3.

49 Daniel Tammet, *Born on a Blue Day: A Memoir of Asperger's and an Extraordinary Mind* (London: Hodder & Stoughton, 2006), p. 209.

50 Tammet, *Born on a Blue Day*, p. 208.

51 Tammet, *Born on a Blue Day*, p. 212.

52 Tammet, *Born on a Blue Day*, p. 81.

53 Quoted in Tammet, *Born on a Blue Day*, p. 226.

54 Tammet, *Born on a Blue Day*, p. 208.

55 It is Tammet's appearance on the Letterman show that causes him to write: 'This experience showed me more than any other that I really was now able to make my way in the world, to do things for myself'. Tammet, *Born on a Blue Day*, p. 229.

56 By 2007, Channel 5 was running its seventh 'Extraordinary People' series, a strand it considers one of its highlights since the channel's launch in 1997. See http://www.five.tv/programmes/extraordinarypeople. Accessed 27 August 2007.

57 Mark Haddon, *The Curious Incident of the Dog in the Night-Time* (London: Jonathan Cape, 2003), p. 268.

58 Tammet, *Born on a Blue Day*, p. 242.

59 *The Musical Genius* was screened on Channel 5 on 19 February 2007, and *The Human Camera* on 26 March 2008. Interestingly, the former documentary, along with *Brainman* and *The Real Rain Man*, the documentary on Kim Peek, were all made by the same production company – Focus Productions, from the UK. Focus also made *Painting the Mind*, a documentary featuring savant artists, in

2006. See http://www.focusproductions.co.uk/Home_Text.html. Accessed 28 August 2007.

60  For details of Wiltshire's work, see http://www.stephenwiltshire.co.uk/index. aspx. Accessed 28 August 2007. Jonathan Lerman is, like Wiltshire, a young artist with autism whose work has received international coverage, especially after the Outsider Art Fair in 2002. See Lyle Rexer, *Jonathan Lerman: Drawings by an Artist with Autism* (New York: George Braziller, 2002) for a full account of his work.

61  Grandin is the subject of chapter 7, 'An anthropologist on Mars', and Wiltshire of chapter 6, 'Prodigies', in Sacks, *An Anthropologist on Mars*, pp. 233–82 and pp. 179–232.

62  For more detail on Paravicini, see http://www.derekparavicini.net/index.html. Accessed 28 August 2007. See also Adam Ockelford, *In the Key of Genius: The Extraordinary Life of Derek Paravicini* (London: Hutchinson, 2007).

63  At the same time, reading Sacks' commentaries on savants he has encountered in various institutional contexts works to remind us that many of these supposed 'abilities' belong to those who have been incarcerated for much of their lives. Sacks' description of seeing an unnamed 'idiot savant' with 'extraordinary bodily skills' in a 1960s asylum 'back ward' is a sobering moment, pointing to the institutionalization that was the common experience for many with autism, savant or not. See Sacks, *An Anthropologist on Mars*, p. 184.

64  See the chapter on Bissonnette in Douglas Biklen, *Autism and the Myth of the Person Alone* (New York: New York University Press, 2005), pp. 168–82. Biklen is also the co-director, along with Zach Rossetti, of a 2005 twenty-two minute documentary about Bissonnette, *My Classic Life as an Artist: A Portrait of Larry Bissonnette*.

65  Biklen, *Autism and the Myth of the Person Alone*, p. 171.

66  Biklen, *Autism and the Myth of the Person Alone*, p. 179 and p. 174.

67  Larry Bissonnette, 'Beyond questions and answers: free expression through art and words', http://suedweb.syr.edu/thefci/7-3bis.htm. Accessed 30 August 2007.

68  'An artist stranded on the island of autism' is part of the title of Biklen's chapter on Bissonnette. See Biklen, *Autism and the Myth of the Person Alone*, p. 172.

69  Bissonnette, quoted in Biklen, *Autism and the Myth of the Person Alone*, p. 170. Images of Bissonnette's art can be found at http://store.graceart.org/store/ productlist/1566. Accessed 30 August 2007.

70  Rosemarie Garland-Thomson, 'Review of *Monsters: Human Freaks in America's gilded Age* and *Extraordinary Exhibitions*', *Disability Studies Quarterly*, vol. 25, no. 4 (2005).

# CHAPTER 3

# Witnessing

I

If looking *for* autism – the processes of assessment and diagnosis – is complex, then looking *at* autism – seeing it in the world – is equally a far from straightforward activity. As a condition that does not automatically signal its presence, and unlike certain other disabilities, autism can go unnoticed, inhabiting an invisibility. Even the most pronounced cases of autistic behavioural difference do not involve a *continual* visual signification of disability. Individuals with autism can, and do, involve themselves daily in activities in which their difference goes unrecognized, a form of passing in the majority world. At the same time, autism can provoke sudden, seemingly inexplicable, behaviour that is highly physical and visual. From tantrums to self-harm, and from playful vocalization to pleasurable acts of physical repetition, autism can be an eruptive force, and – as a consequence – one that invites the gaze of onlookers. And, of course, in thinking through the issues of such gazing, we realize that the processes of looking *for* and *at* autism combine. Clinical diagnosis is necessarily an evaluative process: it requires the person under evaluation to be the subject of methods and procedures that have looking at their centre. The knowledgeable assessment in the hospital is not the glare caused by 'misbehaviour' in the shopping centre, but they share a common thread. To be autistic is often to be the subject of number of different kinds of stares.

It is the nature of these looks and stares, the detail of the gaze and its consequences, which this chapter will explore. In the visual media, the *invitation* to look at autism has never been greater, an invitation that sets out certain rules about the display and consumption of the images in question, and produces particular kinds of narratives as a result. On one level, the stare that autism produces is that generated by disability more generally, and this kind of gaze is one that has been the subject of much work in disability theorizing. There is an inherently visual dimension to the ways in which disability is understood and, even with the complexities of the condition's presence, autism is no exception to this rule. At the same time, there is another kind of visual process with regard to autism, one more difficult to categorize. Looking at someone with autism can be deeply personal, in specific ways. For any parent around the time of initial suspicion and diagnosis, for example, it is impossible not to look, and for that look to constitute some kind of search. This is especially the case with photographs taken *before*: before the knowledge; before it was obvious. And, for some, these photographs can be examined only to look for something that a certain kind of narrative maintains has subsequently been lost, and to frame the experience of the condition in this way. In the photographs taken of my youngest son before I knew of his condition, he looks straight at the camera. He is exactly the right kind of inquisitive – the baby boy dazzled by the magic lantern, the little one next to his brothers. His innocence is here reassuring: it is what it should be. I do not believe for a second that his autism was not present at this stage, but it is often this moment – and this kind of retrospective looking act – that constitutes for many the moment when their child was 'lost'. The baby fixed in a crawling pose, smiling out of the photograph, does not appear out of the ordinary. It is hard to recognize that the autism is there in these glimpses, that it is not latent, but rather present, and that it is simply a question of it not being seen. I should stress that, for all that this kind of description seems a form of acute sentimentality, it is, I would hope, more recognition of what is, in the lives of many who experience autism, a crucial set of events. And these events are to do with an understanding which is based on what is seen.

*Seeing* is vital in any consideration of autism. As writers such as Donna Williams have shown in articulating their lives, visual and perceptual difference is often a key element in the ways in which autism manifests itself, and much medical research has focused on understanding the ways in which the condition influences looking at and processing images. For anyone outside the condition, seeing is initially what you do: you look for it and its signs. If the person with autism is close to you, someone you know well and have known for a long time, you also look for times when it appeared not to be there, and for the subsequent ways in which it has made itself familiar. If it is a stranger you encounter, you look for the ways in which it makes

itself known. And then, when you know, when you're in the *after* world
of knowledge, having read all the books and websites, it is common
to *watch*. Watching here is both exceptional and normal. Personally, I
found that in a relationship where at times there could be little or no
overt communication there seemed no problem with a kind of prying,
despite all I know and feel about privacy. So it became a habit to spend
long periods of time watching a person who didn't watch me, and
seemed to care little about my watching. Watching is less angst ridden
than seeing. It is long term, about learning when seen positively and
constructively, and it is frequently pleasurable and funny – I play games
with my son and his sightlines, me trying to make him catch my eye.
Often when it's difficult to be positive, watching is full of sentiment
and a nostalgia for something that has never been, and an incoherent
fear of the future. At other times it can be a productive way in which
ideas about what it means to be autistic can be pieced together.

The attempt to understand autism through looking at it is central to
many of the most contemporary narratives that deal with the condition.
Especially in film and television, narratives are wrapped around this fundamental invitation to look at the individual with autism, and to try to
see how the condition manifests itself. As Rosemarie Garland-Thomson
has noted, 'In our ocularcentric era, images mediate our desires and the
ways we imagine ourselves'.[1] Since the success of *Rain Man*, autism has
featured regularly in high-profile commercial cinema, while the rise of
public debate over vaccination scares has been paralleled by an increase
in the portrayal of autism in television drama. There is an interesting
tension at the heart of such narratives, caused by the juxtaposition of a
linear idea of storytelling with the public perception of autism as being
a condition that is fixed and static. At a conference on autism in New
York, I met a screenwriter who had recently scripted a highly successful
Hollywood film, complete with an A-list cast. He was at the conference
as he has a nephew with autism, and I had heard that he had ideas to
develop a comedy that centred on an autistic central protagonist. As
we talked, he made it clear that, after his initial enthusiasm, he now
saw no future for the idea. Central to the acceptance of such a story,
he said, would be the necessary development of the character, the journey towards self-knowledge that such a narrative demands. 'They', he
said, generalizing about the decision makers in Hollywood, would not
believe this was possible for a character with autism. He saw all sorts
of potential for the exploration of autism and comedy, but was certain
that the project would never get off the ground.

The perceived impossibility of personal development means that
characters with autism frequently occupy peripheral positions within

film narratives, even if an *idea* of the condition is pivotal to the film concerned. As we shall see, visual narratives that deal with autism – especially fictional ones – oscillate between a concentration on the arresting visual presence of the autistic individual on the one hand, and the placing of that visual moment within the wider movement of the plot and story. The results produce widely differing representations of what autism is and how it functions in the world.

The rise of autism's place in the public consciousness has also seen an increase in the condition as a subject for photography, with a concentration on the representation of children with autism. In discussing any visual representation of disability, but especially photography, it is impossible not to engage with Garland-Thomson's seminal work. Her account of what she terms 'the politics of staring' at people with disabilities, though largely focused on the physically disabled, offers significant insight into the portrayal of autism in both photography and film. My ideas of looking and watching described above, as well as the notion of witnessing I will come to explore later, are informed by her formulations. It is worth quoting her description of the staring process at some length:

> Staring at disability choreographs a visual relation between a spectator and a spectacle. A more intense form of looking than glancing, glimpsing, scanning, surveying, gazing and other forms of casual or uninterested looking, staring registers the perception of difference and gives meaning to impairment by marking it as aberrant. By intensely telescoping looking towards the physical signifier for disability, staring creates an awkward partnership that estranges and discomforts both viewer and viewed. Starers gawp with abandon at the prosthetic hook, the empty sleeve, the scarred flesh, the unfocused eye, the twitching limb, but seldom does looking broaden out to envelop the whole body of the person with a disability. Even supposedly invisible disabilities always threaten to disclose some stigma, however subtle, that disrupts the social order by its presence and attenuates the bond between equal members of the human community. Because staring at disability is considered illicit looking, the disabled body is at once the to-be-looked-at and not-to-be-looked-at, further dramatizing the staring encounter by making viewers furtive and the viewed defensive. Staring thus creates disability as a state of absolute difference rather than simply one more variation in human form. At the same time, staring constitutes disability identity by manifesting the power relations between the subject positions of disabled and able-bodied.[2]

This is a succinct and full explication of the processes inherent in image making as it applies to people with disabilities. As Garland-Thomson goes on to note, the licensed staring that was allowed in the time of the freak shows of the nineteenth and early twentieth centuries may now have gone, but photography, as she puts it, 'has enabled the social ritual of staring at disability to persist in an alternate form'.[3]

Garland-Thomson suggests a 'taxonomy of four primary visual rhetorics of disability ... the wondrous, the sentimental, the exotic and the realistic'.[4] The realistic is, she suggests, the mode that is the least exploitative, but all of them, in one form or another, 'appropriate the disabled body for the purposes of constructing, instructing, or assuring some aspect of a putatively nondisabled viewer'.[5] There is no doubt that looking at the disabled is nearly always a process where meaning is constructed through an idea that the viewer is *not* disabled, and even the most contemporary manifestation of such images cannot escape the long history of disability having been a spectacle and on display. With a neurobehavioural impairment such as autism, however, the contours of the debate are rearranged somewhat. The photograph of the individual with autism does not provide the 'physical signifier' of which Garland-Thomson speaks. Instead, other visual elements come into play. As we saw in the discussion of Jane Bown's photograph in the Preface, the context of the image is often vitally important in any photographic statement on autism. Often, the idea that autism is a condition of withdrawal and solitude – Leo Kanner's early formation of 'aloneness' – prompts photographs in which the subject is framed as though overwhelmed or lost in the surrounding environment. In Rosie Barnes' collections of photographs of her autistic son Stanley, *Understanding Stanley* (2002), Stanley is often figured in this way. In one photograph, 'Mural', from 1998, he sits on a playground toy, a bike on springs, in the bottom right of the image. He is looking away from the camera at a giant, colourful wall mural, in which large figures play above three houses on a vibrant yellow background. The mural itself occupies some three-quarters of the overall frame, with Stanley almost peripheral. As viewers, we see him side on in a three-quarters pose from behind, but because he faces the mural his face is not in view and there is no opportunity to gauge how he is reacting to the images. Barnes herself notes: 'He sat still for a long time on that bike, just sitting still, staring at this kind of madness', but it is arguable whether the mural itself really is 'madness'.[6] In its bright bold colours and large shapes it could equally be fun, or pleasurable, or challenging. We look at Stanley, but are not privy to the way in which he himself is looking.

Two other photographs by Barnes of her son underline similar ideas about autism and the subject. In 'Trampoline' (2001) and 'Stanley on Swing' (2001) Stanley is the single figure in the frame. In 'Trampoline' he stands naked on a trampoline, slightly to the right of centre, facing away from the camera with his hands behind his back. In 'Stanley on Swing' he sits, seemingly passively, on a small swing at a complete right angle to the camera, framed in the middle of the image and in the middle distance. Stanley's hands hold the bars of the swing and he looks down, possibly to the ground or at his clothes. In both photographs there is a clear evocation of distance and solitude. Stanley seems to offer no interaction with the camera; he is potentially 'lost in his own world'. In not bouncing on the trampoline and not swinging on the swing – Barnes' comments on the photographs make it clear that neither image records an 'activity' understood in that sense – he is not using the objects he is on for what most people would consider their primary purpose, namely play. Stanley seems static in these photographs; the implication is that, whatever he might be doing or thinking, he is doing so on his own terms. While this might suggest an idea of agency, of a possible suggestion and portrayal of Stanley's own creation of meaning in the environments in which he is being photographed, the images seem more to function to record a sense of loss. Instead of an idea of presence, Barnes' photographs portray the absence of a connection, a gap (in this case) between mother and son, a problematic difference. One of the other photographs in the *Understanding Stanley* series, entitled 'Cactus', is not of Stanley at all, but rather features a cactus in a large pot, placed in the middle of some grass, with trees in the background. 'Stanley looks like any other child', Barnes comments, 'then you realise that there's this kind of rigidity there. The cactus is about this inflexibility of thinking. It looks like nice soft circular shapes, but it's as stiff as a board.'[7] However effective this might be as a metaphor for her reading of Stanley's condition, it is hard not to see Barnes' image here as a form of erasure. Peripheral in some of the other photographs, here Stanley has gone completely from the frame, replaced by an object that works through a process of analogy. Barnes talks of her photographs as 'me trying to understand what it's like for him'.[8] More than anything else, however, her images seem to record her own anxiety and sorrow.

The other common form of photography featuring autistic individuals (again, predominantly children) as subjects is a portraiture based around close-ups of the head and face. Here, there is a layered and complex set of questions and meanings at work. Given the condition's lack of obvious physical signification, what exactly *is* the detail involved in any invitation to look at the face of a child with autism? In Thomas Balsamo and Sharon Rosenbloom's 2004 collection of images and text, *Souls: Beneath and Beyond Autism*, the photographs (by Balsamo, and untitled) of autistic children are mainly solo portraits, though some

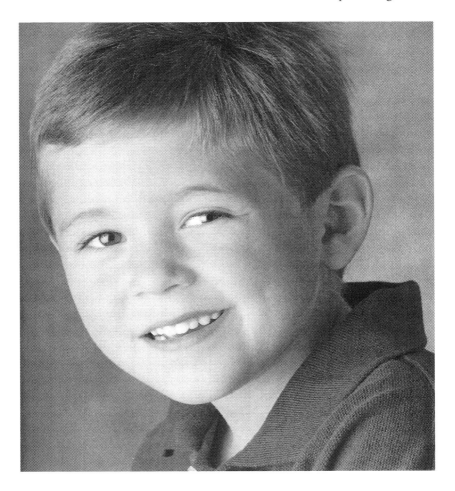

Figure 3. Thomas Balsamo's photograph from page 7 of Thomas Balsamo and Sharon Rosenbloom's collection of images and text, *Souls: Beneath and Beyond Autism* (2004).

feature children with their siblings and parents. The images pose difficult questions. On one level there is nothing to see – the children with autism remain largely undifferentiated from any other children who might appear in photographs and, indeed, from their siblings in the cases where other children are included in the frame. In figure 3, the boy makes direct eye contact with the camera, and his pose is common to many a studio photograph produced for a family or school. Seen without context, this photograph raises the standard questions portraiture produces: for any portrait to have social meaning, it must

Figure 4. Thomas Balsamo's photograph from page 26 of Thomas Balsamo and Sharon Rosenbloom's collection of images and text, *Souls: Beneath and Beyond Autism* (2004).

somehow encode societal expectations, it must somehow typify its subject. Thought of in this way, the photograph raises ideas of child-hood, possibly of family. But the addition of autism – knowing that this boy is autistic – changes the dynamic of the image, especially when aligned with the book's text (mostly written by Rosenbloom), in which it is made explicit that the intention of the photographs lies, in Balsamo's words, in 'capturing the essence of children dealing with autism'.[9] Now looking again at the photograph, and following Balsamo's further advice for the viewer to 'look into the eyes of these beautiful children', it becomes impossible not to look into the face of

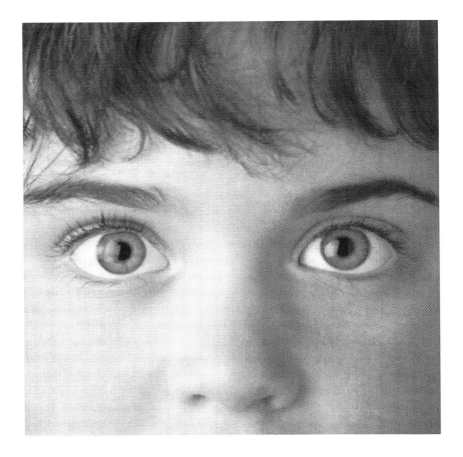

Figure 5. Thomas Balsamo's photograph from page viii of Thomas Balsamo and Sharon Rosenbloom's collection of images and text, *Souls: Beneath and Beyond Autism* (2004).

the boy in the image and to somehow look *for* his autism, even as it is clear that this is an impossibility.[10]

We might feel that this is a conflation of two of Garland-Thomson's visual rhetorics. The realism of the studio portrait becomes overtaken, when the context is supplied, by a suggestion of the wondrous. In figure 4, the invited wonder seems even more pronounced. The girl looks down, below the plane of the camera, possibly aware of its presence, possibly oblivious to it. Her eyes are the focal point of the photograph, and even without the book's accompanying prose, it would be clear here that the idea of the eyes being the window to the soul dominates a sense of the image's meaning. Many of the popular conceptions of autism that focus on notions of withdrawal and isolation invariably invoke the concept of the 'mask' or 'curtain' when contemplating the face, an idea that character is somehow concealed. All the usual associations between the face and personality are, it is assumed, somehow suspended. The girl figure 4 does not so much reinforce or counteract this, but rather seems to allow contemplation upon it. She is, we know from the text, *disabled*. Why? How? What does this mean? Where do we look for her impairment? The invitation in Balsamo's photograph is to wonder upon these questions. That the viewer here is assumed, as Garland-Thomson notes, to be *non*-autistic is taken for granted. The viewing act here is definitely of an outsider looking in.

In figure 5, which is of the same girl photographed in figure 4, the thesis of the eyes providing access to the soul seems to reach an extreme. The close-up is tight and unsettling; here, the studio and portrait familiarities of figure 3 have vanished. What remains is the idea that it might be somehow possible to look *into* or *through* the girl's eyes, that whatever her autism is might reveal itself through the concentrated viewing act. That this is, in fact, impossible only throws the emphasis back on to the *process* of the look. All that we know, or think we know, about autism can be poured into the contemplation of the girl's face. The idea that the condition is inherently enigmatic and mysterious is matched here by the non-disclosure of the eyes. The suggestions for the viewer can be aesthetic – Balsamo's comments about 'the eyes of these beautiful children' – or, indeed, spiritual, even religious. Sharon Rosenbloom's text in the book notes that 'It is written in many holy books that God will transform the world not with the mighty, but with the meek. Perhaps it is this ancient and universal truth that comes to light in the eyes of a person with autism.'[11] What becomes most striking here, then, as with a number of the examples of texts featuring autism in the last chapter, is the *flexibility* that the condition seems to allow. When the viewer looks at the girl's eyes in the photograph in figure 5, autism is as mysterious or profound, or as casual and throwaway, as the imagination allows. Precisely because the condition is seen to lack a specific visual vocabulary of its own, the photographs invite signification as to what exactly autism might be, and all the ideas of the lost child or the redeemed adult flood the images that *Souls* puts before the viewer.

As Garland-Thomson notes in her discussion of the wondrous and photography: 'Photography introduced into the rhetoric of wonder the illusion of fusing the ordinary with the extraordinary'.[12] Although *Souls* does not contain the kinds of examples she uses – such physical 'wonders' as people able to eat or write using their feet – the principle of the juxtaposition is the same. What Garland-Thomson terms the physical 'mark of impairment'[13] might be missing from Balsamo's photographs, but the contemporary general cultural assumptions about autism, the forms of fascination provided by the difference, themselves form a 'mark'. In turn these assumptions and forms supply the detail for the production of the 'extraordinary'. It may just seem to be the face of a boy or a girl that looks out from the pages of *Souls*, but the book is in fact a set of moments that produce an open invitation to speculate about the mysteries of autism, safe in the understanding that the condition is, indeed, one of mystery. *Souls* is a publication committed to increasing understanding of what it is like for children to live with autism. Balsamo and Rosenbloom know that autistic children are often perceived in terms of their external behaviour, and that featuring them in single portraits or family settings offers a different perspective on their subjectivity, but their own methods lock the children in the volume into an objectified account of their autism and present them as curiosities as much as individuals. They are maybe not subject to the exploitative practices of a previous era of display, because we, as a public, would not tolerate that in this particular present, but the manner in which they are shown is an ideological relative of the basic idea that disability is, in part, there to be stared at and wondered about.[14]

Photography of those with autism produces what we should recognize as a key determinant in any understanding of how the condition is understood in the contemporary world. For all the direct nature of the viewing act that is involved when looking at a photograph of an autistic adult or child, the process is not one of *seeing*. In the photographs discussed above, neither the child nor the condition is actually seen – too much crowds in upon the moment and renders it more multiple. Rather, the images constitute a form of *witnessing*, a bringing to bear on the individual photograph of an amorphous and often contradictory set of ideas that stand for what we know of autism at the present time. In part this is a point about the processes of photography, and especially the photography of those with disabilities, namely the contradictions inherent in the need for a portrait to be both singular and yet to inscribe the social meaning of the perceived difference. It is also a specific point about how autism works as a form of such difference, both with its 'invisibility' in the visual image and its wider 'concealment' from the scientific enquiry that might locate exactly what it is and offer treatment – the oft repeated point that, for all our knowledge, we simply don't know the causes of autism. As a result, we don't so much see autism as act as witnesses in the discussion of what we believe it to be. Such witnesses can be experts – from those with autism themselves, to parents and other family members, and to scientific or educational or care practitioners – or they can be largely ignorant, those who know the condition only in a general sense, but might not be surprised to find it in a cultural narrative. Of course, this latter group far outnumbers the former, and so the majority witnessing of autism becomes the processes of engagement, and especially fascination, on which this book seeks to focus. Central to this is the strong visual dimension that many of the most public narratives of autism display. As with other disabilities, autism seems to be most fully the subject of public thought when it can be looked at, the visual engagement providing quick access to a cultural shorthand by which the condition can be contemplated.

In theory, witnessing is positive. We might feel that, as witnesses, we come to any subject with a full sense of what we know. Witnesses are supposed to illuminate, to help in any approach to the truth. But we bear witness haphazardly, and expertise is not necessarily a guarantee of insight. Witnessing cultural narratives of autism is a complex business. As we have noted previously, foundational texts such as *Rain Man* and *The Curious Incident of the Dog in the Night-Time* provide their respective audiences with a degree of knowledge about the condition that appears to work beyond the narratives themselves – they *inform*. A result of this is that the majority audience is made to feel more content in its awareness of what might have been, before the encounter with the book or the film, a subject about which it was wholly ignorant. The members of the audience can now act as witnesses, because they have a model of autism to which they can compare examples of the condition as they find them in the world. Encountering a person with autism in the street thus becomes a situation we might recognize; reading in the newspapers about research on the condition is something with which we can engage. But such witnessing is actually fraught with unease. Based on partial knowledge, it still keeps a demarcated space for a wilful entrance into the fascinating and the enigmatic. The sight of the person with autism, on screen or in a photograph but also in person as well, brings into play the various rhetorics of which Garland-Thomson writes, rendered particular by the nuanced detail of the contemporary obsession with the condition. If it seems that, at times, there is a continual flood of narratives about autism in the present moment, there is an equally continual barrage of invitations and associations that come with such narratives. A lot happens when we start the processes of looking.

II

The visual dynamics of photographing autism produce certain ways of looking at the condition. In film narratives, these dynamics are augmented by the addition of story lines. If *Rain Man* established the type of film in which autism could be central, then many other examples since the late 1980s have expanded upon its basic premise. But, although films that feature autism often feature a great range of emotion and sentimentality, and display noticeable mobility (*Rain Man* is, after all, a road movie in part), they also nearly always provide opportunities to gaze upon autism in ways that replicate some of the ideas about photography outlined above. As we shall see, even the most hectic of filmic autism narratives seems to feel the need to stop and invite its audience to look upon the person with autism, an invitation to contemplation very like that seen in the photographs in *Souls*.

As a paradigmatic example of this, we can cite a key scene in Bruce Beresford's 1994 crime thriller *Silent Fall*. A young autistic boy, Tim Warden (Ben Faulkner), has witnessed the murder of his parents, but seemingly 'locked in' by his condition and unable to talk, he is of no help to the police in finding the killer. Tim's lack of expression and communication becomes the arena for a battle of wills between competing psychiatrists Jake Rainer (Richard Dreyfuss) and Rene Harlinger (John Lithgow). Rainer is a maverick therapist, recovering from a disastrous group home experience in which an autistic child in his care died. Harlinger is a by-the-book medic who believes that the use of drugs will draw the truth out of Tim. In the scene in question, Rainer is reluctantly persuaded to examine the boy in a secure room in a police station. He tests Tim's reflexes – tapping his knees, scraping the soles of his feet – but gets no response: Tim sits immobile, as if carved from stone. As the camera focuses in close on the boy's face, with its wide staring eyes and lack of any movement or expression, Rainer slowly brings his face down until it is level with Tim's, and only a few inches away. 'What are you seeing in there?', he asks quietly, looking straight into the boy's eyes. Rainer is interrupted by Harlinger, whose method is far more direct. Taking drugs out of a cabinet and preparing a syringe, Harlinger asserts 'We'll find out what you have hiding in there'. He, in turn, is prevented from administering the drug by the argument that ensues with Rainer, and the scene ends with Tim still sitting silent on the treatment table, and no indication of how any information might be gained from him.

It would be hard to find a piece of any contemporary cultural narrative of autism that displayed more elements of the orthodox ways in which the condition is represented than this. Firstly, Tim's lack of mobility, indeed his complete immobility, underscores Douglas Biklen's idea that it is an 'autism-inside-the-person' model that dominates prevailing understanding about the condition. He appears trapped, literally locked, by his condition. That Tim has a secret to reveal, and a vital one in a murder investigation, only reinforces this notion of the 'inside'. Secondly, Rainer's question to Tim and his attempt to read the boy's condition *through* his eyes gives detail to this idea of some kind of 'concealment'. The 'unreadable' face, and the passive, catatonic (a word Harlinger uses to describe him) aspect of Tim's presence here act as confirmation that all that can be known about the child is somehow caught within him. Rainer, and then Harlinger after him, both refer to a fundamental idea of interiority – 'in there' – in their attempts to describe or assess how Tim feels or what he might know. As with the children in the photographs in *Souls*, the conception here of the subject with autism is one found in some kind of enigmatic 'beyond', a space free from behavioural characteristics or expressed preferences. Tim is completely still, but the ideas of who he might be are mobile all around him.

Equally, for all that Tim may seem to be the centre of the scene, especially as the object of enquiry, it is in fact the dynamic between Rainer and Harlinger that actually dominates. The competing techniques of the two characters, the ideas of their personalities the clash depicts – the possibility of a caring, child-centred therapy as opposed to a clinical, medicalized model – all these are in play in the argument over how best to approach Tim. As such, and as with so many narrative accounts of autism, what appears to be a comment on the condition is, in truth, an observation about something else, and what might be a depiction of presence becomes rather an example of how easily autism can be rendered absent. Tim's autism becomes a prism through which *Silent Fall* focuses all manner of concerns, whether they be the development of individual characters (Tim is vital to reasserting Rainer's notion of self-worth) or the structuring of wider, generic functions (autism as an obvious variation on the 'silent witness' theme). Whatever the complexities of the film's representation of autism, the condition's ultimate contextualization within the story line is a process that has little to do with disability; and visually, the wonder of autism may be central to certain scenes, but it is easily allowed to convert to a passivity when other elements of the story line are deemed more important. Such processes are, as we have seen in previous chapters, the details of the refractive, prosthetic narrative at work all over again.

*Silent Fall* progresses into absurdities, as Rainer discovers Tim's abilities as a mimic and then uses him to aurally 're-enact' the events of the murder and reveal the killer. The processes of such discovery act to release both man and boy from restrictions which, the narrative asserts, had held them captive. Rainer rediscovers his abilities as a therapist and a wider self-confidence, while Tim begins a partial 'emergence' from his autism, learning to use his own voice by the film's end in place of the mimicry he had displayed up to this point. That this is a 'release' from his condition is made clear by one of Rainer's pronouncements on the nature of autism itself: 'I think autism is a kind of overpowering fear, of the whole world. There's a boy in there, but I think he's trapped behind a wall, and I think that his being trapped makes him terrified.' Terror, murder, entrapment and deceit are grouped together in the film, to be opposed by freedom, enlightenment, truth and justice – and it is clear that autism belongs to the first category.

*Silent Fall*'s misrepresentations of autism are outlandish and border on the offensive, but they should probably not come as a surprise. Mainstream American commercial cinema does not have an especially good heritage of portraying the disabled generally, and the post *Rain Man* interest in autism displays the continuation of a long history of uninformed depictions and problematic spectacularization. As Martin F. Norden makes clear in *The Cinema of Isolation*, his history of physical disability in the movies, the representation of a number of different disabilities in Hollywood feature films bears little actual relation to the experiences of those living with the disabilities in question. Norden notes that:

> the movie industry has perpetuated or initiated a number of stereotypes over the years, … stereotypes so durable and pervasive that they have become mainstream society's perception of disabled people and have obscured if not outright supplanted disabled people's perceptions of themselves.[15]

He generally damns an industry that finds disability most useful as a narrative vehicle for telling stories of the non-disabled and that displays little conscience when engaged in misrepresentation.

Norden's anger is justified, though the situation is not especially unusual. The commercial and narrative formulae driving Hollywood and other commercial cinemas have produced multiple 'others' characterized by their misrepresentation. As E. Ann Kaplan has observed in relation to issues surrounding feminism and the imperial gaze, Hollywood's insistence in its imaginary self-construction as representing 'all human life and behavior', as opposed to that which comes from a limited and bounded culture, has always flattened out the specificities of so-called minority communities.[16] In truth, Hollywood's misrepresentation should probably be taken as a given. As Richard Maltby, one of the best commentators on the industry, has written, Hollywood 'functions according to ... a commercial aesthetic, one that is essentially opportunistic in its economic motivation.... Hollywood movies are determined, in the last instance, by their existence as commercial commodities.'[17] Such commercial opportunism will always, we can presume, involve transforming its subject matter to fit the need for a certain kind of product, and the perceived enigmatic status of many disabilities offers ample opportunities for such a process.

Nevertheless, even within such a paradigm of (mis)representation, there are reasons to view Hollywood's recent fascination with conditions of cognitive impairment, and autism in particular, with a sharp critical eye. In doing so, we find ourselves in a space that is largely free of substantive criticism. Possibly because cognitive impairment itself still occupies a relatively peripheral space within disability studies, and equally because of the general invisibility of any full analysis of disability in popular cultural texts, the critical treatment of the cinematic representation of such impairments lacks rigorous theorizing or discussion. While there is clearly something we might identify as a 'disability film', it is still often absent from most wide-ranging contemporary critical studies of commercial cinema, and Hollywood especially. Steve Neale's 2000 publication *Genre and Hollywood*, for example, contains no discussion of any kind of disability film (as opposed to, say, detective or disaster movies), despite the clear interrelation between filmic representations of disability and well defined and discussed genres such as melodrama. Equally, Neale and Murray Smith's 1998 collection *Contemporary Hollywood Cinema* explores, under the heading 'Audience, address and ideology', issues of the women's picture, the family picture, the relationship between Hollywood and independent black cinema, and the yuppie horror film, but makes no mention of disability movies (intriguingly, *Rain Man* has a single entry in the volume, where it is described by Barry Keith Grant as a 'bland yuppie movie' – a complete erasure of its disability politics).[18] There is no room for disability of any kind in Trevor B. McCrisken and Andrew Pepper's *American History and Contemporary Hollywood Film* (2005), and even a subtle and sensitive reader of Hollywood such as Maltby finds interest in *Rain Man* only as a 'female-oriented picture' in the 1999 collection on Hollywood and its audiences he co-edited with Melvyn Stokes.[19]

Disability is absent, then, from the major book-length critical studies of Hollywood where we might hope to find some sense of its presence, and the often puzzling ways that disability films are glossed in these works (as with the *Rain Man* examples above) makes such an absence only more telling. Equally we might note that a number of critics who have produced studies of disability in film (often as articles or essays) have used methodologies derived from disability, as opposed to film, studies. Writers such as Paul Darke, Tom Shakespeare, and Michael T. Hayes and Rhonda S. Black have published in journals and collections primarily aimed at disability studies audiences.[20] Even within this community, however, there are barriers to a full understanding of how autism features in narrative film. That some disability studies scholars (and, indeed, wider contemporary culture as a whole) seem to think disability is first and foremost oriented around questions of physical impairment adds an extra obfuscatory layer to any desire to look at representations of the condition. Norden's concentration on physical impairment has a perfect logic to it, yet in *his* passing reference to *Rain Man*, he terms Dustin Hoffman's character in the film 'mentally impaired'.[21] While this might not technically be wrong, and while the approach of Norden's study obviously means that *Rain Man* is not a film he will approach in any detail, the lack of specificity here, particularly the absence of the word 'autism' itself, is somewhat surprising. What is it about the condition that people do not know? It seems that even a publication date of 1994 – that of Norden's study – constitutes a point in the pre-history of the contemporary interest in the condition.

If, especially from *Rain Man* onwards, Hollywood has frequently returned in differing ways to depictions of autism, it should be noted that the use of autism as a point of focus for film narrative, or the deployment of autistic characters within films, is relatively recent. It is, however, possible to find films from the 1970s and even before in which characters have clear autistic tendencies, even if they are almost never termed 'autistic'. William A. Graham's 1974 television movie *Larry* – with Frederick Forrest in the title role – is a clear portrayal, based on a true story, of an individual with autism and his struggle with misdiagnosis and the nature of institutional care. Autism is, however, never mentioned, with the film rather promoting a general idea of Larry's 'retardation'. A more high-profile film, Hal Ashby's *Being There* (1979), also features a central character – Chance (Peter Sellers) – seen as retarded, but who we can now see in terms of the specifics of autism. What critic Roger Ebert, in a 1980 review of the film in the *Chicago Sun-Times*, referred to as Chance's 'excruciatingly narrow tone of behaviour' points to the character's autism, as does his use of television narratives to serve as a guide for his social interactions.[22] Indeed, Chance is clearly legitimately read as being autistic, and Sellers' performance creates the kind of interplay between cognitive impairment and comedy that might have been developed as a representational mode, but was not. It is, however, a consequence of the lack of knowledge of autism in the late 1970s that reviews of the film failed to note its presence. This is true even though 1979 also saw the production of *Son-Rise: A Miracle of Love*, an NBC television film directed by Glenn Jordan which dramatized the story of Barry and Samahria Kaufman and their autistic son, Raun, a narrative that inspired one of the most popular autism treatment programmes in the US, something I discuss in chapter 5.

In the 1980s, the increased medical and educational discussion of the condition created a context to which popular cultural narratives could respond, a context in which, for example, autism itself could be named, and it is noticeable that a number of films which figure autism contain scenes set in schools or hospitals in which we see non-acting children and adults who *are* autistic, as if the features are at pains to establish their credentials.[23] For all this desire for verisimilitude, however, it is intriguing that one of the first examples of such 1980s contexts is Lew Lehman's 1981 feature *The Pit*, a feature that marked the perhaps inevitable conflation of autism and horror. A young boy with autism, Jamie Benjamin (Sammy Snyders) takes revenge on those who have taunted him, by luring them to a pit full of man-eating creatures he has found in the woods. *The Pit* is a low-budget horror classic, but its alignment of autism with sociopathic behaviour is extremely disturbing. The juxtaposition of autism and horror was, however, to be something that commercial cinema would find irresistible.

Coming towards the end of the 1980s, the success of *Rain Man* prompted a breakthrough into a wide public consciousness precisely because of the increased sense of context given to autism during the decade, but the film's impact also provided a specific development in terms of a disability film *narrative*, with a new avenue for a particular 'commercial aesthetic' of the kind Maltby describes. From the 1990s to the present there have been numerous examples in film of such narratives concerning autism, operating within a discourse of knowledge of the condition precisely because this period saw the subtleties of the autistic spectrum receive further definition and neuroscientific research begin to understand more fully its biogenetic aspects. The majority of these narratives, however, lack any real exploration of the complexities of autistic agency or subjectivity. The details of witnessing outlined above – the specifics of an essentially *visual* form of fascination – operate in a similar fashion for films as they do for photography, but film narratives have the added dimension of a story line that contextualizes the representation of the condition. As we shall see, in the most commercial cinemas such contextualization usually takes the form of the use of genre. It is the stability provided by generic elements and particulars that often works to contain the potential excess of autistic presence. As with the ideas of the studio portraits generated by the images in Balsamo's photographs in *Souls*, the details of differing generic impulses in films that represent autism – from family melodrama to science fiction – provide frames in which the condition is witnessed. Within the parameters of these frames, the condition usually becomes portrayed in terms of the safe and known stereotypes that inform the bulk of public knowledge of what autism is. At the present time, to witness autism in the cinema is rarely to come across anything new.

The issues outlined above surround and enclose the presence of autism in a number of high-profile commercial feature films, many from Hollywood and starting with *Rain Man*, which feature autistic or Asperger's characters in a variety of narratives. These include *House of Cards* (1993, directed by Michael Lessac), *Silent Fall* (1994, Bruce Beresford), *Relative Fear* (1994, George Mihalka), *Cube* (1997, Vincenzo Natali), *Molly* (1999, John Duigan), *Mercury Rising* (1998, Harold Becker), *Bless the Child* (2000, Chuck Russell), *Punch-Drunk Love* (2002, Paul Thomas Anderson), *The United States of Leland* (2003, Matthew Ryan Hoge), *Mozart and the Whale* (2005, Peter Naess), *Snow Cake* (2006, Marc Evans), *Breaking and Entering* (2006, Anthony Minghella) and *Sparkle* (2007, Tom Hunsinger and Neil Hunter). Other features, such as *What's Eating Gilbert Grape* (1993, Lasse Hallström), *Benny & Joon* (1993, Jeremiah S. Chechik), *Forrest Gump* (1994, Robert Zemeckis), *Nell* (1994, Michael Apted), *Shine* (1996, Scott Hicks) and *I Am Sam* (2001, Jessie Nelson), contain characters, often with complex and overlapping disabilities, that it is possible to read in terms of autistic presence.

The films mentioned here move through a spectrum in the detail of their concentration on autism: in some, such as *Rain Man, House of Cards, Snow Cake* and *Mozart and the Whale*, it is ostensibly an encounter with autism that is central to the narrative; in others we might say that autism is narratively enabling, driving the stories of genre pieces such as the thrillers *Silent Fall* and *Mercury Rising*, the horror/science fiction of *Cube* and the horror of *Bless the Child* and *Relative Fear*. To a degree, then, these latter narratives exemplify the point made by many scholars working in disability studies that disability and impairment often animate narrative while rarely being at its centre, and that, as David Mitchell and Sharon Snyder put it: 'While disabled populations are firmly entrenched on the outer margins of social power and cultural value, the disabled body also serves as the raw material out of which other … communities make themselves visible'.[24] In a twist on the logic of this, we might say that, in the films mentioned above, these 'other communities' can be seen as the ideas and stories that are animated and become possible because of the engagement with autism. At the same time, however, all the films discussed here share a desire to structure at least some aspect of narrative through a specific *use* of the condition. It is the terms of such usage that warrant investigation, as they point to the *desire* of contemporary commercial culture both to be fascinated by the appeal of autism and to fit it into generic, pre-existing narrative concerns. The shifting scale of the focus of these various films on the condition, their differing emphases, from central characters to peripheral presences, is in fact itself a phenomenon that invites critical conclusions, as it clearly speaks of a *range* of potential subject positions for autism within contemporary narrative. Again, what is striking is the ways in which a flexible idea of the condition is at work, and is seemingly so useful to a certain kind of cultural storytelling.

As Garland-Thomson has written: 'Staring at disability choreographs a visual relation between a spectator and a spectacle',[25] and it is this relationship which is key to understanding how the spectacularization of autism works. In their particular display of the condition, *Rain Man*, *House of Cards*, *Silent Fall*, *Mercury Rising* and *Snow Cake* all use the potential for visual eruption within autism. In all five films the characters with autism 'suddenly' produce extremes of behaviour, including screaming, head-banging and other forms of self-harm. Such behaviour often immediately follows periods when characters have been passive, when their autism appears to have rendered them more inert than active. This visual excessiveness is possibly a surprise to the viewer in terms of the specific story line, and is probably designed as such, but this is arguably less the case when contextualized by the popular idea of what constitutes autistic behaviour. It makes sense in terms of the processes of witnessing.

The visual impact of these scenes in all five films is powerful, but – crucially – they also link to a process that is central to the representation of autism in commercial cinema. In the five features mentioned, the sudden explosion of behaviour occurs in the presence of a figure who is largely ignorant of what autism is and who initially misunderstands the meaning of the actions. But the central narratives of the films require that other characters learn from their proximity to the condition. All the films use the refraction narrative of paired impaired/non-impaired characters not only to explore ideas of difference, but also to illuminate for majority audiences questions of individual responsibility, behaviour and knowledge. The most obvious example of this is *Rain Man*'s juxtaposition of the way Raymond Babbitt humanizes his isolated, dysfunctional brother, Charlie. As we saw in the last chapter, Charlie's own clear personal and social limitations are identified and, in part, improved because of his necessary engagement with Raymond. But in the same way, psychiatrist Rainer in *Silent Fall*, mother Ruth Matthews (Kathleen Turner) in *House of Cards*, FBI agent Art Jeffries (Bruce Willis) in *Mercury Rising* and itinerant loner Alex Hughes (Alan Rickman) in *Snow Cake* are all portrayed as dysfunctional characters requiring interaction with an autistic presence in order to change. In an early scene in *Mercury Rising*, for example, Jeffries is interviewed by his FBI boss Joe Lomax (Kevin Conway) following a failed operation. Informing Jeffries that a psychologist has written 'delusional paranoia' on his work file, Lomax also adds that 'all you had to do was act like you belong on the same team as the rest of us'. The details of Jeffries' difference, especially his isolation (and it is intriguing that such dysfunction is often portrayed through possible autistic tendencies), are thus established early on, and it is exactly such a difference that the film seeks to redress through Jeffries' encounter with autistic nine-year-old Simon Lynch (Miko Hughes).

If the above observations make it appear that the films in question focus upon clearly delineated characters *as individuals,* then it should be stressed that all five are structured with clear generic patternings and concerns: as we have seen, *Silent Fall* uses autism to add a twist to what otherwise is a routine crime genre piece; *Rain Man* is a melodrama and an adaptation of the buddy road movie; *House of Cards* and *Snow Cake* are both melodramas; and *Mercury Rising* is a technology-based thriller in which Jeffries' outsider, renegade status affords protection for Simon, who has cracked the government's new, top secret, Mercury defence encryption code. It is worth noting that while this last detail is, on one level, the standard fare of a conspiracy action thriller, it again offers an opportunity to consider the details of the inherently visual underpinning of the filmic narrative approach to autism. Simon first recognizes the code buried within the pages of an everyday puzzle magazine, and in representing this moment of exceptional ability the camera comes in to provide an extreme close-up on his eyes, before zooming in on the close type of the puzzle laid out on the page. As with both *Souls* and *Silent Fall*, the invitation to look at Simon's eyes – here at the very moment he produces a savant deciphering skill – is one that locates his autism in an unknowable space somewhere within him, offered up for an audience to somehow 'see'.[26]

The feature films in which autism is less obviously a narrative concern also use genre conventions. For all of its off-beat concentration on the social impairments of lead character Barry Egan (Adam Sandler), *Punch-Drunk Love* plays out as a variation of the romantic melodrama. As Barry negotiates his way through a world that offers endless problems for all aspects of his life, the manner with which he pursues Lena (Emily Watson) recalls Hollywood's screwball comedies of the 1930s, though in this version seen through an Asperger's filter. Such an idea of an Asperger's identity is also central to the romantic comedy of *Mozart and the Whale*, in which Donald (Josh Hartnett) and Isabella (Radha Mitchell) meet at an autism support group, although the film's representation of the condition is superficially stereotypical. In *Cube*, the hand flapping and repetitive verbal utterances of Kazan (Andrew Miller) clearly mark him as having autism, though the narrative never uses this label. Yet the film uses Kazan's exceptionality to render him one of a group chosen for unexplained reasons to try to escape a deadly cube-like structure in a science-fiction format with generic antecedents in films such as Ridley Scott's *Alien* (1979). For its part, *Bless the Child* employs both a thriller format and the classic horror convention of the innocence of the child (interestingly here – as with *House of Cards* – a girl, something unusual in fictional autism narratives) in a battle against satanic evil.

Characterizing autism within standard generic narratives in this way results in two distinct outcomes. Firstly, it points (again) to a narrative space where the portrayal of the condition's inherent difference animates ideas of absence and presence that, in turn, produce a final focus that ultimately speaks of non-disabled concerns. *Snow Cake* offers a good example of such a move. Alex Hughes, just out of prison in the UK and travelling in Canada, picks up a young hitchhiker, Vivienne Freeman (Emily Hampshire), who is killed when a truck hits the car in which they are travelling. Grieving over someone he barely knew, Alex decides to visit Vivienne's mother Linda (Sigourney Weaver), but is shocked to find her autism means that she appears to register little grief or sorrow herself. The encounter between Alex and Linda becomes the occasion for any number of displays of autistic behaviour, all of which are seen to challenge Alex's existing notion of what constitutes appropriate conduct. Linda flaps and mumbles; she screams when Alex enters her kitchen (a space she has designated off limits to him); she displays memorization abilities, and is also obsessive, literal and clearly sensitive to sensory stimulation; she has comic book interests and is on a gluten-free diet. Linda is a catalogue of a contemporary knowledge of autism, all of which conveys the feeling of accurate research. As the title's 'snow flake' analogy implies, she is unique. Yet, central as her behaviour seems to the film, she is in fact a secondary consideration, since it is Alex's personal journey – the complexities of *his* past and present – that constitutes the film's primary narrative. Alex was in prison for killing the man who killed his own child, and his story unfolds not through conversations with Linda, but rather with her neighbour Maggie (Carrie-Anne Moss), who also provides the narrative's love interest. As *interesting* as Linda might be to Alex, and as much as *Snow Cake* promotes the idea that Alex can learn from her, the film plays out its central thesis in a parallel story line that almost totally excludes her. If she is not quite the fixed embodiment of autism that some films portray, Linda is seen to be sufficiently inflexible (ultimately her concerns are who will take out her garbage on Tuesdays) to be contained within a conventional narrative of personal development.

Secondly, the use of genre allows for one of the most noticeable (and possibly unsurprising) aspects of commercial cinema's representation of autism, namely the focus on the characters' savant qualities. Hollywood narratives in particular indulge in a clear fascination with the supposedly exceptional skills of the autistic individual in a process that both creates and responds to the popular media construction of the condition. In keeping with *Rain Man*'s foundational status, we can see how Raymond's card counting skills in Las Vegas lead to a succession of scenes in the later films that centre plot developments on such abilities. In *Silent Fall*, it is Tim's abilities as a mimic that ultimately lead to the discovery of the truth of his parents' death. In *Cube*, Kazan's mathematical skills allow the imprisoned group finally to escape the complexities of their entrapment, though (intriguingly) he is the sole survivor. In *House of Cards*, the ability of Sally (Asha Menina) to build the card house, an impossibly complex tower of playing cards, leads to her mother's attempts to reproduce the tower in a larger form and a final reconciliation on the structure itself. In *Bless the Child*, the girl Cody (Holliston Coleman) comes to personify an angelic innocence that reveals her to be the chosen child of the second coming who can defeat the presence of the satanic Eric Stark (Rufus Sewell). And in *Mercury Rising*, as we have already noted, Simon's skills with mathematics and word puzzles permit him to break the Mercury encryption code and then allow him to provide positive support in helping Jeffries in the search for justice that follows.

As we saw in the last chapter, this fascination with the savant figure needs proper understanding and contextualizing. Rates of savantism in the autistic population are in the region of ten per cent, a figure much lower than might be expected from any observation of the phenomenon in contemporary culture. Hollywood's concentration on savant skills exemplifies a tangential and misguided understanding of cognitive difference, here used for fictional ends. Autism, of course, does often produce islanded knowledge and differential abilities across a range of activities, but there is no causal connection between this and savant skills. Instead, in the films under discussion here the figure of the savant becomes a peculiarly *narrative*-driven phenomenon, often an opportunity to modify plot or character relations. This sense of narrative then combines with the invited stare of the majority audience to create a visual spectacle of wonder at the cognitive difference that could produce such exceptionality. This wonder can take differing forms, though Hayes and Black, in their account of representations of disability in film, characterize it ultimately as a 'discourse of pity', through which Hollywood uses actual impairments to construct cultural signs.[27] 'Pity' is an interesting appellation here, especially when applied to the depiction of autism. The suggestion is that savant skills, however stunning, are in the last resort seen as an inadequate compensation for the disability that produces them.

Genre allows for the containment of what might otherwise be the worrying disabled difference implied in savant ability or autistic presence. In the narrative world of *Mercury Rising*, Simon's 'abilities' parallel those of Jeffries: the brain that cracks the code is on the same plane as the body that can withstand explosions. In the fabric of the action thriller, the two exceptionalities are equal. Similarly, the notion of the 'innocent' child that is often central to crime or horror features is only enhanced if the child in question adds disabled difference to that innocence, and in both *Silent Fall* and *Bless the Child* autism is contextualized in that way. In turn, such characterization can, within the boundaries of genre, be turned on its head, which is exactly what *Relative Fear* achieves. In a similar fashion to *The Pit*, *Relative Fear* promotes the idea of the vengeful child, the classic horror twist on ideas of innocence. In this case the autism of five-year-old Adam Pratman (Matthew Dupuis) is merely a shorthand that allows for the representation of an idea of 'troubled' child behaviour, since there is little recognizably autistic in anything Adam does. It is the worst kind of example of the prosthetic narrative, where the idea of disability simply becomes part of a generic method.

The continual return to the use of genre, and the interplay between generic structures and an idea of savantism, highlight the ways in which autism is seemingly endlessly subject to narrative construction in contemporary commercial cinema. Part of that construction comes from the additional concentration that is placed on the levels of *performance* of the actors who play central characters with autism. Upon *Rain Man*'s release, it was Hoffman's performance as Raymond Babbitt that gathered numerous critical accolades, including ultimately an Academy Award, and this central portrayal became a key selling point of the film. In a similar fashion, both Sean Penn's performance in *I Am Sam* and that of Sigourney Weaver in *Snow Cake* are seen to be complex and challenging roles for actors considered to be so talented. Here, the actors in question become the focal point for the audience wonder produced by the 'enigmatic' status of autism and disability. The question of how much research the actor in question undertook (something that became central after Hoffman's preparations for *Rain Man*), and the extent to which he or she successfully performs a 'different' humanity, become issues for public debate. Yet we should note that similar responses are not, on the whole, extended to child actors such as Ben Faulkner, Asha Menina, Miko Hughes and Holliston Coleman, whose performances in the films under discussion here are often underplayed, frequently featuring a lack of speech and expression as if they have been directed to *not* act. This range of portrayal, from award-winning performances to representations that are motionless and inert, underscores the presence/absence continuity that is central to the filmic representation of autism. It is also further proof of the complex narrative space the condition inhabits, precisely because it stresses how there are numerous points within this continuum that can provide the starting place for fiction. In film, autism appears as both everything and nothing, with the gulf in between allowing for every kind of portrayal imaginable, from the sentimentality of *Rain Man* to the horror of *Relative Fear*.

These details all underscore the ways in which autistic presence becomes such a variable in fictional narratives, as well as pointing to the specifically visual construction of an idea of the condition in contemporary culture and society. In the majority of the narratives discussed above, the autistic characters (especially the children) alternate between the twin poles of visual absence and presence, where the exceptionality that dominates certain narrative elements can suddenly become a passivity that appears to offer no narrative at all. It is no coincidence that, in *Mercury Rising*, Simon escapes the government-hired contract killers who murder his parents by hiding, and remains hidden even as the police investigate the scene, only to be finally found by Jeffries. Equally, for all of the central narrative interest that appears to be focused upon Sally's withdrawn passivity in *House of Cards*, she is frequently at the periphery of both image and story, as the film concentrates on the trauma of her mother, Ruth, who, it appears, has lost both a husband (killed in an accident, the event that 'prompts' Sally's autism) and now a daughter. The exception to such shuttling between absence and presence is *Punch-Drunk Love*, where Barry's Aspergic subjecthood dominates the film. It is telling, however, that by far the majority of the reviews of the film fail to mention autism/Asperger's at all; rather, Barry is personified as sad, lonely or awkward, and the potential to see *Punch-Drunk Love* as an autistic narrative can become lost in the ways in which it is pulled towards a non-autistic sense of what might constitute character.

Such notions of the active and passive constitute a peculiarly narrativized account of autistic presence, and in so doing they form part of the ways in which the condition has become written in contemporary culture in a wider sense. As we saw in the Introduction, Majia Holmer Nadesan has shown that, for all of its clear status as a neurological impairment, and without denying its biogenetic origins, autism in the contemporary world still frequently operates as a *constructed* idea. As she says, 'perhaps autism is not a *thing* but is a nominal category useful for grouping heterogeneous people all sharing communication practices deviating significantly from the expectations of normalcy'.[28] While Nadesan is analysing medical and sociological narratives that work to achieve such effects, it is clear that filmic narratives like those discussed here are contributors to a *cultural* construction of such a category, and that they inflect the condition with specific terms. The films 'produce' an idea of autism, and themselves add to the wider production practised by medical, social and cultural institutions, that offers a version of the condition for the consumption of a majority audience which has the interest to speculate upon, but not the time to know about, what the ontological questions raised by autism might be. In an era of vaccine scares and exponential increases in diagnoses, themselves events that contribute towards a changing idea of what we think autism is, the narratives of commercial cinema add to the idea that we live in the time of an 'epidemic', an autism 'age', and they do so through the use of stories only tangentially related to the condition itself.

In the films discussed here, autism becomes central in terms of both image and narrative at key moments in the construction of their fictions. At the same time, as we have seen, the ontological questions central to any representation of the condition remain as a surplus. The films present a constant invitation to look at the person with autism, and this look is, ultimately, a moment in which the audience is encouraged to speculate on the very nature of the human condition. At the points at which these invitations occur, however, the films become formless and any meaningful comment on the actuality of autism collapses. Watching a film with an autistic character, when self-consciously looking for how the condition is represented, is a process with a curious pattern of its own. The point in the narrative at which the person with autism appears is almost always followed by the spectacle of watching their behaviour, and the corresponding performance element, before such behaviour becomes less of a narrative centrality and the viewing turns into a question of waiting to see how the end will contextualize the condition. When the fictional film *does* come close to approaching what a character with autism might feel or think, seen in the terms of the individual in question, it largely has nothing to say. There are rare moments when the features under discussion here do attempt to represent what an autistic interiority might be – *Rain Man* contains a number of shots from Raymond's point of view, for example, of power lines or the structures of an overhead bridge as he is driven by Charlie, and these give a brief sense of the pleasure of repetition he might be experiencing – but for the vast majority of all these narratives this kind of character issue is simply not approached.

Instead, the formlessness that is the seeming threat produced by any *actual* engagement with disability is largely rescued by the kind of generic patterning to which the various features resort, or often an overt move towards the sentimental, usually as the narrative redirects the issues of humanity it has raised into more familiar codifications. The majority of the films under discussion here have clearly sentimental endings: Jeffries visits Simon in school at the end of *Mercury Rising* and in response to his demand 'Look in my eyes', achieves both eye contact and a hug that are totally out of character with Simon's behaviour up to this point in the film. In *Bless the Child*, following her abduction Cody is reunited with her caring aunt Maggie (Kim Basinger), who is making plans to adopt her. *Rain Man* and *Cube* contain the most ambivalent endings of these features. In the former, Raymond returns to Wallbrook, the institution from which Charlie originally took him, and an overtly sentimental conclusion is avoided, though Charlie's education in humanity makes up for his loss of the custody battle concerning his brother. In *Cube*, Kazan is the only figure to escape from the cube itself, though the 'outside' into which he might venture is never figured in the film, and he is left on the threshold of safety, a survivor from the horror within. The very lack of any attempt to display the world outside the cube reinforces the idea that, for all his mathematical genius, Kazan's place within the narrative is to solve the problem of how to enact the escape. He is, first and foremost, a function.

For its conclusion, however, *House of Cards* should receive the final comment here. Sally's 'return' from her autism (her autistic behaviour vanishes at the end of the film) is very much seen to be due to the expression of the appropriate degree of love and understanding displayed by her mother, Ruth, a process that dumbfounds psychiatrist Jacob Beerlander (Tommy Lee Jones) and in effect negates the worth of all of his professional work, something we have seen a lot of in the film. The structuring of this narrative conclusion – its emphasis on autism as (firstly) a condition that is *not* connected to impairment but is rather behavioural, and (secondly) as a vehicle for the mobilization of other, non-autistic, sentiments – is a complete evacuation of any idea of the actual expression of autism. The drive to make the Matthews family coherent once again (and it is clear at the film's end that there is a space for Beerlander to replace the absent father) becomes the film's ultimate and final logic. Autism here is simply another occasion to remind parents to love their children properly.

In terms of the kinds of melodrama commercial cinema, and especially Hollywood, practises with regard to autism, such a focus on family as that suggested by the end of *House of Cards* is typical. The full and complex relationship between autism and ideas of the family is the focus of chapter 5, but it is worth noting here that it is the strength of the family unit, with all its perceived moral good, that becomes central in a number of these films. In *Breaking and Entering*, the problematic relationship of Will Francis (Jude Law) and partner Liv (Robin Wright Penn) is explored, in part, through their struggle to cope with the difficulties of dealing with the autism/attention deficit disorder of their daughter Bea (Poppy Rogers). In both *Rain Man* and *Molly*, it is a sibling who must learn the power of family love through an encounter with an individual with autism, and the two have similar conclusions in terms of the family dynamic produced through such a 'learning' process. Sibling relationships are also central to *Silent Fall*, where sister Sylvie (Liv Tyler) seeks to protect Tim following the murder of their parents, while familial dysfunction dominates *The United States of Leland*, where the gruesome murder of young autistic Ryan Pollard (Michael Welch) by central protagonist Leland Fitzgerald (Ryan Gosling), after he establishes a relationship with Ryan's sister Becky (Jena Malone), prompts a narrative enquiry into the dynamics of the American middle-class nuclear family. The murder of Simon's parents is also pivotal in *Mercury Rising*, and in both this film and *Silent Fall* it is the adult male hero who becomes a surrogate father figure, especially as a protector. Maggie's adoption of Cody at the end of *Bless the Child* displays a narrative institutionalization of this impulse. The otherness of autism, it is implied, can be most negated, most made familiar, by its discussion and ultimate incorporation within the structure of family. In being made to function in such a way, autism simply becomes another element (like crime, or drugs, or any number of perceived individual 'abnormalities') that can be characterized and thematized in the dominant drive to create normative narratives of social relations common to the different forms of commercial cinema.

The 'ability' of the disabled figure to overcome (or in the case of *House of Cards* to come back from) adversity, and to take part in the key organizational formations of relationship, family or community, is part and parcel of the kind of specific form of narrative prosthesis representations of autism produce in cultural texts. The consequences of this extend to include social notions of both individual and collective concerns. In particular, filmic ideas of savant ability can be seen to underscore the attempt to stress a disabled individual's worth. Its status as a 'special' skill provides, so the films seem to suggest (and in direct opposition to the Hayes and Black observation of a discourse of pity noted earlier), a suitably compensatory element that offsets the actual impairment itself. For the majority, non-disabled audience of a mainstream Hollywood feature, then (to cite a specific *national* example, for all Hollywood's global reach), such logic is in keeping with the wider cultural politics that utilize an idea of the 'benevolent good' to connect individuals to communities and to the state. 'Overcoming' autism in the context of a Hollywood feature is a narrative that carries the national ideologies of promise and achievement. The misrepresentation is couched within a powerful set of arguments.

Overall, it is debatable how much progress has been made in cinematic depictions of autism since the foundational success of *Rain Man*. 'I know all about autism – I've seen *that* film', says Diane Wooton (Selina Cadell) to Alex Hughes in *Snow Cake*, in what is clearly meant to be a disparaging reference. But, despite such a remark, the sentiment of which is supported by Angela Pell, the film's screenwriter and herself the parent of an autistic son, it is a matter for conjecture as to whether the representation of the condition in the later film really escapes from the limitations set up, in part, from the former.[29] *Snow Cake* may seem to be more accurate in portraying the details of autism than *Rain Man*, and clearly wants to avoid the idea that everyone with autism has savant skills, but this is potentially less important than the fact that, in both films, the prosthetic *narrative* situating of the condition is similar. Despite being made nearly twenty years after Levinson's film, *Snow Cake* doesn't really offer more on how autism can be an everyday part of the world. Indeed, though it is a subjective point, it is arguable that the melodramatic aspect of *Rain Man* – the manner by which the film manipulates the viewer to care for Raymond – is far more successful than the similar process in *Snow Cake*. Equally, there is no sense that Weaver's performance is in any way a progression from that of Hoffman's. The narrative contextualization of the visual nature of the performance – the way we *look* at Weaver – is a practice fundamentally similar to that of *Rain Man*.[30]

An *idea* of autistic presence animates any number of narrative possibilities in the films discussed here. From the championing of an individual's rights through the law, the salvation of a trapped community and resistance to a repressive government to the love of a mother for her daughter, autism provides the raw material for a seemingly endless range of complex fictions. And yet any greater understanding of the presence of autism within contemporary culture eludes the audiences of these texts. Despite the fascination that operates a continual return to the autistic figure in commercial cinema, we are unlikely to find in these stories any sense of a productive disabled agency. The drive of the industry's commercial aesthetic, and the desire for conformity on issues of social relations (such as the family), is too overpowering to allow audiences to move beyond the parameters offered by genre and sentiment. Given the sheer cultural power of an industry such as Hollywood, and the global reach of its products, we might as a result be pessimistic about the results of such portrayals and their influence on audiences. For audiences to find contemporary mainstream portrayals of autism unacceptable will require the kind of civil rights movements, for peoples with disabilities as a whole, that have animated black, ethnic and women's communities. If such a situation doesn't exist at the present moment, or if it might be argued that it is ongoing, there is at least the promise, embedded within all the current attention autism produces, that it will arrive.

In the specific area of film criticism, Peter Bradshaw, writing in the *Guardian*'s arts blog on Anton Corbijn's 2007 film *Control* – with its portrayal of the epilepsy of its central character, Ian Curtis (Sam Riley), the iconic lead singer of band Joy Division – observed that it may signal the arrival of a new kind of disability film:

> the film declines to condescend to Curtis on this score [his epilepsy], with misjudged sentimentality about how 'courageous' he was, and neither does it insidiously romanticise his disability, suggesting an age-old association with creativity, ecstasy or genius.[31]

Such representation might, Bradshaw continued, consign such high-profile features as Jim Sheridan's 1989 feature *My Left Foot* to history, because of what he believes to be the over-romanticization of the disabled condition in Sheridan's film and others like it. Possibly this is premature, and the majority of reactions to Bradshaw's blog were hostile, but it does perhaps indicate that there will be a time when films such as *Silent Fall* or *House of Cards* are considered embarrassing and shameful by everyone who sees them. Equally, we can hope that a commercial cinematic release, aiming for a wide audience, might contain a character with autism not shackled by the stereotypes that dominate the current conception of the condition.

## III

Mainstream cinema audiences may never choose to sit in huge numbers to watch the nearly five hours of Andy Warhol's *Empire* (1964), a film that – with its continual and unedited focus on the Empire State Building – might qualify as a genuine autistic narrative. Given the current interest in celebrity, they are more likely to have watched model and actress Jenny McCarthy's September 2007 appearance on the Oprah Winfrey show, in which she discussed her autistic son, Evan, while promoting her book, *Louder Than Words: a Mother's Journey in Healing Autism*. McCarthy's status as a high-profile figure within American popular culture, and her presence on a show with such huge public power as Winfrey's (she appeared on *Larry King Live* and *Good Morning America* as well), gave her views on autism a distinct platform. Following the show, there was much debate among the various autism bloggers about McCarthy's views, especially her outlining of her son's treatments and her assertions about the possibility of 'recovering' from the condition, or to be 'cured'.[32]

Such is the kind of arena in which the witnessing of autism takes places at the moment. In the US in particular, the power of celebrity has become vital in drawing attention to the condition. Autism Speaks, the highly influential US-based foundation that in 2006 funded research into the condition worth some $20 million, frequently uses sporting or television celebrities in its work to find the 'causes, prevention, treatments, and cure for autism', as its website puts it.[33] The contemporary industry that autism awareness has become, and of which foundations such as Autism Speaks are a major part, has emerged in tandem with the fascination the condition produces. A consequence of this is the way in which autism narratives now have to compete in order to be heard, and celebrity endorsement is an obvious short cut to gaining a profile. Taylor Cross' 2006 feature-length documentary film *Normal People Scare Me*, for example, undoubtedly owes some of its popularity to the fact that it is produced by Joey Travolta, brother of John. Cross' film, made with his mother, Keri Bowers, is a series of interviews in which he asks various questions about the condition of children and teenagers who have autism. In 2006 and 2007 Cross and Bowers toured the US and abroad with the film, giving talks and seminars following screenings. *Normal People Scare Me* made an impact that other, small-scale documentaries made about autism did not, and the weight of Travolta's public profile was an undoubted help.

Celebrity pushes what otherwise can be an unsettling topic into the realm of star biography, and hence to some degree neutralizes the notions of loss and difficulty that are seen to accompany autism and disability more generally. It replicates some of the ideas about performance discussed earlier, creating an additional category of interest that blunts the edge of a subject that a majority audience might find troubling. Without these frames, filmic representation of autism is a very different proposition. In terms of documentary and independent filmmaking, the condition is still a battleground, paralleling the wider arguments that surround the topic. Geraldine Wurzburg's 2004 television documentary *Autism Is a World*, a positive account of autistic student Sue Rubin and her achievements, was shortlisted for an Oscar in 2005, but immediately came under attack because of what was felt by some to be its advocacy of facilitated communication. 'Film resurrects discredited autism tactic', wrote Lisa Barrett Mann as her subtitle in her coverage of the debate in the *Washington Post*.[34] On the other side of the debate, Autism Speaks sponsored the 2006 documentary *Autism Every Day*, directed by Lauren Thierry. The forty-four minute film, which looks at a single day in the lives of eight families with an autistic child, drew substantial criticism from disability rights advocates because of its concentration on the condition as one of problems and difficulties, especially for parents. It created particular controversy when one of the mothers being interviewed, discussing the struggles she had endured in searching for a school for her child, commented that the only reason she had not put her autistic daughter in her car and driven off a bridge was because she has another daughter, who does not have autism.[35]

Wurzburg's and Thierry's films are part on the ongoing arguments that characterize autism at the present moment. Yet the controversy each film created is minor, in terms of public perception, in comparison with the legacy that exists as a result of the multiple portrayals of the condition in the high-profile arena of commercial cinema and media. Here, the stereotypes still dominate. In such fictions, those with autism may have incredible compensatory skills, or may instruct others in valuable lessons about humanity. They may allow other stories to happen. But they rarely have stories which are in any way theirs.

## Notes

1 Rosemarie Garland-Thomson, 'The politics of staring: visual rhetorics of disability in popular photography', in Sharon L. Snyder *et al.* (eds), *Disability Studies: Enabling the Humanities* (New York: Modern Language Association, 2002), p. 57.
2 Garland-Thomson, 'The politics of staring', pp. 56–7.
3 Garland-Thomson, 'The politics of staring', p. 57.
4 Garland-Thomson, 'The politics of staring', p. 58.
5 Garland-Thomson, 'The politics of staring', p. 59.
6 Rosie Barnes, quoted in Dea Birkett, 'See it my way', *Guardian*, 'Weekend', 23 November 2002, p. 33, photographs included.
7 Barnes, in Dea Birkett, 'See it my way', p. 40.
8 Barnes, in Dea Birkett, 'See it my way', p. 35.
9 Thomas Balsamo, 'From the heart of Thomas Balsamo', in Thomas Balsamo and Sharon Rosenbloom, *Souls: Beneath and Beyond Autism* (New York: McGraw-Hill, 2004), p. xiv.
10 Balsamo, 'From the heart of Thomas Balsamo', p. xiv.
11 Rosenbloom, 'The redemption', in Balsamo and Rosenbloom, *Souls*, p. 63.
12 Garland-Thomson, 'The politics of staring', p. 59.
13 Garland-Thomson, 'The politics of staring', p. 60.
14 Rosenbloom's prose is actually more disturbing than Balsamo's images. Talking of leaving the hospital following her son's diagnosis, she writes: 'Driving away from the hospital, the day my child's future was erased, I was suddenly overwhelmed by the weight of reality and was unable to continue to drive. I turned the car into the drive-thru of a fast-food restaurant and ordered the obligatory fries and drink, handing them to the stranger who sat beside me silently strapped in his car seat' (p. 29). Elsewhere, she writes that 'within each of those who bear the label *autistic* lies a human trapped between our world and theirs, screaming to know and be known' (p. 37). The condition is a 'burden' full of 'internal distress' (p. 41); hating the feeling of touch is 'inherent in the nature of the person with autism' (p. 55), and the difference between those with autism and those without is an 'abyss' (p. 60). Noticeably, it is the person without autism (often here the parent) who begins the process of providing the autist with meaning, 'guiding them back' (p. 57) as Rosenbloom puts it. The certainties with which the condition is generalized in Rosenbloom's prose, and her own assumed centrality as an interpreter of the autism she sees around her, creates not only an idea of dependency, but completely elevates the position of the non-autistic adult in any delineation of what the children's autism is and how it functions.
15 Martin F. Norden, *The Cinema of Isolation: A History of Physical Disability in the Movies* (New Brunswick, NJ: Rutgers University Press, 1994), p. 3.
16 E. Ann Kaplan, *Looking for the Other: Feminism, Film and the Imperial Gaze* (New York: Routledge, 1997), p. 57.
17 Richard Maltby, *Hollywood Cinema: An Introduction* (Oxford: Blackwell, 1995), p. 7.
18 Steve Neale, *Genre and Hollywood* (London: Routledge, 2000); Barry Keith Grant, 'Rich and strange: the yuppie horror film', in Steve Neale and Murray Smith (eds), *Contemporary Hollywood Cinema* (London: Routledge, 1998), p. 289.
19 Trevor B. McCrisken and Andrew Pepper, *American History and Contemporary Hollywood Film* (Edinburgh: Edinburgh University Press, 2005); Richard Maltby, 'Introduction', in Melvyn Stokes and Richard Maltby (eds), *Identifying Hollywood's*

*Audiences: Cultural Identity and the Movies* (London: British Film Institute, 1999), p. 9.

20 See, for example, Paul Darke, 'Understanding cinematic representations of disability', in Tom Shakespeare (ed.), *The Disability Reader: Social Science Perspectives* (London: Continuum, 1998), pp. 181–97; Tom Shakespeare, 'Art and lies? Representation of disability on film', in Mairian Corker and Sally French (eds), *Disability Discourse* (Buckingham: Open University Press, 1999), pp. 164–72; and Michael T. Hayes and Rhonda S. Black, 'Troubling signs: disability, Hollywood movies and the construction of a discourse of pity', *Disability Studies Quarterly*, vol. 23, no. 2 (spring 2003), pp. 114–32.

21 Norden, *The Cinema of Isolation*, p. 309.

22 See http://rogerebert.suntimes.com/apps/pbcs.dll/article?AID=/19800101/REVIEWS/1010301/1023. Accessed 25 September 2007.

23 Such scenes occur in *Rain Man*, when Charlie first visits Wallbrook, and in school or hospital settings in *Mercury Rising*, *Silent Fall* and *Bless the Child*. In addition, *I Am Sam* features an actor with Down's syndrome.

24 David T. Mitchell and Sharon L. Snyder, 'Introduction: disability and the double bind of representation', in David T. Mitchell and Sharon L. Snyder (eds), *The Body and Physical Difference: Discourses of Disability* (Ann Arbor, MI: University of Michigan Press, 1997), p. 6.

25 Garland-Thomson, 'The politics of staring', p. 56.

26 This scene is also very similar to one in Ron Howard's biopic of mathematician John Nash, *A Beautiful Mind* (2002), in which Nash (Russell Crowe) is asked by the military to decipher an intercepted code. Here, too, the extreme close-up on the face, and the subsequent camera play on the coded numbers themselves (to a suitably charged soundtrack), is an attempt to enact the workings of the exceptional mind. Though *A Beautiful Mind* is largely about Nash's schizophrenia, it is clear from early scenes in the film in which he displays dysfunctional social skills that the Nash character is seen to have autistic tendencies.

27 Hayes and Black, 'Troubling signs', p. 114.

28 Majia Holmer Nadesan, *Constructing Autism: Unravelling the 'Truth' and Understanding the Social* (New York: Routledge, 2005), p. 9.

29 Writing in *Communication*, the magazine of the National Autistic Society in the UK, at the time of the film's release, scriptwriter Angela Pell noted that 'if nothing else, perhaps [*Snow Cake*] will raise the profile of the condition a little more and maybe, after all these years, offer up an alternative point of reference to *Rain Man*!' See Angela Pell, 'Rain and snow', *Communication*, vol. 40, no. 3 (autumn 2006), p. 21.

30 In addition, while a judgemental point, Weaver's performance does not appear to be an especially good one. Although there are elements of her physical acting – such as her hand flapping – that produce moments when her characterization is convincing, for the most part she disappoints and doesn't convey a believable sense of autism. This is particularly the case with the use of her voice, which is unmodulated throughout, and never really catches the kinds of registers or inflections common to many people with autism.

31 Peter Bradshaw, 'Does Control's take on disability mark a new dawn?', http://blogs.guardian.co.uk/film/2007/10/does_controls_take_on_disabili.html. Accessed 3 October 2007.

32 See, for a single example among the many, Mel's blog at Freak Parade, 'The Hollywood B list and autism', http://ourfreakparade.com/2007/10/05/the-hollywood-b-list-and-autism. Accessed 8 October 2007.

33 See http://www.autismspeaks.org/goals.php. Accessed 12 October 2007.

34  Lisa Barrett Mann, 'Oscar nominee: documentary or fiction?', *Washington Post*, 22 February, 2005, p. HE01.
35  A thirteen-minute version of the film, which includes the clip that caused the controversy, is available on the Autism Speaks website. See http://www. autismspeaks.org/sponsoredevents/autism_every_day.php. Accessed 12 October 2007.

# CHAPTER 4

# Boys and girls, men and women

I

There is a swirl of comment and debate about the causes, manifestations and treatments of autism, but in the midst of the various arguments it is wise to remember that it is properly understood at a general level as being a lifelong condition. 'Autism', Uta Frith noted in *Autism: Explaining the Enigma* in 1989, 'does not go away'.[1] It is, in the more technical language of Laura Schreibman, a 'form of psychopathology ... characterized by a unique constellation of severe and *pervasive* behavioural deficits and excesses' (emphasis added).[2] Pervasive and present, autism is not something one grows out of. And yet, given that this is the case, contemporary cultural fascination with autism nevertheless relentlessly focuses on the figure of the child when seeking to explore what autism is and what it might mean. Neurologist Carl H. Delacato titled his 1984 study of children with autism *The Ultimate Stranger: The Autistic Child*, and this overlapping of autism and the child as some 'ultimate' form of the condition is typical of discourses on the subject.[3] Even though it is obvious that children with autism will become adults with autism, the sense that the condition somehow affects children *more* than adults is itself pervasive.[4] Again and again in contemporary cultural narratives it is the child who carries the weight of what we wish to say or think about the condition, and it is through a focus on children that autism is increasingly being understood. 'This disease has taken our children away. It's time to get them back', says the US Autism Speaks website, in one of the clearest statements of this effect.[5]

Equally, if current ideas about autism seem almost wholly centred on children, they also frequently involve the notion that the condition is, in some way, inherently *masculine*. There are, of course, statistical reasons for this, with more males having autism than females, in a ratio of about four to one, and such figures may well have an underlying neurological foundation; but, at the same time, the more generalized sense that the manifestations of autism, its perceived limitations and expressions are indicative of some form of central masculinity forms a strong cultural impression.[6] In accounts of Asperger's, whether in fiction or memoir, the stress on the male figure is even more pronounced. The kind of interests and obsessions – science, mathematics, calendars and timetables – associated with a figure like Daniel Tammet seem to be paradigmatically male concerns, almost extensions of an idea of male personalities. Autism, it appears, can be understood best when seen in terms of the male character, and while its presence within females cannot be denied, it seems more difficult to map an idea of the condition on to the generalized sense of what we believe girls and women to be. Given that two of the most high-profile figures with autism – Temple Grandin and Donna Williams – are women, this appears especially counterintuitive. But, as we shall see, the urge to discuss autism by seeing it in terms of relationships between men is very strong.

The logical combination of the two observations above is that it is the figure of the boy who, more than any other, speaks to us in the present about what autism might be. It then becomes the faces of *especially* the boys staring out of the pages of *Souls*, or the young male characters of the films discussed in the last chapter, who seem to convey the fullest impression of all that the condition might include. In fictional narratives that depict autism, boys predominate; their autism, their masculinity and their youth combine to form the key contemporary autistic character. Likewise, in the many memoirs produced by parents outlining their accounts of coming to terms with the autism of their children, it is the boy with autism, the son (with all the resonances such a word carries), who is the source of so much emotion.

There are multiple reasons for such a position. In the hard pragmatic world of disability charity fundraising, a focus on children is far more effective than one on adults (and this is especially true if the disability is cognitive). More revenue is generated if autism is 'marketed' by charities as a condition that most affects children than if the stress is on autistic adults. Hence the comment by Autism Speaks noted above, where the emotional language is not only a statement of the foundation's beliefs, but also one carefully directed at would-be donors. In a similar vein, it is worth noting that the National Autistic Society in the UK has had its present title only since 1982. In the twenty years since the Society's formation in 1962 to that 1982 date, all versions of the organization's title included the word 'children'. But the change in title and the overall focus on children also have to be seen as an indication of the contemporary nature of interest in the condition. Historically, much of the energy involved in autism awareness has come from parents seeking to highlight the conditions of their children, and it is precisely the fact that a generation of children with autism, born in the 1960s, are now adults that has caused a shift in the thinking surrounding nomenclature. The two girls in Jane Bown's photograph on the cover of this book, for example, will now be well into their forties.

Possibly perversely, however, the wider *cultural* appreciation of autism and its meaning in the world results in the fact that it is the *current* generation of children with the condition who are now growing into adulthood in the full spotlight of the public eye, something that was not the case for those children born in the 1960s. The generation of children born post *Rain Man*, that is, after the establishment in the 1990s of genetic factors in the condition and at the time of the various vaccine scares, are the children and teenagers of today. The Autism Speaks generation is the contemporary generation of concerned parents and their children. The need for 'early intervention', common to the majority of autism education and treatment programmes and so much the subject of discussion, especially in the US, makes sure that attention is continually brought back to the child. A consequence of this is that, despite the huge exposure of the condition in a film such as *Rain Man*, with its focus on an autistic adult, adult autism has remained something of a secondary concern. It is the children who need to be 'saved', and upon whom most narratives are laid.

The obvious corollary here, though, is that this concentration on autism is then best apprehended as a particular and peculiar *adult* concern. It is driven by a generation of adults, many of whom see autism as a contemporary epidemic that threatens their children. This baseline of fear and worry penetrates deep into all current debates about autism. As we shall see in the next chapter, it carries special resonances in the depiction of families, where the figure of the autistic child is often made meaningful, in a narrative sense, by the way in which it initiates drama or insight in the world of the adult parent. The portrayal of children with autism produces much of the adult meaning of autism, and there is no doubt that this is, in a large part, due to the specific nature of the condition as it exists in the public consciousness at this time.

A similar kind of connection exists in the association between autism and gender. The observation that there are specific connections to be made between the condition and ideas of masculinity is, at heart, a biological as much as a behavioural reflection. As we shall see, the work of a figure such as Simon Baron-Cohen is an ongoing attempt to explore the link between autism and the idea of a 'male brain'. But, at the same time, the explosion of interest in autism comes when there has been a sustained analysis of the concept of the masculine in all manner of social and cultural contexts. The idea that autism is some kind of *form* of the masculine has inevitably fed into such analysis, providing new opportunities for the metaphorization of the condition, and a new context in which it might be depicted through the processes of refraction and prosthesis. Within this logic, autism is a novel explanatory category, one that potentially provides new conclusions in the ongoing debates about male status and behaviour.

To some degree, the above observations come together in a number of recent novels that seek to interrogate the place of the father in contemporary society, and do so through the use of an autistic child, usually male. Though it has not especially been read in these terms, Mark Haddon's *The Curious Incident of the Dog in the Night-Time* falls into this category, and later in the chapter I read this particular dynamic in the novel alongside similar concerns in Nick Hornby's *About A Boy* (1998) and Simon Armitage's *Little Green Man* (2001). All three texts explore ideas of male responsibility, especially through the prism of contact with autism, or autistic behaviour, in children.

But in order to understand how fathers might interact with their autistic children, it is best to be as precise as is possible about exactly how the figure of the child with autism functions in narrative. It was, after all, the specific notion of *childhood* autism that saw the first formations of the condition in the work of Kanner and Asperger. All depictions of autistic children ultimately flow back to those 1940s clinical observations, and all are somehow the heirs of those portrayals. The child has always been at the centre of what autism is thought to be, and by attempting to understand this we can hope to come that bit closer to being able to think properly about the current place of the condition in the world.

## II

In Cammie McGovern's 2006 novel *Eye Contact*, an autistic boy, Adam, seemingly witnesses the murder of his classmate Amelia, in the woods close to their school. Adam's autism affects his sensory perception of his own self. When stressed, he becomes unable to communicate: 'Nothing comes, his mouth doesn't move, because he's almost sure now, his face must be gone. He can't feel anything, can't smell, can't open his eyes to see.'[7] In a plot similar to that of *Silent Fall*, discussed in the last chapter, McGovern's novel plays out the ways in which the evidence of murder must be gently coaxed from Adam, though here it is Cara, his mother, who is the main agent facilitating the revelations of the narrative. But the particular variation of the silent witness theme offered by *Eye Contact* is less interesting than the fact that, as the novel unfolds, its revelation is that the majority of the children central to the story have disabilities. As the details of the murder become clear, Amelia's own behaviour is increasingly questioned. Near the end of the novel, following the final confession of the murderer, a high school teenager named Harrison, Matt Lincoln, the police detective who confides in Cara, tells her that 'there's a lot we don't know yet, a lot of questions we don't have'. When prompted by Cara as to what such questions might be, Matt goes on:

> Like, according to Harrison, she wouldn't back away, wouldn't leave them alone. She kept asking the same questions over and over, and eventually she started singing in his face. But why would a young girl do that to an older kid who obviously looks threatening? Why wouldn't she have backed away?[8]

Cara, who has herself acted as an amateur detective throughout, armed with the knowledge gained from being the parent of a child with autism, has the answer: 'Because she was autistic', she tells Matt, adding to herself that Amelia's mother 'has chosen, even in death, to spare Amelia the taint of labels' as a way of explaining how this information has, up until this point, been a secret.[9]

Both victim and witness have autism. But McGovern's sense of a world of children full of difference extends beyond the protagonists at the very centre of her drama. Morgan, a teenage boy whom the narrative reveals as a potential suspect early in the novel, as he clearly harbours a secret, is withdrawn and aloof, with specific reasons given for his lack of social skills:

> The reason Morgan has gone for thirteen years of his life without making a single friend is simple really: there was never time. His interests made demands on him, filled his days. Trains, for instance, took a lot of time because he had to draw them and then write stories in which trains acted out trainlike dramas: derailments, crashes, tornado encounters. These stories necessitated trips to the library, books to copy from, facts to learn. Eventually he understood that nothing he could write or check out of the library matched the satisfaction of buying things. His Viking ship phase lasted only three weeks because there was nothing to buy, but electricity? Planets? Star charts and telescopes? Every new interest has filled their mailboxes with catalogs full of the surprising products

it is possible to own: a personal planetarium, a cricket-breeding kit, an aquarium for hatching and raising sea monkeys. He's only gotten a fraction of the things he wanted.... In between purchases, Morgan kept busy, filling his notebooks with pages of research, with his coin-collection sleeves, and with the gravestone rubbings he made one summer on a trip to Gettysburg, the vacation he insisted on after reading everything he could find on the Civil War.[10]

If the revelation of Amelia's autism is part of *Eye Contact*'s generic patterning as a thriller, then that of Morgan is kept at the level of textual inference. Morgan, who 'has a hard time judging jokes' and cannot be sure when people are being serious, is undiagnosed within the plot but open to disclosure by anyone following Cara's own detective strategies.[11] He, like a number of the other 'special ed' children who form part of the novel's peripheries, speaks of a school world in which autism, learning disabilities and aberrant behaviour seem more the norm than the exception (what, for example, are we to make of the rage that led schoolboy Harrison to commit murder?). Morgan, guilty of starting a fire that has caused considerable damage, in fact becomes a detective himself, his own idiosyncratic investigations forming a parallel to the more official work of Matt Lincoln and the police.

McGovern's fictional world is, then, one swamped by disability. In the back story to events that actually forms the novel's beginning, Cara's own schooldays are dominated by her relationship with friends Kevin and Suzette. Kevin is a boy upon whom she fixates after he has had a road accident while riding his bike: 'He's had a little bit of brain damage' is part of *Eye Contact*'s second line.[12] As an adult, Kevin haunts the action that surrounds Amelia's murder, a possible suspect himself until it is revealed that he uses a wheelchair and would, as a consequence, have been unable to deliver the fatal blow. For her part, Suzette develops agoraphobia, which keeps her totally confined to her flat. On one level, such a concentration on disabled difference appears to give *Eye Contact* a peculiar disability logic – certainly it is possible to read the plot as one that needs an understanding of autism, manifested in Cara and Morgan, in order to unravel the details of the central crime. Yet the predominance of impaired children seems to speak more of something else. In her acknowledgements at the end of the novel, McGovern writes that 'we are currently in the throes of an autism epidemic that is being fought in Washington, DC, in laboratories, and in a million homes around the world', and if her own writing constitutes part of the fight of which she speaks, it also points to the fear of what the 'epidemic' may entail.[13] The startling manifestation of the autistic spectrum throughout *Eye Contact*, and the notion that it is only one of a wider network of cognitive impairments that suffuse many different types of behaviour, appears as evidence of a deep-seated concern over a generation of children left exposed to autism and conditions like it. Adults, McGovern's fiction implies, have difficulties but will work through them, making connections and resolving problems (solving crimes for example). But for children, it is suggested, the situation is far more threatening. 'His weakest subject is life', Cara says of Adam, 'and everything about moving through it'.[14]

Children with autism, it appears, are both the most typical manifestation of the condition and yet the most extreme at the same time, in the sense that the stakes surrounding diagnosis, education, understanding and acceptance are at their highest when the person with autism is a child. The nightmare scenario is that the child will *not* learn or 'progress', that there will be no overcoming. Writing on the education and treatment of autistic children in 1967, the flat tone of physician Gerald O'Gorman spells out the specific dynamics of this idea of 'failure':

> In the absence of clear ideas of causation, our efforts in the past have been largely empirical, and largely ineffectual. Conventional methods of treatment and orthodox methods of teaching have been tried and found wanting; play therapy and psychoanalysis, conditioning techniques and intensive individual teaching have ended very often in discouragement and disillusionment, and as the child fails to improve after endless hours of treatment, the therapist or the teacher, unable to accept this as a failure of his own personality or skill, tends to regard the child as untreatable and unteachable and to turn his attention to less barren fields. The more conscientious or idealistic one is, the more devastating is the effect of the child's failure to respond.[15]

The field has made vast progress since the time at which O'Gorman wrote – he talks of the move to use 'electric shock treatment, tranquilizers, prolonged narcosis, insulin and other endocrine preparations' following the above failure of treatment and teaching[16] – but the fear conveyed arguably remains. If the challenge to understand autism is a challenge to the workings of modern scientific rationality, then it finds its most obvious location in the search for scientific or educational insight that will help autistic children. McGovern's vision of a childhood full of cognitive disabilities is the end result of a failed search, and a fearful anticipation of the future.

But it is precisely because the implications of autism in children seem so cataclysmic that cultural narratives, seeking to alleviate such fears of profound difference, return time and again to the child with autism who *does* follow a path out of what are seen to be the most horrific limitations of the condition. To return to the films discussed in the last chapter, all the children at the centre of the various narratives 'emerge' in some way from the 'excesses' of autism: in *House of Cards*, Sally's autism appears to simply disappear; in *Silent Fall*, Tim's developing use of his own voice is seen as evidence of a personality that is moving beyond the restrictions of his condition; in *Bless the Child*, Cody is placed in the care of a loving relative as she overcomes her trauma; and in *Mercury Rising*, Simon's embrace of Jeffries at the film's conclusion signals a breaking down of his isolated world. Just as Autism Speaks would wish, these children in some way come 'back'.

Equally, much of the fascination with the savant figure focuses on the *child* savant. Figures like Stephen Wiltshire and Derek Paravicini (discussed in chapter 2) are all the more amazing, it appears, because their prodigious abilities were first noticed when they were children. Such observations reaffirm the compensatory narrative, of course, the 'special' ability that makes up for what is perceived to be lost, though they also invite the sentimental reading that highlights, and then laments, the discrepancy between such talent and the impairment that goes along with it. But figures such as Wiltshire and Paravicini nevertheless occupy a curious position, as their abilities are precisely *not* those usually associated with children. In his chapter on Wiltshire in *An Anthropologist on Mars*, Oliver Sacks notes the comments of one of Wiltshire's teachers in the early 1980s, who talked of Wiltshire's drawings being 'most unchildlike … when other children his age were just drawing stick figures. It was the sophistication of his drawings, their mastery of line and perspective, that amazed me – and these were all there when he was seven.'[17] Wiltshire is both a child and not in such comments, the mature 'sophistication' and 'mastery' transcending the boy who produces them. As a source of wonder, Wiltshire is, in Sacks' words, a 'prodigy' (the title of Sacks' chapter on him); as a child, he is emblematic of a narrative about autism that sees exceptionality overcome disability.

If Stephen Wiltshire is 'prodigious' in his abilities, however, he is not the child figure most renowned for overcoming the perceived limitations of autism. That position belongs to Tito Rajarshi Mukhopadhyay, a boy described as a 'miraculous child' in the subtitle of his book *The Mind Tree*.[18] *The Mind Tree* was published in 2003, and is the revised US edition (it has one extra chapter) of *Beyond the Silence: My Life, the World and Autism*, a book Tito published with the National Autistic Society in 2000, when he was twelve.[19] *Beyond the Silence* contains two autobiographical sections, 'The Voice of Silence' and 'Beyond the Silence', written when Tito was eight and eleven years old respectively, an impressionistic passage entitled 'The Mind Tree', which reads both as fiction and as an extended metaphorical account of Tito's autism, and eleven poems that make up the final section of the book. At the time of writing *Beyond the Silence*, Tito was largely non-verbal and communicated (in English) either through writing or the use of an alphabet board, where he pointed to letters which were then read aloud. Usually it was Tito's mother, Soma, who aided in this process.

The excitement caused by Tito's writing stems from the perceived disjuncture between the severity of his autism and the content of his poetry and prose, a wonder made all the more significant because of his age. Oliver Sacks, commenting in the blurb of *The Mind Tree*, encapsulates the reaction:

> The book is indeed amazing, shocking too, for it has usually been assumed that deeply autistic people are scarcely capable of introspection or deep thought, let alone of poetic or metaphoric leaps of the imagination – or, if they are, that they are incapable of communicating these thoughts to us. Tito gives the lie to all these assumptions.[20]

In a similar fashion, in her Foreword to *Beyond the Silence*, Lorna Wing talks of Tito's 'remarkable skills' arousing 'feelings of wonder, astonishment and intellectual curiosity'.[21] The 'amazing', 'remarkable' Tito has become the central figure for the articulation of what is possible within autism, a phenomenon enhanced because of his youth. He is seen as the producer of creativity from within severe impairment, and thus as proof that the impairment itself can be overcome. In the words of neurologist Mike Merzenich, 'Tito is not only authentic, but also miraculous.... [He] is a beautiful example of the possible'.[22]

In 2001, following the publication and success of *Beyond the Silence*, Tito and his mother moved to the US from India, a move sponsored and facilitated by Portia Iverson, the co-founder of the Cure Autism Now foundation, which itself subsequently became part of Autism Speaks in a merger announced in November 2006. Tito has become a high-profile figure in the various campaigns organized by both Cure Autism Now and Autism Speaks to address the issues of autism in the US. On the Autism Speaks website there is a page specifically dedicated to Tito's biography and writings, giving details of his various publications and noting, in a general introduction:

> Once in a great while, a special person emerges in the history of science and medicine, whose unique set of characteristics shed light upon an entire disorder and sometimes even on entire systems of the human brain, such as language, communication and intentional behaviour. Tito is such a person.[23]

Because of the success of his writing, Tito has become, in effect, the poster child of a specific form of autism campaign located in the US. The consequences of this are considerable, especially in the ways in which they frame an idea of the autistic child.

Rosemarie Garland-Thomson has observed that the poster child of mid-twentieth-century charity campaigns functioned largely within a paradigm of sentimentality. The visual representation of such children, Garland-Thomson notes, presented disability 'to the middle-class spectator as a problem to solve, an obstacle to eliminate, a challenge to meet'.[24] Tito fits the nature of the Cure Autism Now and Autism Speaks campaigns in exactly these terms, because of the ways in which he can be paraded as an example of the 'possible'. As Garland-Thomson goes on to discern: 'In such appeals, impairment becomes the stigma of suffering, transforming disability into a project that morally enables a nondisabled rescuer'.[25] Within this logic, the use of Tito and his family also emphasizes the stress Autism Speaks wishes to place upon the role of parents and their intervention in the care of children with autism. The care and support provided to Tito by Soma, his mother, exemplify the manner in which Autism Speaks renders the condition a non-disabled project. The foundation's web page devoted to Tito also contains a link to Soma's own website, where she gives details of her personal communications method in teaching Tito.[26] The relationship between Tito and Soma thus becomes another example of the 'possible', here not so much an observation on impairment, but rather a narrative of inspiration and guidance, in which parents might see an example of the success that could be brought about by their own actions. Within such an argument, because of Soma, a self-declared 'tenacious teacher' and her son's 'tireless taskmaster' (Garland-Thomson might, however, suggest 'rescuer'), Tito has been spared the 'silence' that autism can impose.[27]

The key point to be made about all the above observations on Tito is that the centrality he has come to occupy as an 'autism celebrity' works through a process of establishing a narrative about his life, family and writing, but this narrative actually has very little connection with the *content* of his own expression, the detail of his presence as he himself writes it. The autism poster child version of Tito is an empty signifier of a declared achievement, a story of struggle and overcoming in which his various books are *markers* on a path towards an undefined state of normalcy and acceptance. Within such a state, the difference of Tito's autism is largely negated, because his writing is read not as an account of living with autism, but rather as a *product*, an uninterrogated (and in fact un*read*) achievement of someone who should not be able to write in the first place. The fact that Tito can write at all is central to the campaigns that point to his ability to overcome; what he might have to say seems of secondary importance.

In fact, Tito's writing presents a highly complex account of autistic subjectivity and presence, and one that – like that of Larry Bissonnette discussed in chapter 2 – does not fall within orthodox boundaries of what autistic production is often seen to be. Tito's 'special ability' as a writer cannot properly parallel the work of other child figures, like Wiltshire and Paravicini, whose talents when they were young existed within certain understood and defined ideas of autistic creativity. Astonishing as is Wiltshire's early artistic renditions of St Pancras Station in London, or Paravicini's ability to copy complex pieces of music on an initial hearing, they do to some degree fall into the recognized forms of memorization or mimicry. Tito's writing, on the other hand, is not any kind of copy. Indeed, in his *literary* ability to work with imaginative creativity and metaphor, Tito is producing the kind of material that is commonly believed to be outside the scope of any individual with autism. As we saw in the discussion of Temple Grandin and Donna Williams in chapter 1, autistic writing possesses the capacity to confound many of the stereotypes held about the condition. In this capacity, Tito is, like Bissonnette, presented as one of the subjects of a chapter in Douglas Biklen's *Autism and the Myth of the Person Alone*, where he corresponds with Biklen in an interview that ranges across ideas of his autistic exceptionality.[28] That Tito can serve as an inspiration for both Autism Speaks and Biklen's thesis of autistic subjectivity only serves to underscore how contested a space his agency has become, and what kind of 'possible' his childhood self appears to promise.

*Beyond the Silence* abounds with the impressionistic conveyance of event and emotion, and is full of extended analogies and metaphors. In the two autobiographical sections Tito moves between third- and first-person perspectives to present his world within autism as a space that is, in his own terms, 'very fragmented'.[29] Like many others with autism who have represented the day-to-day nature of their lives, he stresses the strong spatial dislocations that the condition produces. 'The boy refused to accept the existence of his body', Tito writes of his own sense of his younger self, 'and imagined himself to be a spirit'; and, writing later in his account of his personal growth, he interrupts his narrative to note:

> My readers must be tired of the phrases 'using the body', and 'feeling the body', since I repeatedly use them. But that is unavoidable as I explain every stage of learning and coping with the confusion of relating the mind and body.[30]

Tito's body, as a body in the world, does not make sense to him – 'Am I made up of thoughts or am I made up of my body?', he asks in response to one of Biklen's questions in *Autism and the Myth of the Person Alone*.[31] Its relation with the mundane objects he sees around him is one that, he stresses, is difficult to control. In new environments, he writes, 'he felt that he was not able to find his body. Only if he ran fast or flapped his hands he was able to find his presence.'[32]

The ways in which he might 'find his presence' are central to Tito's autobiographical writings. As he narrates his journey in India with his mother as he undergoes various assessments, a process that sees encounters with numerous experts and schools, Tito writes with an often acute self-consciousness about the disjuncture his agency produces. As with Donna Williams, he has an idea of 'the normal' and is aware that he has his own difference from such a state. Indeed, the parallels with Williams are considerable, even down to the language used to describe the situation in which Tito finds himself. He notes at the beginning of the 'Beyond the Silence' section that 'the boy has definitely reached somewhere and I try to come back from that helpless nowhere'.[33] But, again like Williams, the desire to move from the 'nowhere' to 'somewhere' with Tito is never a simple negation of his autism; for all that Tito's writings obviously constitute autism as a state of 'silence', and posit a space 'beyond' as one of expression, his own articulation of his development into a coherent self is still one in which his awareness of his condition is paramount. As he writes in the epilogue to 'The Voice of Silence':

> Today, the fragmented self of hand and body parts which I once saw myself as, having unified to a living 'me', striving for a complete 'me'. Not in the abstract existence of the impossible world of dreams but a hope for a concrete dream of this book to reach those who would like to understand us through me.... It pains when people avoid us and the schools refuse to take us. I faced it and felt every day there may be others like me who are facing the social rejection like me. I must make the point clear that it is not lack of social understanding which causes the weird behaviour, but it is lack of getting to use oneself in the socially acceptable way, which causes the weird or unacceptable behaviour.... One day I dream that we can grow in a matured society where nobody would be 'normal or abnormal' but just human beings, accepting any other human being – ready to grow together.[34]

Tito's sense of his own completeness, then, which might constitute a form of overcoming, is nevertheless couched within a desire for a tolerant, diverse acceptance of the variety of the human spectrum. The 'us' of whom he talks in the above quote is a statement of belonging in a community that he recognizes as being different. For all that his autism is a difficulty, Tito still represents it here as foundational to his being. Any idea of his 'progress', then, which seeks to eradicate his clear autistic presence operates as an obvious misreading of his own preferred reading of his childhood self contained in *Beyond the Silence*. There is a clear incompatibility between the nuanced presence Tito articulates for himself here and the Autism Speaks representation of a 'disease' that takes children away.

In 'The Mind Tree' section of *Beyond the Silence*, Tito writes a fabular account of a tree that 'cannot see or talk' and 'can do nothing else but wait' for the various visits of men and animals that come to it but are unaware of the full nature of the tree's presence.[35] On one level the analogy is clearly a representation of the disassociation and isolation autism can produce; the tree is unable to communicate with those who use its shade or take its fruit, and can only watch as a non-participant in events. Yet, as the narrating voice notes, the idea of the mind behind the conception of the tree is a 'gift of mind', where 'I came to know that I am a Mind Tree and I was just a tree before'.[36] The Mind Tree, it is stressed here, is an exceptionality. It is also, of course, the narrative voice of creation in this section of Tito's book, the origin of all the observations. There is nothing *dis*abled about Tito's writing here. Instead, it demands to be read as prose that presents an account of what an autistic interiority is like. The Mind Tree is, literally, the surveyor of the space that autism inhabits and the commentator on the possible relationships formed within that space. It is an astonishing survey that is at the same time a powerfully singular statement of presence. If we note that the structure of *Beyond the Silence* places 'The Mind Tree' section (and indeed Tito's poetry) *after* the two autobiographical sections, then it is perfectly justifiable to posit that the 'beyond' the book moves towards is the exceptional creativity that Tito writes in the last third, and *not* some idea of the normal in which his autism is left behind. The eleven-year-old Tito of this particular volume appears to be many things to many people, but he is undoubtedly foremost a chronicler of the complex variability of his own self.

Whether or not Tito will, in the future, be seen as an expressive *writer*, as opposed to a case study for a campaigning cause, is difficult to gauge. He has published a collection of stories, *The Gold of the Sunbeams* (2005), but is still best known as a figure who writes about his self and his life.[37] As I write now, Tito is no longer a child; he is nineteen and a young man. As such, it may well be that his status as a symbol for an idea of the 'possible' with regard to autism has diminished. As with a figure such as Stephen Wiltshire, his childhood difficulties have been resolved into an adult 'success'; the published writer is now a public figure. Within such status, though, there is a curious finality to Tito's situation. The disabled child who is seen to have 'overcome' that disability is projected into a strange adult space. Because of the insistent focus on autism in children, to care – at a public level – about Tito the adult is to invoke a new set of parameters. How does adult Tito, the success, continue for the rest of his life with his autism? What might he have to say himself about this? The questions are real and immediate; they are also *still* centrally about what autism is in the world. But, for some, they will seem less pressing than to reiterate the central question of the moment – 'What is to be done?' – for a new generation of children. The danger is that Tito the example will come to eclipse Tito the person, a process that has arguably already started to happen.

Even the possibility of such a situation tells us much about the current identification of autism as a condition located within a conception of childhood, and the likelihood is that the linkage will continue for the foreseeable future. Certainly, the public focus on the issue continues unabated, with more media coverage than ever devoted to questions of treatment and education. The cultural texts continue to proliferate as well: one of the surprise successes of the 2007 film festival season was Tricia Regan's documentary *Autism: The Musical*, which explores how five children with autism in Los Angeles write, rehearse and perform their own musical called 'The Miracle Project'.[38] Regan's film is both a narrative of what autistic children can do and an attempt to give an idea of the contexts in which such productions might take place – the film deals with the children's family settings in detail. Its sense of being a 'miracle project' in itself is a familial one as much as it is a public statement about the 'possible', but its investment in the idea of transformation is very much part of the contemporary obsession with autism and the terms in which it is understood in the present.

*Autism: The Musical* makes one point clear. The achievements of children with autism today stand in contrast to the expectations made of those groups of children Kanner and Asperger looked at in the 1940s. What Asperger termed, somewhat functionally, 'the social value of the Autistic Psychopath' is no longer necessarily one of, in his words, 'bleak expectations', even for those with severe autism. In truth, Asperger himself stated that he was 'convinced … that autistic people have their place in the organism of the social community', and Regan's film stands as a clear marker of such a possibility. In the conclusion to his own article, however, Asperger noted that it was still difficult to cite medical studies which helped to place the kind of children with autism he had studied in the context of 'personality types'. 'The debate will undoubtedly become more fruitful when we know what becomes

Boys and girls, men and women

of our autistic children when they are adults', he continues, and if this may well be true of a later generation of scientists who went on to study autism in adults, it is surely telling that, at a cultural level, we are still fixated with Asperger's observation. 'What becomes of our autistic children' appears as much a fixation of contemporary cultural fascination as it was a foundational medical question in 1944.[39]

## III

There is a curious link between an idea of childhood and one of masculinity in Barbara Jacobs' 2003 book *Loving Mr Spock*. Jacobs is a novelist and advice columnist, and *Loving Mr Spock* is a confessional account, which also turns into an advice manual, of her relationship with Danny, a man with Asperger's. In the first chapter, entitled 'The handsome stranger syndrome', Jacobs introduces Asperger's in terms of the development of a romance, with Danny as the 'other-wired' seductive stranger she meets while on holiday.[40] As she presents him, Danny is erratic and different: over-direct and annoyingly frustrating, but also endearing and somewhat fascinating. In writing his character early in the book, Jacobs turns Danny into a symbol not just of a child (she finds his appearance childlike) but also of childhood innocence. Upon her return from her holiday, she finds herself unable to forget the strange man she has just met:

> After a week or so, I found I couldn't get him out of my mind. It wasn't so much the memory of his child face which kept returning, but the memory of his voice, the strange sounds he made, the flat pragmatic way he spoke, his mischievous sense of humour, and his vulnerability, an almost feminine vulnerability which made me want to protect and care for him.... And then I realized. It wasn't exactly vulnerability, it was innocence, something I'd lost, and needed to recapture. With him that night I had played at being a kid again, and talked like a kid ... I couldn't let Danny's breath of fresh air go. It had blown away all my adopted media cynicism.[41]

Danny's Asperger's here produces a state of difference. The childlike man is responsible for an idea of innocence that removes Jacobs from the adult world of her employment. Noticeably, Danny's innocence is also defined in terms of a 'feminine vulnerability', an otherness to any orthodox idea of what the masculine suitor might be.

In the end, Jacobs' relationship with Danny falters and fails, and *Loving Mr Spock* turns into an account of the various perils and pitfalls that Jacobs feels such a relationship throws up. Interestingly, it is

Jacobs herself who tells Danny that he has Asperger's; her research into his 'strangeness' provides him with a key to explain himself of which he was unaware. His condition is a 'problem ... a real problem', she stresses to him, but at the same time the style and tone of Jacobs' writing offer *Loving Mr Spock* as a narrative which is itself a curious twist on the classic 'chick lit' conundrum of the difficulties the contemporary professional single girl experiences in trying to find love.[42] Danny's Aspergic difference, initially refreshing and appealing, turns increasingly infuriating when his behaviour continually fails to follow the rules expected in an intimate relationship. Seen as a book specifically about Asperger's, *Loving Mr Spock* posits Danny in a generic position both recognizable and yet different. His masculinity, behaviour and, indeed, his very self become a form of extreme case study; the kind of thing a successful woman needs to deal with in building a relationship, the subject of multiple studies, here receives a particular spin. The 'other-wired' Danny is an example of the kind of difficult man who is out there in the contemporary moment.

As such, Jacobs' book takes its place among the legion of those devoted to the analysis of the idea of masculinity at the present time. The various anxieties and assertions we can find in *Loving Mr Spock* are common articulations, with an especial slant, of a recognizable theme. The idea that masculinity is in some state of transition in the contemporary era is one that occupies any number and manner of expressions and outlets, from public media to cultural theorizing. 'Masculinity in transition' is the name of the introduction to Daniel Lea and Berthold Schoene's 2003 edited collection *Posting the Male*, which analyses the idea of the masculine in post-war and contemporary British writing. What Lea and Schoene call 'the gradual postmodern dismantling of the patriarchal inscription of masculinity as the one subjectivity that remains forever definitively uncontaminated by "difference"' informs not just this volume, but a host of others that see such 'dismantling' of the idea of the male as being one of contemporary culture's obsessions.[43] An influential 1995 collection of essays, including pieces by Judith Butler, Sander Gilman, bell hooks, Eve Kofosky Sedgwick and Stanley Aronowitz, is entitled *Constructing Masculinities*, and in their introduction to the volume, editors Maurice Berger, Brian Wallis and Simon Watson articulate their desire not to 'fix masculinity, to eliminate its formative anxieties, to define its meaning, or reinscribe its strengths'. Rather, they point to the masculine as 'a complex and discursive category that cannot be seen as independent from that of other productive components of identity', and they list the usual trio of race, gender and sexuality as such components.[44] In a similar vein, Bob

Pease's 2000 pro-feminist account of gender change, with its emphasis upon reworking male subjectivities, is entitled *Recreating Men*, another clear textual marker of a discursive approach to masculine identity.[45]

In such studies, men are being posted, constructed and recreated, and the comments and approaches mentioned above will come as no surprise to anyone who has done any kind of work in gender studies in the last ten to fifteen years. They lay out a kind of orthodoxy in stressing both the fluidity of ideas of the masculine, as well as its anxious performativity. But they come into a special kind of relief when we place their concerns next to the ideas that surround autism and masculinity, and specifically next to a text from a different discipline, Simon Baron-Cohen's 2003 study *The Essential Difference: Men, Woman and the Extreme Male Brain*. If the editors and contributors to *Constructing Masculinity* can see the masculine only within the discursive logic of multiple formations, Baron-Cohen, Professor of Developmental Psychopathology and Director of the Autism Research Centre at the University of Cambridge, states his case for an idea of a biological essentialism at the very start of his book, in noting that 'the male brain is predominantly hard-wired for understanding and building systems', in contrast to the female brain's reliance on empathy.[46]

Baron-Cohen extends the idea of the 'extreme male brain' from the work of Hans Asperger, who in his original 1944 paper on the children he was observing noted that: 'The autistic personality is an extreme variant of male intelligence.... In the autistic individual, the male pattern is exaggerated to the extreme.'[47] In using a phrase such as 'male intelligence,' both Asperger and Baron-Cohen, and particularly the latter, point to a number of quantitative and qualitative factors in their assessment. So, for example, *The Essential Difference* follows its chapter on the various tests and clinical observations on individuals with autism and Asperger's conducted by Baron-Cohen in his research with one largely on mathematician Richard Borcherds. In doing so, he gives a narrative (and it might be noted, a *narrativized*) account of an individual who is cognitively exceptional, but also outlines an idea of context, with a range of professions (mathematics, physics, engineering) in which autistic spectrum conditions are seemingly common.

The nature of observation at work in Baron-Cohen's study, then, is both that of the controlled test produced by his research and that of the case study, which he sees, at least partially, as a consequential knowledge of such research. Such movement is typical of his book, which alternates between these two types of observation. As in the writing of Oliver Sacks, there is what we can identify as a critical textual politics at work here, an outline of the details of scientific research that is then extrapolated into specific lives and examples.[48] We might therefore say that the 'essential' idea of the autistic male brain as it is *contextualized* in Baron-Cohen's book is possibly not as far removed from the 'constructivist' notion of masculinity we find in gender studies and the humanities more widely. Baron-Cohen constructs his case for the essential male brain, and plots a certain course through the autistic spectrum, marshalling some examples of evidence and not using others. The result is a form of enquiry that works in set parameters. What if, for example, instead of concentrating, as he does, on Borcherds, Newton and Einstein as examples of the extreme male brain, Baron-Cohen had further discussion of those on the autistic spectrum – such as Andy Warhol or, indeed, Larry Bissonnette – where autism is expressed in other, non-systematized ways? Baron-Cohen's neurological work carries with it the weight of an idea that has all the resources of scientific enquiry behind it, and was thus received as evidence of work being done at the 'forefront' of autism research, but it is intriguing to see it as a form of 'constructing autism' as Majia Holmer Nadesan outlines such a phrase (as discussed in the Introduction). And in the ideas of 'constructing masculinity' and 'constructing autism', we can see how ideas of autism and the male overlap, both as fascinations of our time.

If autism is seen as some form of 'essentialized' masculinity within some quarters, it is rarely explored in terms of male physicality in the various cultural narratives in which it features. For all that there is the potential for violence within autistic behaviour, stemming from frustration or misunderstanding, ideas of aggression are largely infrequent in the various fictional accounts of the condition. Within autobiographical and memoir writing, the notion of force expressed in Bill Davis' 2001 account of his relationship with his son Chris, *Breaking Autism's Barriers: A Father's Story*, is rare.[49] Davis, who has a full chest tattoo of the autism puzzle ribbon symbol (used – especially in the US – as a marker of autism awareness), is unusual in adopting the subject position of a man seeking to 'break' his son's condition. Within mainstream media, there is an increasing creep in the association of autism with violence, as was seen in chapter 1 with the various claims that Cho Seung-Hui, the Virginia Tech student who murdered his teachers and fellow classmates, had autism, but such stories are few compared with those that discuss the 'plight' or 'need' of those affected by the condition. Far more common is the idea that autism offers a particular challenge to an idea of the masculine, an unsettling of male norms that expresses a sense of the dislocation of men in contemporary culture. If the heritage of memoir writing by family members of those with autism is largely dominated by accounts from women – from Clara Claiborne Park's *The Siege* (1967) to Charlotte Moore's *George and Sam* (2004)[50] – then the last decade has seen an increase in fictional narratives in which characters with autism are used to explore ideas of the masculine, especially where adult men are paired with autistic boys.

Such dynamics are certainly true of the novels by Nick Hornby, Mark Haddon and Simon Armitage that I wish to examine here. *About A Boy*, *The Curious Incident of the Dog in the Night-Time* and *Little Green Man* are part of the explosion of literary interest in autism that marked writing at the turn of the millennium. The phenomenal success of Haddon's novel in particular has led to what has been termed 'syndrome publishing' and 'autistic bandwaggonism', in both the US and the UK, with a *Guardian* article of December 2005 noting that Jessica Kingsley Publishers, which specializes in books on the issues of the autistic spectrum, had considered some 900 new proposals in a ten-month period following the public reception of Haddon's book.[51] The three novels occupy different positions on what we might (appropriately) think of as a spectrum of narrative representations of the condition. They deal with the idea of male responsibility inherent in the relationship between an adult male and an autistic/Asperger's boy, and reflect upon the learning process produced by an engagement with autistic presence. That said, the novels are very different; if Haddon's book has been celebrated for its immersion in the world of fifteen-year-old narrator Christopher Boone, Hornby's novel makes no mention of autism at all, and Armitage's narrative occupies a position outside the condition, in which autism is rather looked upon from a distance. Such detachment is possibly best expressed in a scene from Armitage's novel in which the father, Barney, photographs Travis, his autistic son:

> I studied his features, noticed the smallness of his mouth and his dry, bloodless lips. And the strain across his forehead, and the tiredness under his eyes, and a tension in each eye, enclosing or guarding a darkness, there, in the pit of the eye, that could only be fear. He was peeping out of his own head. Not looking with his eyes, but looking out from somewhere behind. That blackness, when I found it in the lens, made me jump. As if I'd lifted a stone. Such a contrast as well with his face, not flesh-coloured at all but white in the proper sense of the word, without colour or shade.[52]

This central idea here of a space that is 'somewhere behind,' or of being 'locked-in' (this last phrase is used in David Lodge's 2001 novel *Thinks*, another that uses a boy with autism to explore an idea of adult male masculinity[53]) is, of course, a virtual orthodoxy in narrative depictions of autism; and the structured nature of this scene, with

Travis seen through the viewfinder of a camera, highlights the power of the gaze in terms similar to those discussed in the last chapter in relation to photography and commercial cinema. The narrative dynamic established here lays a clear emphasis upon the potential of the non-autistic adult to read, or work towards the capacity to read, the meaning of the child with autism (Travis' 'darkness ... could only be fear'). In *Little Green Man* such a process involves no real analysis of, or reflection upon, the condition of autism within the narrative itself, but rather a recontextualization, often in terms of a clear sentimentality, of the issues of masculine behaviour and appropriate adult responsibility. In a highly symbolic scene at the very end of the novel, Barney jettisons all the material markers of his immaturity – 'Balls, toy cars, comics, soldiers, badges, plastic guns' (p. 245) – over a cliff and into the sea as he embraces an appropriate level of parental responsibility. Similarly, at the end of *The Curious Incident*, the father, Ed, suggests a 'project' to Christopher whereby: 'You have to spend more time with me. And I ... I have to show you that you can trust me. And it will be difficult at first because ... because it's a difficult project. But it will get better I promise.'[54]

In both novels, an idea of male accountability, and subsequently one of appropriate behaviour, is outlined because of the relationship that develops between single father and son with autism; yet, possibly curiously, this idea of a sentimental humanity, conveyed through such a narrative of refraction, is most explicit in the relationship between Will, the adult, and Marcus, the teenager, in Hornby's *About A Boy*. Marcus, presented as being wise beyond his years, is depicted early in the novel with a virtual catalogue of autistic traits. He couldn't 'spot the difference between inside and outside, because there didn't seem to be a difference'.[55] Like Christopher in Haddon's novel, Marcus likes mathematics, and his mother is a music therapist (a traditional therapy used with autistic children). When Marcus first meets Will, he is 'humming tunelessly' (p. 46), and Will observes that 'Marcus had shown no interest in him whatsoever' (p. 49). Marcus is consistently literal: 'Are you always this bloody literal-minded?', Will asks him at one point (p. 108). 'Being Marcus' (p. 163) is a clear condition of ontological presence for Marcus in the novel, and one that is heavily associated with autistic behaviour. The force of such representation is, however, that these traits become refracted through the character of Will, the selfish bachelor with no sense of responsibility and the one character in the novel with no *true* conception of others' feelings. It is very noticeable that, as the narrative progresses and the relationship between man and boy develops, Will becomes more responsible and

Marcus is seen to have acquired a new degree of social awareness where
the autistic tendencies he has fall away – he becomes genuinely perceptive about his mother's relationship, for example (p. 249), something
impossible beforehand. However, in keeping with the workings of the
kind of gendered sentimentality narrative *About A Boy* constructs, this
is clearly a secondary characterization that follows the novel's central
preoccupation, Will's progression to mature adulthood. In a telling
phrase near the end of the novel the narrative notes:

> Will couldn't recall ever having been caught up in this sort of messy
> sprawling chaotic web before; it was almost as if he had been given a
> glimpse of what it was like to be human. It wasn't too bad, really; he
> wouldn't even mind being human on a full-time basis. (pp. 264–5)

Such a moment of realization for Will helps in an understanding of the comments Hornby has made about the novel and the
place of autism within it. In *31 Songs*, his 2003 reflection on popular
music, Hornby goes out of his way to assert that autism is, in fact,
unconnected to *About A Boy*, that he made no link between his own
autistic son and the novel he was writing during its composition,
and that therefore readings which invoke such a frame are to some
degree illegitimate.[56] While this is understandable in terms of the
way Hornby may wish the novel to be read, the textual evidence suggests that a clear idea of Marcus' difference (and it is a difference we
can, and should, read in terms of autistic characteristics) is vital to
the wider workings of the novel's narrative. The force of the narrative overall may well lie in the conversion that Will undergoes, and
Marcus is clearly secondary to this – so in this sense it is possible to
note that the novel is not 'about' autism at all. But Will's conversion
is the product of his interplay with what is projected as the 'humanity'
of other key characters in the novel, especially Marcus, and Marcus'
(clear) autistic tendencies work exactly to provide material (and, in
narrative terms, an obvious textual space) that makes this conversion
possible. Seen in this way, *About A Boy* follows the rules of countless
disability narratives – the encounter with difference forcing the positive re-evaluation of the central male protagonist.

For its part, *Little Green Man* revolves around Barney's careful manipulation of a group of childhood friends he contacts again in adulthood.
Using the green man of the title, a jade figure with a 'bulging cranium'
which depicts wisdom and which the group had seen as a lucky talis-
man when they were boys, Barney engages the friends in an elaborate
version of boyish dares, at the end of which the final winner will
keep the jade figure, initially thought to be extremely valuable, but

ultimately seen to be worth only £7500. Barney's cruelty towards his friends, his controlling of the terms of the game, is presented as an almost pathologized version of the playground, and exactly the kind of behaviour that he needs to lose in order to function as a fully socialized individual. It is in such a context that Travis operates as a character, offering (through the perceived humanizing qualities of his disability) a corrective to Barney's own aberrant actions. The novel makes clear reference to various well known markers of autism – both *Rain Man* and Bruno Bettelheim are cited or alluded to, and it is interesting that the jade figure itself is deemed to be 'impaired' by the specialist who evaluates it – but the predominant display of the condition in the novel is based on the descriptions of Travis' behaviour, which often work to combine his supposedly antisocial actions with an idea of other-worldliness common to many contemporary accounts of autism. In an early scene when Barney has to care for Travis, the boy's behaviour is linked to images of malnourished Africans in an attempt to provide an explanatory context:

> He squatted on the kitchen floor, crouching with his elbows between his knees and his fingers interlocked above his head, covering his ears with his wrists. The only other people I've seen in this position are starving Ethiopians, hundreds of them, usually sitting beside a crusty river bed or an army tent, their huge eyes looking straight down the camera and out through the *Ten O'Clock News*. But they're silent and patient. Travis, in this mood, is frantic and noisy and rolls his eyes upward, looking for a fly buzzing around in the top of his skull. (p. 54)

Similarly, later in the novel, as Travis is swimming in the sea, Barney observes:

> He looked like something out of a fairy story, a skinny little sea-elf with blond hair and blue eyes, who'd come ashore from the deep. At any moment he might slide back under the waves and disappear into the underworld. (p. 167)

In both these scenes, Travis is subject to a process of over-determination from without. As a figure who is presented in the novel primarily through the cumulative sum of his behaviours, Travis *performs* autism for both his father and, as a consequence of the book's invited sense of sympathy, the reader. When Barney is astounded on seeing Travis read for the first time, a potential scene of revelation turns into one of irony, as Barney's ex-wife points out, with undisguised scorn, that he has been doing so for six months. As with all the scenes concerning Travis, here the effect is ultimately to stress details concerning Barney's character and its limitations. When, late in the novel, some of Barney's friends kidnap Travis as a reaction to Barney's manipulation of the games they have been playing, Travis literally becomes part of the plot's mobility – enacting in actuality what he has performed figuratively for the book as a whole.

The explanatory category that autism has become in *Little Green Man* and *About A Boy* is one that, on the whole, is only tangentially related to the condition itself. That tangent is, as we have seen in previous chapters, the narrative space through which autism is increasingly becoming represented in the contemporary moment. By way of contrast, *The Curious Incident of the Dog in the Night-Time*, as narrated by Christopher, constitutes a genuine, though highly stylized, attempt to present the workings of an autistic mind. It is not only an idea of fidelity that marks Haddon's novel out as different, however, as disability narratives are full of prejudices that come in the guise of well meaning liberalism. Rather, as we stressed in chapter 1, Haddon's novel centres Christopher's version of the world in terms that inscribe his narrative as rational and, crucially, customary. His difference thus becomes – within the created world of the fiction – normal, the ultimate goal for much study in contemporary work on the representations of disability and impairment, where, in the words of Michael Bérubé, it is hoped that 'disability studies will be widely understood as one of the normal – but not normalizing – aspects of study in the humanities, central to any adequate understanding of the human record'.[57]

Christopher's normality is a set of subtle observations about autistic presence, and the careful fictional construction of that presence – Christopher's uniformity of expression and reaction for example – is central to the novel's powerful portrayals. But one of the areas where Haddon does deviate from a consistency in Christopher's characterization is in his treatment of the novel's central relationship – that between Christopher and his father, Ed. In terms of its representation of parental responsibility and masculinity, it is noticeable that *The Curious Incident of the Dog in the Night-Time* takes the unusual step of making the father the main provider of care. As noted earlier, the majority of high-profile accounts of caring for autistic children have been written by mothers, often (as in the case of Moore's *George and Sam*) with fathers who are either absent or peripheral. In terms of the gendered nature of such memoirs, and the manner in which they construct ideas of love, energy, effort and commitment, it is nearly always the mother's responsibility and expression that are the source of the 'overcoming' narrative contained in these texts. In Haddon's novel it is arguably more the force of the mother's absence, rather than the father's presence, which unsettles ideas about disability and parenting, given the orthodox idea of care and the concept of 'love' that comes from this. Such revisionism does not detract from Ed's status as a troubled male, however; he is still a liar, and still insecure in his role as a father. He shares in a number of the insecurities we have identified in the central protagonists of Armitage's and Hornby's novels, and Haddon's representation, for all the unique qualities of its construction, does also participate in the examination of the anxiety seemingly foundational in contemporary masculine behaviour.

In *The Curious Incident of the Dog in the Night-Time*, the mystery of the missing mother takes over from that of the murder of Wellington the dog, the original case to be solved and the catalyst for Christopher's detections, and it is the emotional complexity of his relationship with his parents that sits in subtle juxtaposition with the supposedly 'straightforward' nature of Christopher's narration. One of the key textual spaces in which these two come together is in the representation of Christopher's relationship with his father at the crucial point when Ed's central deceit, his assertion that Christopher's mother is dead, is discovered. When Christopher creeps past his father to escape the house, he displays a range of sophisticated thought processes – wondering if Ed is pretending, imagining whether trust now exists between the two (pp. 152–4) – which are part of the fictional creation of a strong bond between father and son, but which also indicate the performative range the novel at times applies to Christopher's behaviour. Precisely because this relationship is pivotal to the narrative, it is here that Haddon's display of autism fully utilizes its fictional licence. So, Christopher can, and does, assess situations from his father's point of view, as with his reasoning when he finds his book that Ed has hidden (pp. 117–18), for example, despite this being the kind of 'mind reading' that other parts of the novel present Christopher as being unable to achieve. These moments in the book are subtle, and they can go unseen because of the ways in which they are surrounded by the paraphernalia of a more obvious construction of an autistic persona, but it needs to be stressed that they work to foreground a sophisticated relationship between the two males in the novel.

Haddon's novel resists the obvious narrative conclusion that would reunite Christopher's family and, as happens in so many disability narratives, produce a new social unit empowered by an encounter with disabled difference. Christopher becomes the successful detective and asserts his agency – 'I was brave and I wrote a book and I can do anything' (p. 268) – but the wider issues of care and his relationship with his parents remain provocatively unresolved. By way of contrast, the novels by Hornby and Armitage are fundamentally melodramatic, and reach conclusions of reconciliation and suitable adult responsibility based on the utilization of the enigmatic space autism is seen to offer within fiction: a 'properly human' Will knows that Marcus 'would be okay' in the final lines of *About A Boy* (p. 277); and, free from the material of his youth that he has 'scattered to the wind', Barney is ready to face the 'big, wide world' (p. 246). This underscoring of a new idea of presence for Will and Barney does, however, render the respective novels' representation of autism as a form of peripheral absence. It is the moral education of the non-impaired male that triumphs here, although to say this is not necessarily to suggest that the novels themselves are profound interventions in these debates. Rather, it is to note how a specific disability narrative, utilized precisely because of its perception as describing a condition of ambiguity, can connect with the workings of culture more generally, and in loose, inchoate ways ultimately become a marker of identity for a non-disabled majority.

Given the success of Haddon's novel, and the status of Hornby and Armitage as popular writers whose works have reached wide audiences, we might conjecture on how these issues might impact upon a readership. In *Pulp*, his 1998 study of the processes of reading popular fiction, Scott McCracken advances the idea that the reading of popular novels allows for the creation of a 'workable, if temporary, sense of self' in the reader. He goes on: 'It can give our lives the plots and heroes they lack. While the same can be said for all fiction, narratives read by large number of people are indicative of widespread hopes and fears.'[58] McCracken's work exemplifies that strand of cultural studies that seeks to stress the agency of the reader, to assert that audiences do not simply consume the ideologies in the texts they read, but rather work as critical receivers and can project positive, utopian conclusions as a consequence of the reading process. But the optimism in such a position seems misplaced. In the wide media representation of disability generally, and autism in particular, there is such a distinct lack of knowledge of the nature of impairment that any idea of a genuinely constructive interaction with its forms by a reader should be read as largely being an impossibility. Rather, the audience for *Little Green Man* and *About A Boy* in particular will, on the whole, potentially receive a stereotypical idea of autism as a way of being in the world, and narratives that talk more of a vulnerability and insecurity about the business of being masculine than of disability or exceptionality. As with much of the popular fiction that features characters with autism, the condition becomes a prop, a prosthetic device, for the discussion of a range of issues – masculine identity, family cohesion, adult responsibility – that ultimately have their meaning in non-disabled contexts.[59]

## IV

In August 2007, the *New York Times* magazine ran an article that specifically discussed issues of autism as they relate to girls and women. Entitled 'What autistic girls are made of', and written by Emily Bazelon, the main focus of the article was on the difficulties girls with autism experience because of their numerical minority within the wider autism population, and because of the expectations that come with the general cultural association between autism and masculinity. Because there are fewer females than males with autism, Bazelon notes, there is a tendency for their experiences not to be properly registered, or understood. She quotes Ami Klin, the director of the autism research programme at Yale University, who has termed girls and women with autism 'research orphans', because of the difficulty in finding sufficient numbers of autistic females to use in large-scale research.[60]

The phrase 'research orphans' is an arresting one. It reminds us that, for all the advances in scientific research on autism in the last fifteen years, there are still considerable and significant omissions in what we know about the condition. It is also an idea we can translate into any assessment of the place of autism within narrative, where depictions of autistic girls and women are equally rare. Their status as 'orphans' here is, in part, because of the desire to use the condition to explore what it means to be male, and it is instructive that in a rare example of the portrayal of an adult woman with autism – Sigourney Weaver's character Linda Freeman in *Snow Cake* (see chapter 3) – the overall arc of the narrative is still more concerned with a central male protagonist. In the business of fiction, the combination of women and autism seems to be a complicated conjunction that can, at best, be seen as some form of add-on to the core concerns of how an idea of autistic masculinity might shape our thinking about men. The irony is, of course, that this supposed central concern is itself a kind of floundering in the complexities of contemporary gender politics, and often has little to say about autism itself. As long as the condition is seen in terms of some form of 'essential' maleness (to return to Baron-Cohen's terms), then it is highly likely that the orphan status of autistic girls and women, whether in the realm of the scientific study or the commercial feature film, will remain. And possibly when those involved in investigating ideas of the male through autism tire of this particular prism, they will go elsewhere.

There is, however, a space where an investigation of the interaction between adult women and autism does have a high-profile centrality, and this is, of course, where the woman in question is a mother. If a scientific idea of the 'autistic male' has filtered down into various kinds of fictional narratives, as I have looked at here, then the cultural concerns of what autism means to a notion of family can be seen to be an obvious extension of this. Arguably, however, ideas about family have become even more common and central to an idea of what autism is in the present than the traditional association between the condition and gender. A focus on what autism means within families, of course, can continue the stress on children that this chapter has seen to be a principal manifestation of the contemporary fascination with the condition, but it can also stress the contextualization of that fascination as a specific *adult* concern. In addition, it can project a sense of what autism means within a *community*, where those communal demands take shape within what is the preferred normalized unit of social organization. In terms of both how autism can be figured as a threatening and destructive force, and how it can be presented as a catalyst for love and connection, it is the family that has emerged as the dominant arena through which we want to discuss the condition in the present.

## Notes

1 Uta Frith, *Autism: Explaining the Enigma* (Oxford: Basil Blackwell, 1989), p. 15.
2 Laura Schreibman, *The Science and Fiction of Autism* (Cambridge, MA: Harvard University Press, 2005), p. 2.
3 Carl H. Delacato, *The Ultimate Stranger: The Autistic Child* (Novato, CA: Arena, 1984).
4 In recognition of this, in February 2008 the National Autistic Society in the UK launched, as part of its 'Think Differently About Autism' campaign, a set of advertisements proclaiming 'Autism also affects adults'. Using the central phrase 'I exist', the advertisements sought to draw attention to adult autism precisely because the dominant paradigm is clearly one in which the condition is associated with children.
5 See http://www.autismspeaks.org/founders.php. Accessed 25 October 2007.
6 Most organizations agree on the sex ratio of four to one. See, for example, the UK's National Autistic Society at http://www.nas.org.uk/nas/jsp/polopoly. jsp?d=235&a=3431 and the Autism Society of America at http://www.autism-society.org/site/PageServer?pagename=about_whatis_home. Accessed 29 October 2007.
7 Cammie McGovern, *Eye Contact* (London: Viking, 2006), p. 31.
8 McGovern, *Eye Contact*, p. 275.
9 McGovern, *Eye Contact*, p. 275. Although Amelia has been described as being 'learning disabled' earlier in the novel (p. 22), the disclosure of her autism is particularly important, and revelatory, given the links it sets up with Adam.
10 McGovern, *Eye Contact*, p. 82.
11 McGovern, *Eye Contact*, p. 72 and p. 230.
12 McGovern, *Eye Contact*, p. 1.
13 McGovern, *Eye Contact*, p. 291. The biography of McGovern on the novel's dust jacket notes that her own eldest child is autistic.
14 McGovern, *Eye Contact*, p. 9.

15  Gerald O'Gorman, *The Nature of Childhood Autism* (London: Butterworths, 1967), p. 112. O'Gorman was the superintendent of Borocourt Hospital in Reading in the UK.

16  O'Gorman, *The Nature of Childhood Autism*, p. 112.

17  Chris Marris, quoted in Oliver Sacks, *An Anthropologist on Mars* (London: Picador, 1995), pp. 189–90.

18  Tito Rajarshi Mukhopadhyay, *The Mind Tree: A Miraculous Child Breaks the Silence of Autism* (New York: Arcade Publishing, 2003).

19  Throughout my discussion of Tito's work, I shall refer to him as 'Tito', rather than use his surname. This is largely the accepted practice in discussions of his writing, and stems from Tito being his Bengali family name, the use of which is common in familial circumstances.

20  Oliver Sacks, blurb, *The Mind Tree*.

21  Lorna Wing, 'Foreword', in Tito Rajarshi Mukhopadhyay, *Beyond the Silence: My Life, the World and Autism* (London: National Autistic Society, 2000), p. 3.

22  Mike Merzenich, blurb, *The Mind Tree*.

23  See http://www.autismspeaks.org/tito.php. Accessed 8 November 2007.

24  Rosemarie Garland-Thomson, 'The politics of staring: visual rhetorics of disability in popular photography', in Sharon L. Snyder *et al.* (eds), *Disability Studies: Enabling the Humanities* (New York: Modern Language Association, 2002), p. 63.

25  Garland-Thomson, 'The politics of staring', p. 63.

26  See http://www.halo-soma.org/about.php. Accessed 8 November 2007. Soma Mukhopadhyay's instructional method is called 'rapid prompting'.

27  See http://www.halo-soma.org/about_soma_tito.php. Accessed 8 November 2007.

28  Tito Rajarshi Mukhopadhyay and Douglas Biklen, 'Questions and answers', and Larry Bissonnette, 'Letters ordered through typing produce the story of an artist stranded on the island of autism', in Douglas Biklen, *Autism and the Myth of the Person Alone* (New York: New York University Press, 2005), pp. 117–43 and pp. 172–82.

29  Tito, *Beyond the Silence*, p. 9.

30  Tito, *Beyond the Silence*, p. 15 and p. 40.

31  Tito and Biklen, 'Questions and answers', p. 121.

32  Tito, *Beyond the Silence*, p. 20.

33  Tito, *Beyond the Silence*, p. 59.

34  Tito, *Beyond the Silence*, pp. 57–8.

35  Tito, *Beyond the Silence*, p. 79.

36  Tito, *Beyond the Silence*, p. 87.

37  Tito Rajarshi Mukhopadhyay, *The Gold of the Sunbeams, and Other Stories* (New York: Arcade Publishing, 2005). He also has a new book, *How Can I Talk If My Lips Don't Move: Inside My Autistic Mind* (New York: Arcade Publishing, 2008).

38  See www.autismthemusical.com. Accessed 2 November 2007. The documentary was an official selection for the Tribeca Film Festival in New York and the Vancouver Film Festival, among others.

39  Hans Asperger, '"Autistic psychopathy" in childhood', in Uta Frith (ed. and trans.), *Autism and Asperger Syndrome* (Cambridge: Cambridge University Press, 1991), p. 87, p. 89 and p. 90.

40  Barbara Jacobs, *Loving Mr Spock* (London: Michael Joseph, 2003), pp. vii–viii.

41  Jacobs, *Loving Mr Spock*, pp. 9–10.

42  Jacobs, *Loving Mr Spock*, p. 35. *Loving Mr Spock* is only the most high-profile account of relationships with Asperger's partners. Maxine Ashton's *The Other*

*Half of Asperger Syndrome: A Guide to Living in an Intimate Relationship with a Partner Who Has Asperger Syndrome* (London: National Autistic Society, 2001) and *Aspergers in Love* (London: Jessica Kingsley, 2003) are books with a similar focus.

43 Daniel Lea and Berthold Schoene, 'Masculinity in transition: an introduction', in Daniel Lea and Berthold Schoene (eds), *Posting the Male: Masculinities in Postwar and Contemporary British Literature* (Amsterdam: Rodopi, 2003), p. 9.

44 Maurice Berger, Brian Wallis and Simon Watson (eds), *Constructing Masculinity* (New York: Routledge, 1995), p. 3 and p. 2.

45 Bob Pease, *Recreating Men: Postmodern Masculinity Politics* (London: Sage, 2000).

46 Simon Baron-Cohen, *The Essential Difference: Men, Women and the Extreme Male Brain* (London: Penguin/Allen Lane, 2003), p. 1.

47 Hans Asperger, quoted in Baron-Cohen, *The Essential Difference*, p. 149.

48 For more on the method of Sacks' writing, see Leonard Cassuto, 'Oliver Sacks and the medical case narrative', in Sharon L. Snyder *et al.* (eds), *Disability Studies: Enabling the Humanities* (New York: Modern Language Association, 2002), pp. 118–30.

49 Bill Davis (as told to Wendy Goldband Schunick), *Breaking Autism's Barriers: A Father's Story* (London: Jessica Kingsley, 2001).

50 Clara Claiborne Park, *The Siege: A Family's Journey into the World of an Autistic Child* (Boston, MA: Little, Brown, 1967); Charlotte Moore, *George and Sam* (London: Viking, 2004).

51 Sarah Adams, 'A curious phenomenon', *Guardian*, 7 December 2005.

52 Simon Armitage, *Little Green Man* (London: Penguin, 2002), p. 120. Subsequent references are in parentheses in the text.

53 David Lodge, *Thinks* (London: Penguin, 2002), p. 86.

54 Mark Haddon, *The Curious Incident of the Dog in the Night-Time* (London: Jonathan Cape, 2003), p. 265. Subsequent references are in parentheses in the text.

55 Nick Hornby, *About A Boy* (London: Penguin, 2000), p. 14. Subsequent references are in parentheses in the text.

56 Nick Hornby, *31 Songs* (London: Penguin, 2003), pp. 98–9. No doubt this is, in part, because Hornby fears easy biographical readings, given that he is himself the parent of a child with autism.

57 Michael Bérubé, 'Afterword', in Sharon L. Snyder *et al.* (eds), *Disability Studies: Enabling the Humanities* (New York: Modern Language Association, 2002), p. 343.

58 Scott McCracken, *Pulp: Reading Popular Fiction* (Manchester: Manchester University Press, 1998), p. 2.

59 It might be observed, however, that the phenomenal success of Haddon's novel has actually created another type of text, in which individuals with autism or Asperger's feature as a kind of generalized signifier of quirky 'difference', but where any idea of the actuality of autistic presence remains unexplored. Margot Livesey's *Banishing Verona: A Novel* (New York: Henry Holt, 2004) seems to fall into this category, with its central Asperger's character Zeke providing an idea of eccentricity or idiosyncrasy that marks the novel as possessing a narrative difference. This could well be as much a commercial decision – making a text distinctive in a very competitive market – as anything to do with the context of seeking to explore individual agency, but Zeke's Asperger's is little beyond a collection of behavioural traits.

60 Emily Bazelon, 'What autistic girls are made of', *New York Times*, magazine, 5 August 2007. Available online at http://www.nytimes.com/2007/08/05/magazine/05autism-t.html. Accessed 3 December 2007.

CHAPTER 5

# In our time:
# families and sentiments

I

In April 2006, Alison Davies drove with her son Ryan from their home in Stockport in Greater Manchester to the Humber Bridge near Hull in the UK. Following a phone call to the local Humberside police, she is alleged to have taken her son's hand and jumped from the bridge to the river below. 'I have failed as a Mother' was the subsequent front-page headline of the *Daily Mail* on 18 April, reporting on the two deaths and picking up on the words of Davies' sister, Lindsay Cook: 'She feels a failure as a mother. She thinks she's a burden to us and that to save us all the worry she'll take herself and Ryan away and we'll never have to worry about them again.' Ryan, as the newspaper made clear in the subheading on the front page, was autistic. He was, according to Cook, 'very friendly and trusting but completely unable to cope on his own', while according to the other family friends the paper talked to he was an 'increasingly difficult only child'.[1]

Ryan Davies' death was not a unique event. There are a number of cases each year, often given high-profile coverage in the media, where children with autism die at the hands of family members, usually parents. Kathleen Seidel, who organizes neurodiversity.com, a web-site that covers a multiplicity of autism-related issues, has a section entitled 'Murder of Autistic Persons', which lists numerous instances of such deaths.[2] As with the *Daily Mail*'s coverage of Ryan's death, in the majority of these cases the focus of the media coverage is not on the child who has died, but rather on the parent. In August 2003, Daniela Dawes suffocated her autistic son Jason in Sydney, Australia. After pleading guilty to murder, the charge against Dawes was reduced to manslaughter and she was ultimately sentenced to a five-year good-behaviour bond by a district court judge in June 2004. Reporting on the case, Australia's national broadcast radio, ABC, noted that 'neither the State Opposition nor a national carers' group have any quarrel with the judge who let her go free' and that 'District Court Judge Roy Ellis said the circumstances were so exceptional as to justify a bond instead of a jail sentence for Daniela Dawes.... He was also highly critical of the services that were supposed to be available to help her care for her son.' The ABC report went on:

> Jason Dawes was diagnosed as autistic when he was 18 months old. At the age of 10 he had the mental age of a 3-year old. He couldn't speak and he needed constant help to eat, bathe and go to the toilet. Most of that responsibility fell to his mother, Daniela Dawes. The court heard that her husband Craig had a drinking problem, was sometimes violent towards her, and later suffered a breakdown and didn't work for two years. Mrs Dawes became the sole breadwinner. To compound all of that, she suffered severe depression. It all got too much for her on August the fourth last year. That day she suffocated her son and then tried to kill herself.[3]

As was the case with Ryan Davies, Jason Dawes here becomes a peripheral figure in the narrative of his own death, reduced to the presence of some form of 'cause' in the actions of his mother and no more than the summary of his own behavioural difference. Reflecting on the deaths of Alison and Ryan Davies in *The Times* a few days after the event, novelist and journalist Debbie Taylor made it clear that the full force of the story lay in the way it shed light on the pressures faced by mothers suffering from depression. 'The deaths of Alison Davies and her autistic son Ryan highlight the tragedy of maternal depression' ran the subheading to Taylor's article, 'The dark side of mothering'. In Taylor's account, Ryan (the 'friendly and trusting' son, 'unable to cope on his own') jumps to his own death from the Humber Bridge, while at the end of her article she makes her priorities plain: 'If particular attention could be paid to the mothers of disabled children, the tragic deaths of people like Alison and Ryan might be averted'.[4] Reading Taylor's account of the event, and the narrative places in which she stresses her interest, it is impossible not to conclude that one of these two deaths appears more tragic than the other.

We should pause when considering the deaths of Ryan Davies and Jason Dawes, and the others like them. In all the issues relating to autism there is no more emotional subject, it appears, than that produced by the condition within the family, and especially in the central relationship between mother and child. If, to repeat the point made in the last chapter, the image and idea of the child have become the focal point for what autism *is*, then it seems that the *impact* of the condition is most seen in the ways in which it affects the contemporary family. In all the various forms of the vaccine scares which have dominated discussion of autism in the US and the UK over the last ten years, it has always been an idea of the family – often beleaguered and unsupported – that has been at the centre of 'the need for answers'. To judge from much recent comment about autism that circulates in the media, the condition appears to affect families more than it does individuals. At specialist publishers such as Jessica Kingsley, the number of books devoted to autism as seen through the eyes of parents or siblings, or volumes that are intended to aid families that have an autistic member, form a significant part of the catalogue.[5] The specific *representation* of autism within the family has become a common feature of television drama in recent years, possibly as the format is thought to lend itself to such analysis of the domestic in a way that feature films do not. And in both fictional prose and memoir, ideas of autism and the family abound, part of the processes of narrative usage that we have seen in this study up to this point.

But family occupies another vital point in the contemporary discussion of autism, one that brings many of the concerns of this book together. It is families, and especially parents, who are the target for the many foundations and programmes that offer therapies for children with autism, and in so doing produce a particular language of achievement and hope that fills the pages of many books aimed at parents who wish to 'treat' their child. Arguably, it is nowhere more than here that the economy of autism is at its most obvious, an economy that includes the costs of programmes and advisors and the full range of materials and resources that come with treatment. Later in the chapter I shall focus on one of the most well known and influential of these programmes, Son-Rise, both because of its international scope and because Barry Neil Kaufman, one of the co-founders of Son-Rise, has written extensively about its development out of the strategies he and his wife, Samahria, created when working with their autistic son, Raun. In both *Son-Rise* (1976, published in the UK as *To Love Is To Be Happy With: The Miracle of One Autistic Child*) and *Son-Rise: The Miracle Continues* (1994), a sequel which rewrites and extends the first text, Kaufman outlines a narrativized idea of the treatment of autistic children in which the family unit and all that it stands for is central.[6] In the words of the website of the Autism Treatment Center of America, the main umbrella organization that oversees the provision of Son-Rise: 'The program places parents as key teachers, therapists and directors of their own programs and utilizes the home as the most nurturing environment in which to help their children'. It is, the description continues, 'respect and deep caring' that is 'the most important factor impacting a child's motivation to learn'.[7] In *Son-Rise* and *Son-Rise: The Miracle Continues*, Kaufman's prose outlines the principles that came to underpin such sentiments, sentiments that in many ways dominate ideas about autism and the family.

Thinking back to Ryan Davies and Jason Dawes, we might feel that here were cases where the idea of the 'nurturing' home environment, for whatever reason, failed to materialize, or to help. Potentially, these deaths show the limits of the 'caring' programme, though – as we saw above – one of the issues that always emerges in the aftermath of such deaths is state provision of care and support systems for families with disabilities. But, for all its merits, such a conclusion would miss the dominant drive behind the ways autism in families is represented, namely that the focus is *still* on questions of home, caring and familial love, whether the event is considered a 'tragedy' or a 'miracle'. To say that Alison Davies 'failed' as a mother is to invoke a very specific paradigm, and to direct discussion about her death in a certain way. It also, of course, necessarily positions Ryan in an all too familiar space, the disabled figure on the margins of a story. To find Ryan's presence in this narrative, we have to make an effort to look for him, to conjecture as to his version of events, and to campaign for his inclusion. He was, after all, a family member as well.

## II

The contemporary fascination with the relationship between autism and the family, and especially parenting, has a clear source. It lies in the early clinical formations of the condition that emerged in the mid-twentieth century and came to dominate the ways in which autism was understood. In 'Autistic disturbances of affective contact', his foundational 1943 article, Leo Kanner appears at times to be as interested in the parents of the children he analysed as he was in the children themselves. As he introduces each child in his research study, usually through the contact he has with their families, Kanner lists the professions of the parents, as if compiling a secondary archive of evidence relevant to his study. All this material is then brought together in two key passages towards the end of the article. In the first, written after the detail of all the children has been presented and just before the concluding 'Comment' section, Kanner's compulsion to record family details finally emerges as a kind of subtextual thesis:

There is one other interesting common denominator in the backgrounds
of these children. *They all come of highly intelligent families.* Four fathers
are psychiatrists, one is a brilliant lawyer, one a chemist and law school
graduate employed in the government Patent Office, one a plant patholo-
gist, one a professor of forestry, one an advertising copywriter who has
a degree in law and has studies in three universities, one is a mining
engineer, and one a successful business man. Nine of the eleven mothers
are college graduates. Of the two who have only high-school education,
one was a secretary in a pathology laboratory, and the other ran a theatri-
cal booking office in New York City before marriage. Among the others,
there was a free-lance writer, a physician, a psychologist, a graduate
nurse, and Frederick's mother was successively a purchasing agent, the
director of secretarial studies in a girls' school, and a teacher of history.
Among the grandparents and collaterals there are many physicians,
scientists, writers, journalists, and students of art. All but three of the
families are represented either in *Who's Who in America* or in *American
Men of Science*, or both.[8]

Upon reflection, it should probably come as no surprise that
the majority of families who were able to bring their children to a
university-based research project, in a discipline that was, at that
time, still emerging, might contain a high proportion of academics
and professionals, but as he makes the above observations Kanner's
rising excitement is almost palpable.[9] In turn, it leads to the second
central observation that he makes about families, one that comes at
the very end of the article. Though Kanner states that 'It is not easy to
evaluate the fact that all of our patients have come of highly intelligent
parents', he immediately goes on to add: 'This much is certain, that
there is a great deal of obsessiveness in the family background. The
very detailed diaries and reports [produced by the various parents to
aid his research] ... furnish a telling illustration of parental obsessiveness.'[10] The observation of this obsessiveness then itself becomes the
lead-in to a further comment, one that has had profound consequences
for the understanding of autism in the last sixty or more years:

> One other fact stands out prominently. In the whole group, there are
> very few really warmhearted fathers and mothers. For the most part, the
> parents, grandparents, and collaterals are persons strongly preoccupied
> with abstractions of a scientific, literary, or artistic nature, and limited
> in genuine interest in people. Even some of the happiest marriages
> are rather cold and formal affairs. Three of the marriages were dismal
> failures. The question arises whether or to what extent this fact has
> contributed to the condition of the children.[11]

Kanner's 'question' projected the idea that parents might in some way
be responsible for their children's autism into the future, and it became
a hypothesis that dominated ways of thinking about the condition

for over thirty years. That this comment about adults came in such a speculative mode from a *child* psychiatrist, seemingly throwing out unfounded ideas that were peripheral to the main focus of his research, and towards the conclusion of his writing, seemed not in any way to influence those who picked up on it. Crucially, the observation established the family unit, and an idea of parental care and love, as one of the prisms through which autism might be understood. With the kind of neurology that would later develop to aid in understanding autism still in its infancy, the fields of psychiatry and psychology instead offered multiple avenues to explore the mysteries of the condition.

Reading Kanner retrospectively, it is clear that his comments about families and parents here are secondary concerns to the detail in which he discusses the children, but at the same time, as intimated above, the idea of parental causation forms a definable thread that runs, trace like, through the article as a whole, as if Kanner is looking for causation even as he realizes he needs to attend to the specifics of studying the children. In his later work on autistic children, Kanner continued to stress what he clearly felt to be the unusual and 'obsessive' nature of many of the parents of the children who came to his clinic, but he combined this with the use of his central theory of 'autistic aloneness' and the observation that the 'pure-culture examples' – the children who came to be seen as having 'early infantile autism' – might relate to objects but did not do so to people.[12] As such, his question as to the potential responsibility of the parents in the 'creation' of the autism experienced by their children was, to some degree, blocked by the answers provided in his own work. If children with autism did not relate to people, then what did it matter what their family circumstances might be?

The unravelling of this particular question came in the most notorious study to explore possible theories of causation with regard to autistic children, Bruno Bettelheim's 1967 book *The Empty Fortress*. Bettelheim was a Freudian psychologist who had been an inmate of a Nazi concentration camp in the late 1930s, an experience which, as he puts it, 'led me to introspect in the most personal immediate ways on what kinds of experience can dehumanize.... It was an experience of living isolated from family and friends, of being severely restricted in the sending and receiving of information.'[13] It is ultimately a matter of conjecture as to exactly how this experience of isolation and restriction informed Bettelheim's interest in autism and his idea of being human, but it is impossible to think that it did not play some part in the ideas that came to inform his work. Certainly, his incarceration informed his understanding of psychology and of the self, something he writes about in the early pages of *The Empty Fortress*. With regard to Kanner's question about the place of parents in childhood autism, Bettelheim believed that 'autism is basically a disturbance of the ability to reach out to the world', and concluded that the truth about children with autism was that they did indeed relate to people, but that the 'fortress' displayed by the condition was the product of a failure of parental response at a key moment of childhood development.[14] Picking up on two terms in a 1956 article co-written by Kanner that surveyed research on infantile autism from the mid-1940s to the mid-1950s, Bettelheim commented:

> It is difficult to see how the 'emotional configuration in the home' can play 'a dynamic role in the genesis of autism' if the child does not respond to it because he does not relate to people. The only way these two statements can be reconciled is to assume that the parents' behavior does not permit or induce the child to come out of his shell. That is, the only way one can accept Kanner's thesis that the home affects the disturbance and still hold his view that the child cannot relate would be to assume that the parents fail to evoke any response in the child and that he therefore remains in his original autistic state.[15]

Within the logic of this thinking, Kanner's somewhat casual question receives its seemingly authoritative answer. It is the dynamics of the family, the manifestations of parental love, care and behaviour, which finally provide the clues to the nature of autism. For Bettelheim, autistic children want to 'reach out to the world', but the nature of the caring relationship they receive prevents a 'normal' self from developing. The major figure in any familial caring situation was understood, of course, to be the mother, and so it was the mother–child relationship in particular that became the focus of Bettelheim's analysis. The reaction of the child to the mother, especially seen in terms of emotions, came to dominate ideas about the development of an autistic self. As Bettelheim noted, 'In those children destined to become autistic their oversensitivity to the mother's emotions may be such that they try, in defense, to blot out what is too destructive an experience for them'.[16] And it was irrelevant exactly *when* the first signs of autism might appear in the child, for, as Bettelheim observed: 'I believe that stories about autistic children being unresponsive from birth do not, in and by themselves, suggest an innate disturbance. Because it may be a very early reaction to their mothers that was triggered during the first days and weeks in life.'[17] Whichever way one looked, and whether they were aware of their emotions or not, mothers now appeared to be the triggers for the development of autism in children.

Bettelheim was wrong, although this knowledge must have been little comfort to the mothers of autistic children in the period from the

1950s to the 1970s. As the 1970s progressed, research in neurology continued to suggest the relationship between autism and the physical make-up of the brain, and the critique of psychoanalysis that emerged as the method began to lose some of its clinical and cultural central-ity pointed out the inconsistencies in the psychoanalytic account of the origins of autism. Yet for all the sense that Bettelheim marks a particularly dark stage in the history of autism in the contemporary period, which has now been overcome, there are still clear traces of his ideas in the most recent articulations of how the condition operates in, and is apprehended by, the world. One of the most obvious is in the continued resonance of his idea of autism being a kind of 'fortress', or a state of siege. The multiple metaphors that emanate from this – of battles and breakthroughs, and attack and defence – are still dominant in the public perception of what autism is. The suggestion that there is a need to break in to the isolated autistic child, to find and save him or her, can be seen in the titles of many books on the subject, ranging from a volume published in the same year as Bettelheim's own book, Clara Claiborne Park's *The Siege* (1967), to contemporary accounts, such as Karen Zelan's *Between Their World and Ours: Breakthroughs with Autistic Children* (2003), Barbara Lasalle's *Finding Ben: A Mother's Journey Through the Maze of Asperger's* (2003) and Howard Buten's *Through the Glass Wall: Journeys into the Closed-Off Worlds of the Autistic* (2004). More generally, these ideas now form the currency of much public debate on autism, metaphors that function as an effective reality in the way that they are understood and transmitted.

More pertinent for the concerns of this chapter, however, is the fact that the consequences of Bettelheim's concentration on the role of the mother have created a legacy in which the mother–child relationship remains pivotal in discussion of autism. As we have seen in previous chapters, mothers abound in all forms of representations of autism, from the obvious form of the family memoir to fiction and film. It is the mothers in texts as different as Joseph Conrad's 'The Idiots' and Cammie McGovern's *Eye Contact* who channel much of the meaning of autism in their respective narratives, the mother in Rosie Barnes' photographs of her son Stanley who, possibly inadvertently, reflects a deep sense of maternal loss, and the mother in *House of Cards* who becomes the saviour of her daughter. And it is noticeable that, even when the mother is not the central figure in such narratives, familial relationships predominate: sibling concerns in *The Secret Agent*, *Rain Man* and *Silent Fall*, and fathers in *The Curious Incident of the Dog in the Night-Time* and *Little Green Man*. Bettelheim's idea of the self that has been impaired by the family might have been relegated to the realm of the pseudo-scientific, but it appeared impossible to forget the idea that autism somehow *belonged* to the dynamics of the family. The trajectory from Bettelheim to the concerns of Autism Speaks, with its stress on the need for parental involvement, in particular in any treatment of autism, is real and obvious.

So, when the vaccine scares erupted in both the US and the UK at the turn of the millennium, the parameters of the opposing groups established themselves quickly: an emotionless empirical authority as embodied in governmental health services set against the collective ranks of families who asserted the truths they felt their experiences had taught them. In the media profile of Andrew Wakefield, the lead author of the notorious 1998 *Lancet* article that led to the suggestion of a possible link between the vaccine for measles, mumps and rubella (MMR) and the rise in cases of autism in children,[18] he was presented as the champion of those families who appeared to be excluded from the scientific consensus stressing the safety of inoculation. Wakefield, ostracized from the medical community in which he worked, became rehabilitated as the hero of family support groups, who demanded that their stories be heard. As we shall see, such a status even made its way into the fictional narratives of the period, both in prose and in television drama.

Similarly, in his *Evidence of Harm*, the study of the development of the debate over the use of thimerosal (also known as thiomersal in the UK, a preservative used in vaccines and which contains a quantity of mercury) in the US, David Kirby's central figures are all embattled parents, fighting the stresses of looking after their children even as they struggle to learn the language of clinical medicine that will allow them to take on the doctors and university professors. For Kirby, these parents are awe-inspiring modern-day heroes, and it is intriguing to note how his book slides into a form of fiction as he recreates historical dialogue between real people he has met and interviewed for his study. In his first chapter, entitled 'Mothers on a mission', Kirby introduces Lyn Redwood, Sallie Bernard and Liz Birt, figures who come to act as characters throughout his text, and who are primarily *characterized* through their roles as mothers. In the ways in which his narrative enters into the minds of the various women he discusses, recreates their thoughts and emotions, and even speaks their words, Kirby sets up a clear sentimental dynamic about the position they hold within their families:

> By this point Lyn had stopped working altogether in order to devote more time to Will [her son]. Like many parents of autistic kids, she learned how destructive the disease can become for the entire family ...

> Lyn had not slept an entire night in weeks. She was exhausted, guilty, and overwhelmed. Her house, her home, her whole family seemed to be fraying at the edges. She was so bankrupt of energy, it was nearly impossible to hold it all together. For a second, she considered walking out the door, never to return, then quickly put escape out of her rattled mind. Lyn needed to be the strong one. She needed to be the mom.[19]

'Being the mom' is here conceived of exclusively in terms of the domestic. The idea of strength it encapsulates, of energy and care, is one of a love that can counter the destruction that autism brings. It is a role based on commitment and responsibility, a singular rooted presence set against the perceived chaos of autism. In *Evidence of Harm*, parenting is seen as the ultimate profession of emotional honesty and truth.

The vaccine debates became all about parents. The children concerned were strangely only adjuncts to the community of mothers and fathers who demanded to have their say. I remember listening to a BBC national radio phone-in show on the MMR debate one morning in 2003, and it struck me that it was clear that no one involved in any aspect of the programme had conceived of the possibility that anyone with autism might actually be *listening*. The whole tenor of the various conversations seemed to repeat the singular theme: that autism was a tragedy, that people who did not have children with autism could not imagine the hardship involved for the family that did contain an autistic child (almost, indeed, that it was the very *worst* thing that could happen to a family) and that official denials over vaccines were the final torment for those whose lives had been blighted by the condition. For all its centrality to this debate, autism was curiously peripheral. Autistic children could occasionally be heard in the background as parents called in to contribute, but the idea that these children would grow up to become adults, that they would *develop*, was almost totally absent from the various arguments. It was a particular form of the present that dominated proceedings, a present in which parents were always parents of small disabled children, about whom – in a set of moments that seemed to belong squarely with Bettelheim – all worries seemed to be extensions of ideas of love.

I make these points not to belittle the parents involved in these various debates. I understand how they felt. It was, in this instance, the BBC that seemed to lack an adequate understanding of how to frame the discussion, something true more widely in the media coverage of the vaccine issue. But there was no doubt that it was the idea of the parent, and especially the mother, as a kind of category that animated many of these conversations. This was something grasped by those who wanted to assert the safety of vaccines as much as the families

who saw them as the problem. Michael Fitzpatrick, a general practitioner working in London who is also the father of an autistic son,
entitled his 2004 book *MMR and Autism: What Parents Need to Know*. In it,
he made the case clear that faith in the vaccine needed to be reinstated
because of the effect that doubt and suspicion had created in parents:

> The key moment in my decision to become more actively involved in the
> MMR–autism controversy came in early 2002 when the mother of a boy
> newly diagnosed with autism came into the surgery to tell me how guilty
> she felt that, by agreeing for him to have the MMR, she had helped to
> render him autistic.... I want to reassure parents faced with decisions
> about vaccinations that they have nothing to fear in MMR and every
> reason to welcome the protection it affords their children. I particularly
> want to reassure parents of children with autism that they have no cause
> to blame themselves over MMR. There is no good evidence to support
> a causative link between MMR and autism and strong evidence that it
> protects children against serious infectious diseases.[20]

Fitzpatrick would become a vocal figure in the criticism of Andrew
Wakefield and what he termed 'the anti-MMR bandwagon'.[21] Crucially,
he would voice his concerns about the validity of Wakefield's scientific
research not only in the terminology of the published medical literature, but also on the effect the arguments had on parents and the ways
in which the media reported them. For Fitzpatrick, a family doctor
himself, the most effective way to combat what he saw as Wakefield's
distortions was on the ground that the anti-vaccination supporters
sought to make their own: that of parental responsibility and care.

It is not, of course, the case that it is somehow wrong to say that
autism needs to be understood in terms of the family. The condition,
like other disabilities and especially those with behavioural differences, still inhabits an uneasy space in the public or social realm,
where it often invites numerous stares and disapproving comments.
As a result, articulating autism is often a process where a family
understanding predominates, and it is usually family members who
are the main carers of those who have autism. Rather, it is the *shape* of
the narratives that come with this idea of family that stresses certain
features, elevating some moments and characteristics and ignoring
others. At a most obvious level, a dynamic of family continually articulated by adults continues the impression that those with autism are
predominantly children. In all the literature that represents dealing
with autism in the family, it is rare that there is any consideration
of adults with the condition. Equally, narratives of family may stress
the notion that it operates as a unit, but in fact there are often crucial
differences ascribed to the roles of parents and siblings, and – within

this – between mothers and fathers. As the fascination with autism began to produce increasing numbers of representations of the condition, the ways in which families were portrayed became a site for an outline of what, in some formative way, it was thought to be.


III


In her 2006 novel *Daniel Isn't Talking*, Marti Leimbach not only has her central character, Melanie, the mother of the autistic Daniel, debate the possibility that MMR caused her son's autism, but she also has her write a letter to Bettelheim during a period of anger and grief following Daniel's diagnosis. Melanie is an American living in the UK whose world is turned upside down by her son's autism; her marriage to husband Stephen falls apart and she is projected into what the novel portrays as a grey world of social misunderstanding and fraught emotional uncertainty. The conversation about MMR takes place between Melanie and some other mothers as she waits to pick up her daughter, Emily, at the pre-school her husband has demanded that Emily attends so that she can then move on a private prep school. Melanie is out of place with the middle-class mothers and nannies who pick up their children, both in terms of her natural sensibilities and because of the stares she receives when Daniel is with her:

> 'It wasn't the MMR, was it?' asks another of the mothers who wait at the gate, as I do, each afternoon at twelve thirty. It's one of my least favourite moments of the day – not that I can't wait to see Emily – but it is all I can do to stand among the crowd of nannies telling children Daniel's same age to shut up, stop making so much noise, while I try desperately to get Daniel to imitate me as I make faces, or point at a red bus, or laugh when I blow raspberries on his tummy.
> 'I don't know,' I say honestly.
> 'They say the doctor who claimed it was the MMR is a fraud, you know,' says another. She's only here because she's waiting with her friend. Her children are older, both at St. Paul's School – the sort of place that makes me shiver.
> Now I realize that the MMR is a good, solid medical precaution that has nothing to do with autism. That's true and right. I have heard the radio shows, the TV reports, all of which assure me that my feeling the MMR is to blame for Daniel's autism is something I've completely made up. But you know, there is this part of me that understands with absolute certainty that I didn't make it up. I could have been hallucinating and still I wouldn't have missed the signs that after that shot my baby changed.
> 'I don't think that doctor is a fraud,' I say.[22]

In this exchange, it is ultimately an idea of motherhood that is the explanatory category both for what the consequences of the MMR might be in terms of autism, and for the ways in which Melanie experiences this. She 'wouldn't have missed the signs', a statement of proof that mothers know their babies best, something that was a key argument that families put to healthcare officials when discussing the safety of vaccinations. But, at the same time, it is the *difference* here between Melanie and the other mothers, her emotional scepticism set against their cruel certainty, which marks her reaction as a form of honesty. 'He lied', says one of the other mothers, referring to Wakefield, 'He joined the parents who just want someone to blame'. As Melanie looks at this mother, she thinks: 'She is a woman whose hands have never cleaned her child's excrement from walls, never waited through hour-long temper tantrums, never hurt for anything, I imagine. But she wants to hurt me. Of that, I'm certain.' Her response is, interestingly, a statement of fact, almost of a kind of subject position: '"My son has autism and he has problems with his bowels," I say to this lady, who doesn't give a damn'.[23]

For the American Melanie, the privileged English middle-class mothers whom she interacts with here replicate the vacuous health bureaucrats – speech therapists and psychologists in particular – who can offer no help with or understanding of Daniel's autism. In both cases it is an exceptionality – Daniel's autistic behaviour, and Melanie's form of emotional mothering – that others cannot recognize or deal with. It is especially the hurt that Melanie feels as a mother that prompts much of her anger: 'I want to be a good wife. A good mother', she says, 'The glue that keeps a family together, a sign of permanence and peace in our lives. Isn't that what a woman is?'[24] The letter she writes to Bettelheim (a figure she knows is dead, and whom, she notes, she came across in her university sociology classes) is full of this particular pain:

> *Dear Dr. Bettelheim,*
>
> *Were you there when I rocked my baby to sleep, or held his rattle for him before he could hold it himself? I didn't know I could love so much as I have loved my son, my daughter. Why do you insist that this isn't the case? Why do you openly despise me, despise all mothers of children with autism? I am twenty-nine years old. I would give my life publicly if I thought I could lift from my baby this appalling diagnosis. If it were that he could be normal – just ordinary like other children – I would climb the scaffold and tie the noose myself, smiling as I waved away the pain of watching him unable to speak or play or look at people. You would not hear me complain. You'd have to beat me away from those steps.*[25]

Here, the offer of the sacrifice is one that, it appears, only a mother can make, the product of an intense love that seeks to have Daniel as

an 'ordinary' and 'normal' child. Tellingly, however, Melanie folds the
letter and puts it away in an ornamental wooden jewellery box that was
a present from Stephen on their first wedding anniversary, a sign of
love from a figure who no longer has that emotion to offer. *Daniel Isn't
Talking* promotes an argument that became almost an orthodoxy in the
various narratives depicting autism at the time of the vaccine debates,
that while mothers will do all that they can to help their disabled
children (including the kind of sacrificial love outlined above), fathers
are unable to cope. If mothers cannot contain their love, fathers close
theirs off. Stephen, Melanie's husband, is a complete caricature of an
emotionally retarded, work-obsessed, unfaithful and deeply inarticu-
late man. 'Remarkably', Melanie notes in her narration, 'after the
announcement of Daniel's diagnosis, Stephen dropped us back at the
house and went to work. I have a meeting, he said. Try not to worry,
he said. Take a pill if you have to.'[26] Stephen, Melanie says, 'will not
talk to me at all…. He goes to work early, comes home late, retreats
into his laptop and is unavailable for comment.'[27] Worst of all, in the
arguments the couple have, Stephen accuses Melanie of knowing but
not acting with regard to Daniel's autism:

> I am lying face down on the couch while he sits at the other end, poking
> his keyboard, answering emails.
>     After a very long while he says, 'If you knew there was something
> wrong, why didn't you get help?'
>     'So it's *my* fault?'
>     'I asked why you didn't get a doctor. Sooner. Obviously, you *knew*.'[28]

Here, in a perverse version of Bettelheim's thesis, the mother's ability
to care is questioned by the father, an act of cruelty that marks Stephen
out as a character flawed to a point beyond salvation.

Melanie's emotions lead her to gravitate towards Andy O'Connor,
a 'maverick' Irish behavioural therapist who has 'no qualifications
other than an undergraduate degree' and 'no formal training in working with children'. Andy is initially described as a 'cornball rip-off
artist, swindler of the first degree', and it is pointed out that 'No
decent university or health authority would have him. And he charges
the moon, too.'[29] But everything that Andy lacks in terms of appropriate paper qualifications, he compensates for through an intuitive
emotional understanding of what autism is and how it affects both
those with the condition and their parents. 'How do you know he's
not retarded?', Melanie asks Andy the first time he meets Daniel. 'I
just know right away', he replies, 'all those stupid tests they give you
are shit'.[30] Melanie's final rejection of Stephen for Andy at the end

of *Daniel Isn't Talking* is a move that embraces the intuitive and the unconventional at the expense of the orthodox, as such orthodoxy is ultimately seen to be hollow. This conclusion is, of course, one that both resolves a personal romantic narrative and promotes an idea of how autism is best understood. In Leimbach's novel, that understanding is one produced through a sense of unconditional love that allows for none of the boundaries that a social idea of medical professionals or healthcare might impose. Within such a scheme, it is the bond between parent and child, here between mother and son, that takes centre stage. The romantic narrative, however, has also to be viewed in *generic* terms. It is no coincidence that Andy, the maverick outsider, is a recognizable stereotype, and *Daniel Isn't Talking* concludes with devices taken straight out of popular romantic fiction: the heroine choosing the independent, handsome, individualist rebel over the staid and repressed alternative. As we have seen in so many of the narratives this book has looked at up to this point, genre offers a safe contextualization for the ending of an autism story.

In *Daniel Isn't Talking*, it is not that autism provides an *excuse* for the telling of a romantic narrative – the questions surrounding the condition are too central to the novel for that – but it is nevertheless true that the dominant trajectory of the story is one that combines Melanie's coming to terms with Daniel's autism with her appreciation of the 'right sort of man' who will aid her in providing the familial support she needs. Daniel himself is a peripheral figure in the novel, something that prompts an ironic reading of the title. Though he does come to talk (even to use pronouns correctly, an act that frequently produces bursts of emotion in autism narratives), he is still more talked about, still the subject of the considerations of others.[31] The narrative patterning of Leimbach's novel, especially its concentration on the respective roles of mothers and fathers, is typical of those accounts of autism within families that have been produced since the height of the vaccine scares, between 2001 and 2003. In particular, it was television drama that returned time and again to the dynamic of the 'family with autism', seeking to explore how the condition affects families and what version of domesticity is produced as a consequence.

*My Family and Autism* was the title of a documentary, produced and directed by Fran Landsman, which screened on BBC 2 in January 2004. The family in question was the Jacksons, single-parent Jacqui and her seven children, three girls and four boys. All four of the boys, aged between six and nineteen at the time of the making of the film, are on the autistic spectrum. If autism had become the condition of contemporary fascination by 2004, then no family seemed more fascinating than the Jacksons, where all the issues of living with autism appeared to have been taken and magnified due to the prevalence of the condition in the family. Landsman's film, structured round an interview with Jacqui and a narration and video diary provided by fourteen-year-old Luke, the second oldest of the boys, captures what the Jacksons all describe as their 'normality', a seemingly chaotic range of different characters and behaviours. The four boys – Matt (diagnosed with dyslexia, dyspraxia and PDD–NOS),[32] Luke (diagnosed with Asperger's), Joe (diagnosed with attention deficit hyperactivity disorder) and Ben (diagnosed with autism) – encapsulate a spectrum of autistic difference. Matt's quiet reserve is counterpointed by Joe's inability to keep still, and his obsession for collecting and hoarding his siblings' and mother's possessions. Luke, who, despite his age, is an author of two volumes on living with Asperger's, is shown speaking at a conference organized by an autism charity, whereas Ben (the youngest of the boys, who learned to walk and talk only when he was five) has such sensory sensitivities that he chooses not to wear clothes when at home.[33] All four boys are seen interacting with their three sisters, but it is the figure of Jacqui who dominates the film. Whether endlessly having to clean the house, negotiating the complexities of multiple dietary requirements (the boys are on gluten- and casein-free diets, the girls are not), taking Joe for various appointments with educational psychologists and optical specialists, or participating with the whole family in regular taekwondo training, Jacqui's ability to normalize the day-to-day life of her family is presented as an exceptionality in itself. 'I still have moments of weeping', she confesses when being interviewed about Joe, 'There must be something that I've done wrong. There must be some reason that I can't get through to him, because – to me – that's a parent's job'; but the film suggests such self-criticism is misplaced, as Jacqui's 'job' is seen to be undertaken with a heroic perseverance that is presumably unimaginable for most viewers. As if to underline the point about her capability, Luke mentions in passing during his narration that his mother is studying for 'a master's degree in forensic psychology, whatever that is…'.

If Jacqui Jackson's capacity for care is astounding, then the public image of her that was produced by the documentary and other media interest has to be seen in terms of a tension. Though she stresses the normality of what she does, and remarks that she is happy to come home to it after being away, it is impossible not to see her actions within a paradigm of 'coping', even as Landsman's film seeks to remain understated and neutral about the life it records. 'Difference is cool', say various members of the Jackson family during the film, and as Luke observes near the end, 'I wouldn't want it to be any different…. You can never underestimate human potential.' At the same time, however, it would be difficult to imagine a family with *more* autism than the Jacksons, and there is something about this sense of scale that projects the world of the family, and especially the figure of Jacqui herself, into an excess beyond any intelligible social expectations of a parental carer. If Jacqui and her family do not 'overcome' their autism – and she is at pains to stress that, though Luke obviously has a talent for writing and computers, some of her other sons equally clearly do not – then her (and their) management of it is still near miraculous. As we will see in relation to the various foundations and programmes that offer treatments for children with autism, the creation of guilt is a highly effective means of pressuring parents into participating, and the extent to which Jacqui Jackson functions as an autism 'super mother' does work to produce such sentiments, for all that she also commands admiration and respect. In addition, moving away from the actual lives of the Jacksons themselves, it is difficult not to conceive of the decision to focus on *this* family as being one that constitutes a form of disability inflation, in which the extent of the autism produces a narrative where the difficulties of the condition are made more meaningful precisely because they are multiplied.

The life of the Jackson family was dramatized in a television feature entitled *Magnificent 7*, made in 2005, and shown on BBC 2 in December of that year. Drawing on material from *My Family and Autism*, *Magnificent 7* presents the Jacksons interacting in a series of non-autistic contexts, and this differentiates it from Landsman's film, which is largely an internal portrait restricted to Jacqui and her children. In tone, *Magnificent 7* is a light comedy, in which the difference of the Jackson family is set against the world outside of its boundaries. Starting with a Christmas in which the Jacqui character, Maggi (Helena Bonham Carter), promises her fearful sons that Santa is not coming, the film juxtaposes the 'normality' of the Jacksons against a social world whose rules demand conformity but are exposed as actually being arbitrary. At the next-door Christmas party to which Maggi takes her whole family, the talk surrounding the food abounds with an excess of metaphors and analogies – 'what's your poison?', 'this one might just have your name on it!', 'they won't bite', 'you frightened me to death'. Mishearing the word 'artistic' for 'autistic', an elderly neighbour attempts to start friendly conversation with Maggi by observing that her children are 'handy with a paintbrush I hear'. By way of contrast, the school caretaker, Dmitri (Bruno Lastra), when asked by the Luke character, Christopher (Christopher Parkinson) what he does, observes that he 'takes care of the school'. Such linguistic playfulness effectively reinforces a sense of autistic subjectivity, and sets a context for the film's account of the difficulty Maggi faces in loving and caring for her children.

Maggi is even more of a centrepiece in *Magnificent 7* than Jacqui Jackson is in *My Family and Autism*. The fictional account replaces the narration provided by Luke Jackson in the documentary with a voice-over by Maggi herself, underlining the sense that it is predominantly her story. In a key scene, following the destruction of a school sports day flower display by the Joe character, Davey (Joshua Thurston), Maggi takes to the stage to apologize for her son's action. Faced by a sea of disapproving parental faces, she follows her apology with a speech that encapsulates the heart of the film's affirmation of a sense of disabled difference:

> My children aren't like yours. No, they're not normal, like yours. They don't have the normal standards and preoccupations. No. Well thank goodness really, because my children surprise me every day – one thing after another. One thing I know for sure is that they will never, ever do any real harm, that is do any real damage to anyone. They will never murder anyone. They will never cheat anyone. They will never knowingly and deliberately cause harm to another living thing. It's a privilege actually, because how many of you – honestly – how many of you can say the same?

The 'privilege' that Maggi identifies in living with her autistic children is generated by the internal dynamics the family itself produces. The world of 'assessment and experts', to which Maggi takes her sons once a year, is seen as remote and lacking in any kind of usefully applicable knowledge. As with most narratives that represent families and autism, that which is most valuable is seen to originate within the family unit itself. By virtue of the expert status she holds as a mother, Maggi regulates how her family works. As such, it is perhaps a surprise that *Magnificent 7* includes a romantic narrative in which Dmitri comes to slowly fill the position of the absent father; he notes that Maggi runs her house as if it were 'a prison' (interestingly, with a reference that suggests the script's awareness of Bettelheim, Davey calls it 'a fortress – Fortress Jackson') and suggests ways in which she might give her sons greater independence. In *My Family and Autism*, Jacqui Jackson makes it clear that she and her ex-husband increasingly had separate worlds, and that she always looked after the children and assumed she worked alone in doing so. In *Magnificent 7*, however, the possibilities of fiction seem to leave writer Sandy Welch and director Kenny Gleenan unable to resist the temptation to qualify Maggi's independence, and the suggestion of romance strikes an odd note given the otherwise faithful way in which the film works with the material inherited from Landsman's documentary.

*Magnificent 7* could be seen to function as what David Mitchell and Sharon Snyder refer to as a 'disability counternarrative', in that it 'does not seek to fully repair or resolve a character's impairment, but rather delves into the social, personal, political and psychological implications of impairment as bequeathing a social awareness'.[34] Certainly the film refuses to operate any policy of 'repair' and creates a clear narrative space that asserts the legitimacy of an autistic presence. But, at the same time, its configuration of an idea of maternal care and the centrality of the familial complicate Mitchell and Snyder's thesis. The film creates a definite 'social awareness', but that perspective is itself framed within, and perpetuates, the legacy of a representation of autism as one contained within the central relationship of mother and child. 'Christopher is vulnerable', Maggi says at one point in the film, 'all the boys are, and it's my job to protect them'. As with the point made by Jacqui Jackson herself in *My Family and Autism*, and as with the mothers represented by Kirby and Leimbach, the care and love of an autistic child are here employment for the mother figure. The manner in which this relationship exists across texts again suggests that the responsibility identified by Bettelheim continues to cast a prominent shadow over the depiction of the child with autism.

There is never a suggestion at any point during either version of the Jacksons' story that the autism in the family has any kind of connection with MMR. At the same time, there is no doubt that both the documentary and the drama gained clear currency with a UK audience that understood autism was a condition in the spotlight precisely because of the debate over vaccination. The major drama that did focus directly on the issue of MMR and autism was a two-hour special entitled *Hear the Silence*, written by Timothy Prager and directed by Tim Fywell, which screened on Channel 5 in December 2003. Such was the explicit link between the drama and the issues connected to MMR that Channel 5 immediately followed the programme with a studio debate, called *MMR: The Debate*, that featured actors and members of the *Hear the Silence* production team alongside parents and scientists, including Andrew Wakefield and Michael Fitzpatrick, in discussion over topics raised by the film.

*Hear the Silence* follows two separate stories. The first is of Christine Shields (Juliet Stevenson), who becomes convinced that her son Nicky (Jamie Martin) developed autism as a result of his MMR vaccination. Christine's narrative follows the trauma that comes with Nicky's diagnosis, the break-up of her marriage to husband Martin (Andrew Woodall), and her subsequent determination both to respond to her son's condition and to fully articulate her conviction that the vaccination was to blame for its onset. The second narrative is that of Wakefield (Hugh Bonneville). It depicts the publication of his original *Lancet* paper and the consequences that come from it, including the tapping of his phone, the withdrawal of his research funding and the eventual closure of his research project by the Royal Free Hospital in London, where he works. The final scenes of the drama draw the two narratives together, with Christine hosting a gathering wishing luck to Wakefield as he is about to leave to continue his career in the US.

In the overall trajectory of its concerns, *Hear the Silence* parallels the kind of material Kirby covered in *Evidence of Harm*. Like the mothers in that account, Christine becomes an obsessive expert on the issues of vaccinations following Nicky's diagnosis. She leaves her job as a high-level researcher for a major bank, consults a range of specialists in seeking to understand what has happened to her son, and joins a pressure group composed of other mothers in similar situations to hers. 'He's just withdrawn into himself', Christine tells one doctor when talking about Nicky, 'He's not the same as he was…. He's not right.' 'Something happened to him. That's what I know in my heart', she tells Martin, and when she makes the link between Nicky's autism and the MMR she states that 'The boy I knew disappeared' to her new family doctor. These questions and concerns are seen in the drama to be completely bound up with Christine's status as a mother. 'You work full-time don't you?', asks one doctor Christine consults early in her search and, on hearing that the family uses a nanny, adds, 'Sometimes nannies who are overbearing can provoke language delay', in a bizarre but explicit reference to the heritage of Bettelheim. In one of the many arguments she has with Martin, Christine counters his assertion that 'No-one's blaming you' with the simple assertion 'I am'. Martin responds: 'It's all about you…. It's you against the world. You're right! You're the only one who cares! Because you feel guilty about it!'

Christine's primary characterization is one that invokes the quality of her love and the depth of her emotion. Unlike *Magnificent 7*, *Hear the Silence* conveys autism in the family as a source of trauma and heightened drama. In the very first scene of the film, Nicky escapes from Christine while they are out shopping and runs into the traffic, narrowly avoiding being hit by a bus. A shocked Christine gathers him into her arms and sits weeping on the pavement. Such a moment sets the tone for the first half of the drama in particular, in which Christine is traumatized by Nicky's behaviour and illness and is forced to cope more or less alone while Martin spends long hours at work. As with the husband Stephen in Leimbach's *Daniel Isn't Talking*, Martin's response to his son's diagnosis is to do nothing, even collecting only his other son Max (Stefan Mervyn), and leaving Nicky with Christine, when it is his turn to care for his sons at the weekend. Husbands are, the narrative implies, useless. 'When did yours walk?', Christine is asked acerbically by Valerie (Denise Black), one of her friends in the mothers' campaign group shortly after she joins. The centrality of Christine as a mother is also, however, the catalyst for the process that sees Nicky 'emerge' from the worst excesses of his autism. It is Christine's adoption of the gluten- and casein-free diet that cures the worst elements of his various gastric illnesses, and her discovery of an applied behavioural analysis (ABA) tutor that leads to an educational programme that, by the end of *Hear the Silence*, sees Nicky with a place in mainstream school. 'Don't trust me', Christine shouts at a male consultant doctor in the Royal Free Hospital towards the end of the film, when she has an impressive array of knowledge and achievements, and he stands belittled by her arguments, 'I'm just a mother!' Fittingly, when Nicky does return to talking after losing his language, the first words we hear him say are the name of his brother (Max) and the repeated 'Mah' sound he makes on his way to saying 'Mum'.

If an emphasis on maternal care might be expected in Christine's narrative in *Hear the Silence*, it is revealing to see that it is also dominant in that of Andrew Wakefield's story as well. Early on in the drama, as he works in the hospital, a woman arrives unannounced in his office asking for his help and remarking that she has read his research. 'Are you a doctor?', he asks, somewhat puzzled. 'No', she replies, 'I'm a mother'. Throughout the developments that follow, Wakefield is portrayed as a figure who uses the anecdotal evidence he receives from mothers as one of the bases for his own research. His theories are, he tells his fellow hospital researchers, 'consistent with the mothers' stories'. 'I can't censor the parents' stories', he says to his wife just before the press launch of the *Lancet* article, 'all the parents believe there's a connection to MMR'. 'Why wouldn't I believe you?', Wakefield says to Christine after hearing her story on their first meeting, a simple question that causes her to burst into tears following the complete lack of belief she has met from every other health professional up to this point in the narrative. If, as is common to virtually all the other autism narratives examined here, medical and health practitioners are portrayed as cold, uncaring and deceptive in *Hear the Silence*, Wakefield is the exception, someone driven by 'the truth', as he remarks to one of his colleagues who leaves his research team in order to secure a promotion. That 'truth', in turn, is seen to lie not within institutional and governmental systems whose responsibilities are to care for citizens (the drama does not state that Wakefield's research is stopped because of his discovery of an inconvenient truth about vaccines, but definitely hints at this reading), but within the microcosm of the family, where emotion provides the adequate barometer of how autism should be understood and dealt with. Even Martin comes to understand this at the end, awkwardly arriving at what had been, up to his entry, a mothers-only campaign group, to voice his support both for Christine and Wakefield. That he does this immediately after he has been shocked to find Nicky talking and Christine implementing the ABA programme only confirms a strong sense within the film that Christine's judgement has been correct all along.

Ultimately, *Hear the Silence* functions as a piece of emotional propaganda. Following the conclusion, a statement lists the number of US institutions that support Wakefield's work, while quoting the UK Department of Health that 'There are no plans to fund a study into the effects of MMR because there is no credible scientific evidence showing a link between MMR and autism'. The programme's implicit support of Wakefield's position reflects the public theories prevalent between 2002 and 2004, when it was assumed that autism was beyond the understanding of scientific experts and institutionalized health systems. In place of such understanding, it was easier to believe in the arguments of a maverick outsider who, it appeared, dared to challenge the hegemony of drug companies and health departments. In *MMR and Autism: What Parents Need to Know*, Fitzpatrick talks of 'the metamorphosis of Andrew Wakefield', a media-driven process by which Wakefield's 'self-consciously humble posture' offers 'a popular departure from the traditional images of the paternalistic doctor', but ultimately blinds the public to the fact that 'he has no background in immunization or child psychiatry'.[35] If various newspapers and documentaries provided much of the material for this 'metamorphosis', then *Hear the Silence* is undoubtedly its key *dramatic* iteration.

*Hear the Silence* buys into the Wakefield myth without a murmur, presenting autism on his terms and dramatizing the condition within a paradigm created by a concentration on family. 'Everything I know about autism', Wakefield told a Canadian interviewer in 2000, 'I know from listening to parents', and it is to an idea of parenting that the drama returns again and again.[36] In Christine Shields, with her journey from the trauma of Nicky's diagnosis, through her stubborn resistance to authority, to her successes in creating contexts for her son's individual and social learning,[37] autism found its contemporary emblem.

The irony of this, that it is a characterization so close to the concerns of Bettelheim's causation thesis, should not be lost. If further information has emerged about the various conflicts of interests Wakefield had at the time of his research into the twelve children who formed the basis of his team's *Lancet* article, and if his reputation has suffered as a result, then the centrality of parenting he championed nevertheless remained.[38] In Autism Vox, her excellent blog which covers all aspects of autism awareness, Kristina Chew noted in July 2007 that the Wakefield affair tapped into a central desire for a voice that many parents of children with autism feel:

> People, I think, are hungry for their experience – for their story – with their autistic child to be heard. I see the numerous memoirs about autism by parents, not to mention the ever-growing count of blogs, as testament to this hunger. But are we parents so hungry that we take the first food offered? Is it that we have no other choice?[39]

Chew's questions do not negate the desire of parents to seek answers, but in stressing the notion of choice she asks for an appropriate consideration of an agency *within* families. For those families who have found themselves the viewers of the recent representations of autism on television, who have (to continue Chew's metaphor) consumed the narratives, it is difficult not to feel that the ghost of Bettelheim is alive and well.

## IV

In her 2006 book, *Could It Be Autism? A Parent's Guide to the First Signs and Next Steps*, Nancy D. Wiseman interrupts her narrative of how she has cared for her autistic daughter, Sarah, and struggled to find appropriate treatments for her, firstly to take stock of the cost such care has incurred and then to put such an idea of cost into the context of the relationship she has with her child:

> By then, Sarah's treatment had cost our family well over $100,000, much of it for experimental biomedical therapies that insurance companies didn't cover. I'd gone literally years without enough sleep or leisure, had given up my well-paid career and my suburban dream house. I'd spent every available moment finding, paying for, or providing my daughter's therapy.
>     And every bit of it was worthwhile.
>     I am repaid every time I see my daughter laugh at a joke or sympathize with a playmate who's been rejected by another child. I am repaid many times over every time that she hugs me and says, 'I love you, Mom.'[40]

Wiseman's comments here display the very obvious overlap of two central economies through which autism functions in the contemporary world. The first is a literal one of finance, in which treatments (especially within the context of healthcare in the US) run to thousands of dollars; the second is one of maternal love, in which children 'recover' from the condition to the extent that they can reciprocate such love. Wiseman is divorced from her husband (she notes that Sarah sees her father, who is nameless and absent for the majority of the book, for one weekend a month), and employed full time as an 'Autism Mom';[41] her story is the kind of narrative of success gestured towards in *Hear the Silence* and the countless memoirs referred to by Chew, many of which parallel the structure of *Could It Be Autism?* The aggressive optimism behind the entirety of Wiseman's book stands as a marker of hope and inspiration for those readers, parents of children with autism, who form its target audience.

But we should understand this approach less as the natural process Wiseman represents it to be and more as a particular concept of care operating at a specific time. It is instructive to juxtapose Wiseman's comments with those of Ann Lovell in her 1978 book *In a Summer Garment: The Experience of an Autistic Child*. If Wiseman's battle and breakthrough produce the reciprocated love of her daughter, then Lovell's story of her son Simon has no such conclusion. At the end of *In a Summer Garment*, Simon is a young adult and is still severely impaired. 'For Simon there can be no choices', Lovell writes:

> He has no say in the ordering of his days.... As a child, as an adolescent, and as an adult, he has been, and will be denied free will. He is totally dependent on the will of others. He is completely innocent. And he is vulnerable. The whole texture of his life is created by the rest of us, by our thoughtlessness, our neglect, our cruelties, our incompetence, and by our care and our love.[42]

Lovell's observation here is, just as with Wiseman, that of a parent. It is still the context of familial love and care that produces the 'texture' of Simon's life, but it is unlikely that Wiseman would ever see her daughter as 'weak and helpless', as Lovell sees Simon towards the end of her book.[43] For Lovell, there is a potential happiness in Simon's impairment, in that she feels he does not see the difference between himself and other children. By way of contrast, less impaired children face potential suffering precisely because of their ability to recognize their difference from others: 'I wondered if any autistic people, those with the highest degree of mental ability and verbal ability, could understand their own deprivation, and difference. I hoped not, for their sakes.'[44]

Here, the possible breakthrough between an autistic and a non-autistic state is a process fraught with worry, and one possibly best avoided.

The key difference between Wiseman's and Lovell's accounts arguably lies not in any discrepancies in their concept of mothering, but rather the respective publication dates of their studies. Lovell's story of Simon dates from a period which was, in effect, the prehistory of the presentation of autism in narrative. Her book reads as one that lacks points of reference to any articulation of autism in the world, so Simon becomes pushed into the dynamics of the family because, in many ways, it is *only* in such a space that he is understood. For Wiseman, by way of contrast, an idea of extended family is one of a mobilization of love and care, with the figure of the mother as the foot soldier leading an often ruthless process of organization and dedication in the assault on Sarah's autism. Both books issue from the same source, namely a recognition of the responsibility of parental care, but their dissimilarities serve as a reminder of the cultural construction of such care at different times. That Wiseman's narrative is more common on the relevant 'Parents' shelf of the local bookshop in our time does not mean that Lovell's is any less true.

The context for the rise in the role of the parent as the figure who 'treats' the autism of their child comes, ostensibly, in the transformation of the negative idea of family in the theories of Kanner and Bettelheim into a positive notion of parenting that forms the centre of many educational and treatment programmes that are now well established as part of an orthodoxy of caring for autistic children. In fact, there is a certain disingenuousness in such reasoning, as many autism societies (such as the UK's National Autistic Society) were founded a number of decades ago by parents committed to providing care for their children; but the rise of the parent as a personal instructor definitely parallels the increasing acceptance of the treatment programme. Of these, Son-Rise is the most well known, with a base in the US and outreach programmes in a number of other countries. Son-Rise is the extension of the system used by Barry and Samahria Kaufman with their son Raun, who was diagnosed with severe autism in the early 1970s and for whom long-term institutionalization was thought to be the only option. The Kaufmans now run The Option Institute, a 'personal growth' education centre in Massachusetts, which is the home for both the Autism Treatment Center of America and Son-Rise itself.

The language that surrounds all elements of the Son-Rise programme is one of converting negatives into positives. In the narrative of coming to terms with his son's autism, Barry Kaufman makes clear such an idea of transformation:

A little boy set adrift on the circulation of his own system. Encapsulated behind an invisible and seemingly inpenetrable [*sic*] wall. Soon he would be labeled. A tragedy. Unreachable. Bizarre. Statistically, he would fall into a category reserved for all those we see as hopeless ... unapproachable ... irreversible. For us the question: could we kiss the ground that others had cursed?[45]

For the Kaufmans, kissing the ground meant an acceptance and understanding of their son's autism, a process of constant observation and interaction with Raun. The 'marathon sessions of observation' and 'endless hours' of identification with their son produced the basis for what Barry Kaufman presents as a real knowledge that counters the medical logic of the time:

> With each passing day, we came to know our son more and more, to know also about the labels, the inferences, the prophecies and confusions. Indeed, there were professionals who in their way were trying to say something, trying to do something, but who were constrained by their own limiting theories and dogma. Even now, they continued to have difficulty analyzing and synthesizing an approach for themselves, for their 'patients' and for the distressed parents. Two generations of research and energy had produced elaborate systems of judgments and predictions. And yet, for all this effort, little had transpired that was meaningful for this small boy and others like him.[46]

In place of any conventional framework of support and development for Raun, the Kaufmans supplied their own, and the book *Son-Rise* charts the growth and expansion of the care programme they devised through what they term the 'moment-to-moment mastery' of his condition.[47] In *Son-Rise: The Miracle Continues*, Barry Kaufman notes how a byproduct of this was that their work with Raun came to dominate their whole lives:

> Every aspect of our lives had been transformed by our work with our son. We had learned to draw on our own humanity. We pulled closer together as a family. Our daughters, although still young, became our dearest friends and coworkers. Samahria and I grew ourselves stronger to meet Raun's challenge and we both felt blessed by the opportunity.
> Finally, one night I suggested what I thought might be perceived as the 'unthinkable.' My business in the city no longer seemed relevant. Our work with Raun felt so meaningful. Although I could not guess where the road might lead eventually, I wanted to change the direction of my life and devote all my efforts to our son's program. That meant closing my business down.... I held my breath, feeling like a parachutist about to take the first leap out of an airplane. I sighed. My whole body let go and eased into the decision. 'I'll do it. I'm done with my company. I'm done with the city. This will be my life now.'[48]

Within this passage lies the genesis of many of the concepts about family and care that we have observed in the other texts in this chapter: the *total* commitment to the care of the child with autism, conceived of as a project of 'work'; the rejection of a life outside of dealing with the condition; the consolidation of the idea of the family unit as a caring whole that can combat autism; and the spiritual sense of a 'blessing', which allows for the discovery of a love that extends beyond autism to regenerate all those who are willing to open themselves to it. The Kaufmans present autism as their ultimate challenge, but also their ultimate salvation.

The Son-Rise story contains many elements. The Kaufmans' description of their commitment to Raun is a narrative juggernaut of self-belief, and a refusal to accept that their child was in any way disabled. Their establishment of a programme of care devised from their own observation and intuition is presented as a spectacularly successful alternative to a confused medical profession that cannot deal with the fact of autism. The evangelical zeal of this narrative of achievement is, in all honesty, somewhat disturbing. Not only did Raun 'emerge' from his self-stimulating autistic muteness, but he went on to the kind of career in education that is the dream of every middle-class American parent for their child. As the Autism Treatment Center of America notes in its web page 'History of the Son-Rise Program®':

> The Kaufmans' unique program, which marked a complete departure from existing methods of treatment, transformed Raun from a mute, withdrawn child with an IQ of less than 30 into a highly verbal, socially interactive youngster with a near-genius IQ. Bearing no traces of his former condition, Raun graduated from an Ivy League university and went on to become the director of an educational center for school-aged children.[49]

The trajectory here, from disability to supreme *ability*, is an example of a resurrection that can be grasped only in spiritualized language. In the world of Son-Rise, 'coming back' from autism is a question of belief, and a form of belief that transcends any notion of medical or scientific evidence. As Raun Kaufman himself puts it, in his own foreword to *Son-Rise: The Miracle Continues*:

> The word *expert* is the misnomer of the century. The pessimistic outlook that the 'experts' show many parents need not be taken seriously. Whatever you've been told about the severity of your child's condition, don't buy it. You and your child can do a whole lot more than any 'expert' could possibly know. No matter how much evidence a doctor can show you, it will never be enough to prove that something is impossible. You want to know something? Evidence is a sham. It can always be defied or

demolished. If you really believe in evidence, use it to prove the possible instead of the impossible.[50]

There could be no clearer statement of the distrust of health professionals that characterizes contemporary narratives of autism than this, and the sentiments here are foundational in thinking through the kinds of representations of clinical assessment presented in the fictions of *Daniel Isn't Talking*, *Magnificent 7* and *Hear the Silence*, as well as within the scepticism of the case histories in a book such as *Evidence of Harm*. Raun Kaufman is, so the logic runs, himself the proof of the 'demolishing' of medical evidence. His 'recovery' is self-reflexively indicative of the 'whole lot more' that can be achieved.

The tension here lies in the understanding of what autism itself is thought to be. On one level, Raun Kaufman's opposition to the workings of clinical diagnosis parallels the work disability activists undertake to have their subjectivity recognized as valid and legitimate, and not as some form of deviance from a standardized norm. 'Refusing to accept the age-old view of autism as a terrible catastrophe', writes Raun, 'my parents came up with the radical idea that my autism was a chance – a great opportunity'.[51] Such sentiments are not so dissimilar from those of a figure like Amanda Baggs, examined in chapter 1, equally a proponent of 'radical' ideas in terms of an idea of autistic living. But the 'opportunity' of which Raun Kaufman speaks is, in fact, 'to try to reach a child lost behind a thick, hazy cloud', to allow for what he describes as 'a spectacular metamorphosis' that meant he could 'emerge from the shell of my autism without a trace of my former condition'.[52] This last phrase in particular (and 'bearing no traces of his former condition' is used in the 'History of the Son-Rise Program' web pages quoted above) is all-important. For the Kaufmans, engaging with autism, to come down to its level, is ultimately the catalyst to defeat and banish it. There is no conception in this thinking that, in working outside clinical and scientific frames of thinking about the condition, one might find a way of seeing the world, or an idea of subjectivity, that could be of value. Rather, autism is (to use appropriate language) to be exorcised or vanquished. It is presented as the language of 'recovery', but in fact it is the language of cure.

'Without a trace of my former condition' is, then, the desired subject position of the process that seeks to overcome autism; and, as seen by the success of Raun Kaufman's career, it is one declared as being *possible*. The importance of this, of course, is that Son-Rise is a treatment programme with an international platform. Here, again, we see the economies of autism combine. The trajectory that saved Raun Kaufman, thanks to what he terms 'a passionate relentlessness on the

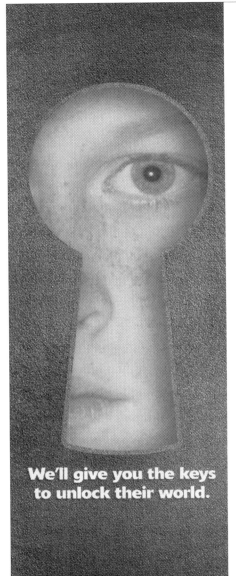

# Autism does not have to be a life sentence.

*The Autism Treatment Center of America™ Presents*

## The Son-Rise Program® START-UP

**16–20 January 2005**
The Royal Chace Hotel • Enfield, England

A 5-day group training program for parents, relatives and professionals caring for children challenged by Autism, Autism Spectrum Disorders, PDD, Asperger's Syndrome and other related developmental difficulties. This primary course delivers comprehensive instruction in the fundamentals of **The Son-Rise Program**. **The Son-Rise Program Start-Up** is designed to help those with children of varying ages, from 18 months to 60 years old, with a wide range of diagnoses.

**You'll Learn:**

- Attitudinal training and empowerment—having a child with developmental difficulties can feel very challenging; we will give you the tools to overcome obstacles that may sometimes feel insurmountable.

- To help your child build meaningful social interaction—move beyond repetitive "stimming" behaviors and encourage sincere affection and expressions of joy and caring.

- To motivate and teach your child—find your child's motivations and interests and create a dynamic curriculum so that your child can acquire skills, from using the toilet to reading a book.

- To increase (or develop) speech and language abilities—implement functional strategies to increase verbal communication that will help your child interact, make requests and express themselves.

**Call 001-413-229-2100 to register for The Son-Rise Program START-UP or visit us online at www.son-rise.org**

Register before 1st of November for our discount rate of $1,695 (US funds). After 1st of November the rate is $2,385 (US funds). Space is limited. Book early to reserve your place!

We can help.

**Autism**
TREATMENT CENTER OF AMERICA™

The Son-Rise Program®

2080 South Undermountain Road
Sheffield, MA 01257-9643 USA
Telephone: 001-413-229-2100 • E-mail: sonrise@option.org

## www.son-rise.org

Call for a free 25-minute initial
consultation • 001-413-229-2100

**We'll give you the keys to unlock their world.**

Figure 6. One-page advertisement for the Son-Rise programme, taken from *Communication*, the magazine of the National Autistic Society, vol. 38, no. 3, autumn 2004, page 14.

part of my parents', is itself one that is attainable for other families.[53] Son-Rise holds regular 'Start-Up' sessions, across the world, in order to introduce parents to the workings of the Kaufmans' techniques. The advertisement for such a session, in figure 6 here, took up a full page in the autumn 2004 issue of *Communication*, the magazine of the UK's National Autistic Society. The idea of autism conveyed here is familiar, if somewhat extreme. Children with the condition are locked away, shut up or incarcerated, and Son-Rise offers the promise of release. The striking nature of the key-hole image, however, and the metaphor of criminality that accompanies it, especially in the idea of the 'life sentence', seem a worrying and potentially irresponsible formation, given the increasing juxtaposition of autism and crime discussed in earlier chapters. And the child's face, the eye that offers itself up to be read, is again an invitation, as with the photographs discussed in chapter 3, to speculate on the depths of what autism might be.

In many ways, the subtleties of the advertisement's prose are more interesting than its visuals, however. 'The Son-Rise Program Start-Up' is, the reader is informed, 'designed to help those with children of varying ages, from 18 months to 60 years old, with a wide range of diagnoses'. The mistake is surely unintentional, a typographical error that replaces '6' with '60', but there is something fitting in the idea that the programme infantilizes adults with autism, since, in the language of curing autism, all those with the condition are, in some way, children waiting for the liberation into a 'beyond' of normalization that can be also read as an 'independent' adult existence. But it is, arguably, the advertisement's other figures that should command the most attention. For the 'parents, relatives and professionals' who might attend the start-up session, the list of what they will learn is an impressive outlining of motivational and attitudinal training, skills that may well be genuinely beneficial in helping them to work with the autistic children in their care. But the costs that follow the list – $1695 for early registration and $2385 thereafter – mean that only certain parents and professionals will be able to access such benefits. Remembering that this course is an initial induction, and that the full Son-Rise programme will incur significant additional costs, the reality of the treatment is that it is outside the budgets of the majority of families who have an autistic child. Freedom from the life sentence comes at a considerable price.

In June 2005 a short documentary entitled *The Twin Who Could Only Scream* screened on BBC 1. It followed Dawn and Stuart, British parents of Thomas – their non-verbal, autistic son (and twin brother to non-autistic Amy) – and their implementation of the Son-Rise programme. Dawn and Stuart undertook all the required training, committed themselves to spending four hours every day working with Thomas, and redesigned their garden shed as a suitably neutral play space in which he could learn. As with the majority of autism narratives involving families, the force of *The Twin Who Could Only Scream* lies in the presentation of the parenting couple; Stuart breaks down as he reads a letter he has composed to Thomas (part of the ritual that accompanies the end of the training programme) and the couple discuss their hopes for Thomas following the treatment. After six weeks of sustained interaction with Thomas, his behaviour is still more or less at the level it was before the programme started. A Son-Rise helper, William, visits the couple to help with the development of Thomas' language but, following his departure, the documentary ends ambivalently, with the Son-Rise experience less a narrative of change for Thomas than a marker of difficulty for Dawn and Stuart, who affirm that the programme was 'worthwhile', but who struggle to keep the level of optimism that they displayed at the onset of the initial training.

*The Twin Who Could Only Scream* feels like a documentary that was made with the hope, and maybe the expectation, that it would be possible to record significant changes in Thomas' behaviour and abilities. When this turns out not to be the case, the film becomes rather a story of parents willing to do everything they can to help their autistic son, and an account of an emotional journey. A potential narrative of fascination thus becomes one portraying the difficulties and virtues seen to be inherent in the family that contains autism and, somewhat uneasily, this is then projected into an uncertain future. The Son-Rise programme and others it like have many testimonials that pay tribute to their successes, stories of recovery and dramatic change, but it is fair to assume that the history of the programme's implementation also contains many accounts like those of Dawn and Stuart, where the end result is not so clear cut.

In *The Science and Fiction of Autism*, Laura Schreibman includes a short discussion of the Son-Rise programme in her chapter 'Miracle cures or bogus treatments?' She stresses the lack of any scientifically valid data or hard evidence that might be used in establishing its effectiveness, notes that 'the program just does not make sense' in its advocacy of parents mirroring the actions of their child, and observes that there has been speculation as to whether Raun Kaufman was, in actual fact, ever autistic.[54] In addition, she describes as a 'serious problem' the potential effect the programme can have on parents who feel that they do not have either the time or money to follow its schedule (she notes that the 'intensive program involves both the parents and the child and costs \$11,500 for one week'). 'Does it work?', she asks in conclusion – 'Probably not'.[55] Schreibman's opinion is usefully succinct, and even though she is, of course, exactly the kind of figure the Kaufmans distrust because of her supposed reliance on 'evidence', her almost casual dismissal of Son-Rise is highly effective. There is little doubt that Son-Rise's recourse to vacuous notions of belief, love and commitment means that its idea of autism is ultimately fanciful. It encourages a spiritual and holistic approach to the condition, an approach that is almost completely abstract and has, as Schreibman notes, never been subject to the processes of systematic analysis that might see whether it is effective in any way. This much is unsurprising. What *is* surely worthy of comment, however, is the question of how such an empty and speculative programme can command such a centrality in ideas relating to the treatment of autistic children, and how the shape of its beliefs and methods can find such broad resonance in the many cultural narratives that discuss the place of autism within the family. It is one thing to see the Kaufmans as exponents of a peculiarly American brand of personal motivation, but quite another to see how the kind of attitudes they exemplify continue to dominate much received wisdom about how autism and the family coexist. The more one looks at Son-Rise and programmes like it, the easier it becomes to dismiss them; but, equally, the further one explores the central tenets of such 'treatments', the more it becomes apparent that, stripped of their overt new-age spiritualities and workshop psychobabble, their ideas about autism are still commonly held to be viable, and frequently represented as such.

V

Possibly what the Kaufmans do more than most in the arena of the autism debate is to remind us that families, and especially families as represented through narrative, are units suffused with sentimentality. The 'family with autism' has, in the contemporary era, become a certain kind of cultural product. In the narratives in which they feature, such families are dominated by either the excess of love and care, or the absence of these. As we have seen, the space of the family also becomes one where the by now familiar processes of narrative prosthesis and refraction can play out their dynamics, with autism used as a vehicle to discuss an idea of marriage or the capacity of a mother to love her child. In all these stories, it is assumptions of emotional sentiments and truths that form the core of how they work on their audiences. If autism destroys families, a sentiment that appears as a common extension of the notion that the condition is a tragedy, then this actually manifests itself as a subset of a wider concern that families might just be being destroyed by a variety of *other* processes as well. As with the point made about masculinity in the last chapter, autism here provides a lens for a particular contemporary fear. In an era in which there is much discussion about the 'break-up' of the family, autism becomes a peculiarly focused example of what this might mean.

At the same time, there is a strange kind of voyeurism at work in watching or reading representations of autism in families. This is something that, in all probability, is attributable to the juxtaposition of the familiar with the fascinating but strange. If autism is, still, a condition of such mystery, an alien embodiment of difference, then it undoubtedly produces specific resonances when placed within something as 'ordinary' as the family structure. And the ways in which representations show that it disrupts such ordinariness – destroying marriages, making work impossible, isolating individuals – take on a curious appeal for viewers and readers presumably safe in their family units where such disabling forces do *not* occur. I sense that the interest in the drama of the autism family stems, to a large degree, from such a dynamic, and it does so because, ultimately, the figure in the fiction or memoir with which the audience connects is not, of course, that of the person with autism. Rather, it is the traumatized, or inspired, parent who is the dominant presence, the mother whose emotions triumph over adversity, the couple who stay together through all the difficulties.

So runs the orthodoxy. It is good to know, however, that perceptive, clever and funny observations of autism in families do indeed exist, and that they might be held up to counter the seeming dominance of some of the narratives we have encountered in this chapter. Thinking of all that has gone before, for example, it is revealing to look at Charlotte Moore's account of her autistic sons, *George and Sam* (2004), and read, in Nick Hornby's introduction, why he suspects people may have picked up her book in the first place:

> I'm guessing – I can't know for sure, of course, but this seems a reasonable assumption – that you have picked this book up, if not with a heavy heart, then with an oppressive sense of duty. Perhaps you have an autistic grandson, or nephew – most autistic kids are boys – and you feel that the least you can do is to find out more about his condition, especially since you don't know him as well as you'd like to.... Or perhaps you're more directly affected: perhaps your own child is autistic, as

mine is, in which case your need to read a book on the subject might feel more urgent…. Maybe something in these pages will help to alleviate the panic you feel when you're told that your child has a condition for which there is no cure; indeed, maybe you're hoping that *George and Sam* will tell you that there *is* a cure, contrary to all the information you've been given by health professionals. Books tend to need narratives, after all, and the most popular kind of narrative for books about disability is the kind that takes us from the darkness into the light, from despair to hope, from disaster to triumph.[56]

Hornby's foregrounding of the ways in which he knows most family narratives on autism work is effectively disarming. His assumption of the questions readers might bring to the book neatly undermines the possibility that Moore might well produce a narrative that leads to the kind of conclusions outlined above. And Hornby is right. Moore's book does not offer the possibility for cure, or redemption, or spiritual insight. It does, however, offer a picture of a family in which there are, as she neatly puts it in the title of her final chapter, 'Compensations'. 'Have I made life in an autistic family sound like hell?', she asks.

> That hasn't been my intention. There are moments of extreme stress, but isn't that the case in most families? Our tensions, our flashpoints, are different from those of your average family, but who's to say they're more intolerable? … Our family life has its own rhythms, its own compensations.[57]

Inherent in such compensations, Moore notes, is the recognition that they stem precisely from the various things that make her sons autistic in the first place: their 'incorruptible innocence', or the fact that 'it's actually quite relaxing to be around people who ask so little socially'.[58] And when Moore concludes her point that 'many of the most aggravating habits of normal children are refreshingly absent' from her sons, she does so with the observation that 'they haven't the least notion of "cool". They are immune to peer pressure. They are always completely themselves', and, as a result, we are back to the idea of autistic presence outlined in chapter 1.[59] George and Sam are themselves, and Moore's book acknowledges that this makes her family different and at times difficult, but she acknowledges it as the reality in which she finds herself.

Similarly, near the end of Robert Hughes' 2003 memoir *Running with Walker*, his account of family life with wife Ellen and autistic son Walker, there is a revealing passage in which ideas of fantasy and reality are juxtaposed:

> This book has not told the story I sometimes dreamed of telling when Walker's autism first hit our family with all its force. The other story was

a secret fantasy that ran through my head as I fell asleep at night. In it, a mother and father possessed of ultra love and ultra brains, together with fierce independence and persistence, found a cure not only for their own son but for all children with autism.... Over the years this story receded from the repertoire of soothing scenarios that helped me fall asleep at night.... Every other day or so some one thing would occur that made the story seem too far-fetched, even for a fantasy.... But in place of the fantasy, a story with more solidity and reality gradually took hold. Ellen and I have both learned the lesson, to paraphrase Bette Davies, that hope is not for sissies. We've learned to accept – even expect – the electric shocks of disappointment as the necessary consequences of keeping hope aloft. We're able to do this because others are willing to do it too – willing, even, to risk looking like chumps when they fail.[60]

The balance of hope and disappointment that Hughes articulates here, even the contemplation of the possibility of failure, is a long way from the remorseless drive to success that seems a demand of writers like Nancy D. Wiseman and Barry Kaufman. Crucially, in Hughes' narrative, as with that of Moore, autism is not *denied*. It takes, undoubtedly, many forms, but to make such an observation is really to observe what is true about any family. As we have seen before in this book, spending time with disability is often a route to seeing it not as alien and distancing, but as routine and everyday.

Possibly most interesting in the contemporary narratives of autistic families are those which include the contribution of the person with autism. Barbara Lasalle's *Finding Ben* (2003) includes an introductory section, entitled 'In Ben's words', which also provides links to an informational website on Asperger's. In addition, Lasalle's text itself is interwoven with italicized passages that form Ben's own commentary on the story his mother tells.[61] Similarly, Ralph James Savarese's 2007 *Reasonable People: A Memoir of Autism & Adoption* leaves the final chapter, entitled 'It's my story!', to DJ Savarese, who ordered and composed it entirely according to his own preferences. DJ's story is one that could easily lend itself to the canon of 'overcoming' disability narratives, in that it follows his journey from an abusive familial setting, through adoption, to an ability to express himself through typing and eventual success at school. In addition, *Reasonable People* is an unusual text even without DJ's contribution, as it expands the idea of family and autism precisely because it deals with the adoption of an autistic child. But for all of the drama that the story might contain, it returns finally to an idea of the reasonable. In the final chapter, DJ includes a letter he wrote to the principal of the middle school he attends, in which he notes:

> You treat me very well very much of the time. Now testing me is over, untested in free real world. Underinstructed great. Nice fresh start

helped me get fresh understanding. Reasonable, free dear heartfelt fresh start helps me getting better.

Underneath the letter DJ notes:

> I'm reasonable. Polite people make me feel comfortable. Which by the way isn't very often. Reasonable people promote very very easy breathing…. Unhurt, responsible, persevering, humorous, mighty people are helping my real, kind, mighty, very smart self.[62]

In his own words, and anticipating his entry into the 'free real world' beyond testing and categorization, DJ articulates something both exceptional and ordinary. The comfort of 'easy breathing' is not an aspiration that demands the world be overturned, but it still might be significant when voiced from within an autistic presence.

An idea of the 'reasonable' might be a suitable point on which to end a consideration of autism and the family. So much connected to the topic seems distinctly 'unreasonable', full of a manic desire for success or achievement that distorts ideas of parenting, marriage and love, that being 'reasonable' can be seen as a position worth attaining. If a reasonable idea of autism were allowed – if autism itself was allowed to be a form of the reasonable – and if it were reasonable to know and understand that there are families that contain autism (in children, but in adults as well), then there might be less of the absence of reason that seems so prevalent now. This appeal to an idea of rationalism might sound odd, given the damage that has been done to those with autism in the name of the rational or empirical, and understanding that (for example) those who argue for or against an idea of 'curing', or the place of vaccines, will equally see their position as being reasonable. But it is precisely this rational sense of the reasonable, the assertion that it *is* acceptable to have autism in the family and that it is *not* a stigma that somehow blights familial life, that can and does help. Those who know this to be true may have to argue for its acceptance, but it is worthwhile knowing that it is right.

## Notes

1 *Daily Mail*, 18 April 2006, p. 1 and p. 7. The story was also reported as front-page news in the regional paper the *Yorkshire Post* on the same day.
2 See http://www.neurodiversity.com/murder.html. Accessed 11 December 2007.
3 See http://www.abc.net.au/pm/content/2004/s1121667.htm. Accessed 11 December 2007.
4 Debbie Taylor, 'The dark side of mothering', *The Times*, 23 April 2006. Available online at http://www.timesonline.co.uk/tol/news/article708206.ece. Accessed 11 December 2007.

5  See http://www.jkp.com/catalogue/index.php/cat/autism. Accessed 11 December 2007.

6  Barry Neil Kaufman, *Son-Rise* (New York: Harper & Row, 1976), published in the UK as *To Love Is To Be Happy With: The Miracle of One Autistic Child* (London: Souvenir Press, 1976), and *Son-Rise: The Miracle Continues* (Tiburon, CA: H. J. Kramer/New World Library, 1994). The latter volume is an updated and extended version of the earlier book.

7  See http://www.autismtreatmentcenter.org/contents/about_son-rise/what_is_the_son-rise_program.php. Accessed 11 December 2007.

8  Leo Kanner, 'Autistic disturbances of affective contact', *Nervous Child*, no. 2 (1943), p. 248 (emphasis in original).

9  A number of other researchers into autism working after Kanner's initial publication noticed this fact. In response to a remark from Kanner that his Baltimore clinic saw autistic children from all over the world and that they frequently were the offspring of intelligent parents, in *The Empty Fortress* Bruno Bettelheim noted that, 'If children are brought to him from the four corners of the earth, doesn't it suggest that a preponderance of them are the children of highly educated or successful parents? How else could they have learned of Dr. Kanner and made the trek to Baltimore?' Bettelheim also quotes child psychiatrist Lauretta Bender, who referred specifically to the issues of the 'family background of his colleagues, professors and intellectual sophisticates who have selected his [Kanner's] service'. See Bruno Bettelheim, *The Empty Fortress: Infantile Autism and the Birth of the Self* (New York: Free Press/Macmillan, 1967), p. 420.

10  Kanner, 'Autistic disturbances of affective contact', p. 250.

11  Kanner, 'Autistic disturbances of affective contact', p. 250.

12  Kanner, 'Autistic disturbances of affective contact', p. 250. In his second publication on autism, Kanner dropped the term 'disturbances of affective contact' and replaced it with 'early infantile autism', which became the standard phrase used to describe 'classic' autism in children. See Leo Kanner, 'Early infantile autism', *Journal of Pediatrics*, no. 25 (1944), pp. 211–17.

13  Bettelheim, *The Empty Fortress*, p. 8.

14  Bettelheim, *The Empty Fortress*, p. 393.

15  Bettelheim, *The Empty Fortress*, pp. 389–90.

16  Bettelheim, *The Empty Fortress*, p. 398.

17  Bettelheim, *The Empty Fortress*, p. 399.

18  A. J. Wakefield, *et al.*, 'Illeal–lymphoid–nodular hyperplasia, non-specific colitis, and pervasive developmental disorder in children', *Lancet*, vol. 351, no. 9103 (February 1998), pp. 637–41.

19  David Kirby, *Evidence of Harm – Mercury in Vaccines and the Autism Epidemic: A Medical Controversy* (New York: St Martin's Press, 2005), p. 76. For an account of how Kirby came to write the book see, http://www.thoughtfulhouse.org/0405-conf-dkirby.htm. Accessed 16 December 2007.

20  Michael Fitzpatrick, *MMR and Autism: What Parents Need to Know* (London: Routledge, 2004), pp. x–xi.

21  Fitzpatrick, *MMR and Autism*, p. 165.

22  Marti Leimbach, *Daniel Isn't Talking* (London: Fourth Estate, 2006), p. 112. Like Cammie McGovern, Leimbach is the parent of a child with autism.

23  Leimbach, *Daniel Isn't Talking*, pp. 112–13.

24  Leimbach, *Daniel Isn't Talking*, p. 98.

25  Leimbach, *Daniel Isn't Talking*, p. 98 (italics in original).

26  Leimbach, *Daniel Isn't Talking*, p. 59.

27  Leimbach, *Daniel Isn't Talking*, p. 63.

28  Leimbach, *Daniel Isn't Talking*, pp. 63–4.

29  Leimbach, *Daniel Isn't Talking*, p. 107.

30  Leimbach, *Daniel Isn't Talking*, pp. 131–2.

31  Leimbach, *Daniel Isn't Talking*, pp. 254–5. It is instructive that Daniel's correct pronoun usage comes in the same moment as he tells his mother that he loves her.

32  Pervasive developmental disorder – not otherwise specified.

33  Luke Jackson is the author of *Freaks, Geeks and Asperger Syndrome: A User Guide to Adolescence* (London: Jessica Kingley, 2002) and *A User Guide to the GF/CF Diet for Autism, Asperger Syndrome and AD/HD* (London: Jessica Kingley, 2002). Since the making of *My Family and Autism*, he has also written *Crystalline Lifetime: Fragments of Asperger Syndrome* (London: Jessica Kingsley, 2006).

34  David T. Mitchell and Sharon L. Snyder, *Narrative Prosthesis: Disability and the Dependencies of Discourse* (Ann Arbor, MI: University of Michigan Press, 2000), p. 165.

35  Fitzpatrick, *MMR and Autism*, p. 160 and p. 158. Fitzpatrick glosses the moment in *Hear the Silence* when the character of Wakefield meets Nicky for the first time as an introduction from a 'caring, listening doctor' (p. 158).

36  Wakefield, quoted in Fitzpatrick, *MMR and Autism*, p. 160.

37  In the US, the verb 'recover', as in 'fighting to recover children with developmental disorders', is used to describe this process. This phrase is taken from the 'Welcome' page of the Thoughtful House Center for Children, an educational and research practice in Austin, Texas, where Wakefield is now executive director. David Kirby is one of the Center's advisors. See http://www.thoughtfulhouse.org/index.html. Accessed 16 December 2007.

38  On 31 December 2006, under the headline 'MMR doctor given legal aid thousands', the *Sunday Times* reported allegations that Wakefield was paid over £400,000 in fees and expenses by lawyers attempting to prove that the MMR vaccine was unsafe, that the work for which he received these payments started in 1996, some two years before the publication of the *Lancet* article, and that some of the children used in the 1998 study were also claimants in the lawsuit. Wakefield, along with two colleagues from the Royal Free Hospital, is also the subject of a hearing by the UK's General Medical Council (GMC), which is enquiring into allegations of serious professional misconduct during the 1996–98 research period. The GMC panel is looking specifically at issues of ethical approval relating to the research. The *Lancet* has said it would not have published the 1998 paper had it known about the potential conflict of interest.

39  See http://www.autismvox.com/petition-for-wakefield-who-do-you-believe. Accessed 17 October 2007.

40  Nancy D. Wiseman, *Could It Be Autism? A Parent's Guide to the First Signs and Next Steps* (New York: Broadway Books, 2006), p. 180.

41  Wiseman, *Could It Be Autism?*, p. 215.

42  Ann Lovell, *In a Summer Garment: The Experience of an Autistic Child* (London: Secker & Warburg, 1978), pp. 137–8. The book was republished, also in 1978, as *Simple Simon: The Story of an Autistic Boy* (Tring: Lion Publishing). The pagination of the two books is identical.

43  Lovell, *In a Summer Garment*, p. 140.

44  Lovell, *In a Summer Garment*, p. 131.

45  Barry Neil Kaufman, *To Love Is To Be Happy With: The Miracle of One Autistic Child* (London: Souvenir Press, 1976), p. 2.

46  Kaufman, *To Love Is To Be Happy With*, p. 38 and pp. 47–8.

47  Kaufman, *Son-Rise: The Miracle Continues*, p. 148.

48  Kaufman, *Son-Rise: The Miracle Continues*, pp. 189–90.

49  See http://www.autismtreatmentcenter.org/contents/about_son-rise/history_ of_the_son-rise_program.php. Accessed 17 December 2007.

50  Raun Kaufman, 'Foreword', in *Son-Rise: The Miracle Continues*, pp. xiv–xv.

51  Raun Kaufman, 'Foreword', p. xiii.

52  Raun Kaufman, 'Foreword', p. xiii.

53  Raun Kaufman, 'Foreword', p. xiii.

54  Laura Schreibman, *The Science and Fiction of Autism* (Cambridge, MA: Harvard University Press, 2005), p. 224. Doubts over Raun Kaufman's autism are also expressed in Bryna Siegel's *The World of the Autistic Child: Understanding and Treating Autistic Spectrum Disorders* (New York: Oxford University Press, 1996).

55  Schriebman, *The Science and Fiction of Autism*, pp. 224–5 and p. 223.

56  Nick Hornby, 'Introduction', in Charlotte Moore, *George and Sam* (London: Viking, 2004), p. ix.

57  Moore, *George and Sam*, p. 234.

58  Moore, *George and Sam*, p. 236.

59  Moore, *George and Sam*, pp. 237–8.

60  Robert Hughes, *Running with Walker: A Memoir* (London: Jessica Kingsley, 2003), pp. 233–4.

61  Barbara Lasalle, *Finding Ben: A Mother's Journey Through the Maze of Asperger's* (New York: McGraw-Hill, 2003), p. xiii–xiv. The web link is to http://aspergerjourney. com. Accessed 16 November 2007.

62  DJ Savarese, 'It's my story!', in Ralph Savarese, *Reasonable People: A Memoir of Autism & Adoption* (New York: Other Press, 2007), p. 435.

# Conclusion:
# causing/curing/caring

In *An Anthropologist on Mars*, Oliver Sacks writes 'Autism, clearly, is a condition that has always existed'.[1] His comment is the product of a life spent as a neurologist caring for those who are cognitively different, and his relationship with autism has led him to investigate the historical record in a search for cases that, as a clinician, he might recognize. But we can use his observation in order to face another direction. Just as autism has always existed, so it *will* always exist. It is here, as part of the grand patterning of humanity, and will continue to be so for as long as there is variation in the condition of being human. If thinking about autism takes certain forms at the moment, it is likely that these will not last, and other, as yet unimaginable, ideas about the condition will circulate in the future. This book has attempted to look at how autism is being framed and discussed across a wide range of narratives, most of them contemporary, and has sought to explain the ways in which it operates as a curious fascination of the present. The stories and events about autism that increasingly unfold all around us are markers of a particular desire to engage with human difference, but it is probable that, as it always has done, this desire will change over time. Possibly autism will experience a fate similar to that of schizophrenia, once thought of as a possible spring of creativity and wonder, but now more commonly related to media stories about crime or state health policies.

The difference between the respective images of schizophrenia and autism at the moment is one of a perception about neurology. The science, so we seem to feel, has advanced to such a degree that the mysteries of the schizophrenic no longer hold any appeal. Autism, however, appears to be different. The scientists hold up their hands and admit to a lack of knowledge about the cause or the various forms the condition might take, and this coincides with the idea that autism appears to be everywhere, exploding in an epidemic that is about people and yet that also seems, even in its most general formations, to be somehow easily apprehended as a metaphor for a version of the present, as some kind of cultural and social mirroring. The central point to be made about such a linkage is that it will create very real dangers if the conception of autism as a metaphor floats completely free from the actuality of the condition itself. In the suggestion that we are all, in some way, autistic, or that the term might be usefully applied to other contexts (listening to the radio while working one morning, I heard adolescence described as 'temporary autism'), there is a chance that the word will become meaningless. For this to happen at a point when so much is still unknown about the condition would be a disaster, and yet there have been many times during the research for this book that it has seemed to me as if it is a process that is already occurring to some degree.

The search for the cause of autism is, by and large, a scientific one. Few of the narratives that have come in the preceding pages have had much to say about cause, and this is even true of the MMR stories, where an *idea* of a cause has provided the platform to discuss what might come next. On occasions, for example where a revelation about a supposed origin of the condition carries some sort of shock media value, a debate about autism's cause will briefly animate news narratives. So, recent theories that autism might be brought on by different manifestations of contemporary technology, from cable television to wi-fi, all play into our neuroses about our immediate environments and the ways in which we don't know how they affect our lives.[2] At different times, similar ideas have been suggested about other technological forms, from power cables to computer use. And there is also, of course, the suggestion that diet is all-important, that the connection between digestion and the brain in the growing child is a vital and vulnerable one in which autism somehow waits, like a kind of predator, to exploit the wrong connections. Possibly what unites all these scenarios is an idea of toxins, of the problem being some form of poison, be it physical and somatic or environmental. At times, we seem to worry that we cause autism by living the wrong way.

So, identifying causes might be about pinpointing the problem, and of course such an idea fits with the broad medical notion of dysfunction. Medical research will continue to look for what might be supplemental or lacking in the autistic brain and, in all probability, all sorts of progress will be made. It still would be productive,

Figure 7. Poster images produced by Ralph Smith, 2001.

however – even if it seems utopian – to wish for an idea of cause that did not see it as aberrant or an anomaly, but rather as a consequence of human diversity. Because, of course, the conception that the cause of autism *is* an aberration can lead only to the desire for a cure, for something that rectifies the mistake. This study has seen an extended idea of 'curing' at work in all manner of narratives, from the 'compensation cure' of savantism to the devotional love of a parent producing miracles. Whether overt or implicit, curing autism seems to be something we cannot help but want. It is, in this manifestation, something like cancer, that other great medical demon of our times. Like cancer, autism is often seen as a remorseless attacker of innocents, a destroyer of lives and families.

Yet, of course, the two are nothing alike, and the ideas that surround 'curing autism' take up positions of much greater complexity than exist for most medical conditions or diseases. There is a vocal autistic community that sees the cure campaigns as narratives that amount to a kind of genocide, a desire to eradicate cognitive difference. In the photographic posters of Ralph Smith (examples are shown in figure 7), the power of the argument against a cure is ultimately augmented by that inherent in the statement 'we are autistic adults', with its adoption of a rhetoric of rights familiar from any number of causes.

In the specific context of autism, of course, such a claim to collective subjectivity acquires a particular resonance, given the multiple metaphors about being 'locked in' that accompany the condition. Smith's posters are aggressive and opinionated. They challenge the viewer's perception of what autism is, and they voice the demand that those with the condition have the right to shape their own lives.[3] As we have seen, set against the arguments of the advocates are other communities, usually parents, who see autism as a condition that afflicts their children, and that causes pain, illness and fear. For this community, curing is paramount and an obligation, and the research funding capability of an organization such as Autism Speaks is a reflection of the powerful belief with which this argument is held.

The two approaches clash frequently. In November 2007, the National Autistic Society (NAS) in the UK launched a new campaign, entitled 'Thinking Differently About Autism', with the aim of increasing public awareness of the condition. The president of the NAS, actress Jane Asher, made the case for such awareness:

> The lack of understanding about autism among we so-called 'normal' people is one of the major causes of the unhappiness and isolation of those affected by this potentially devastating condition. It would be wonderful to think the NAS's campaign could change attitudes.[4]

In response, Asher and the NAS were immediately attacked in a letter to the national newspaper *The Independent* from parents who make up the pressure group Treating Autism. Lara Hawkings, a spokesperson for the group, noted: 'Hope for people with autism does not lie with celebrity endorsement and a pretence that autism is normal but in the torrent of medical research that is pouring out of the United States'. Rather ironically, given the associations sometimes asserted between having autism and being an alien, the Treating Autism letter accused the NAS of being 'on another planet'.[5]

'Curing' is here a battleground, as it is in so many forms in which it is discussed, especially when care and treatment are involved. There is no sign that either side in this particular battle will give ground to the other. Interestingly, there are few fictional texts in which narratives seek to imagine what life either side of a cure for autism might be like. In one of the few that does, Elizabeth Moon's 2002 near-future novel *Speed of Dark*, the juxtaposition of the two states ultimately ruins the book's effectiveness as a work of fiction. *Speed of Dark* builds up an insight into the life of Lou Arrendale, its central protagonist, showing his life at work and at home, and part of the fiction's accomplishment is to show the challenges and pleasures of Lou's independence. But, able to take advantage near the end of the novel of a trial treatment that will cure his autism, Lou agrees to the change. The results, as Moon presents it, are a surprise even to Lou himself:

> When my counsellor, a cheerful young man with a bright red beard, explains what they did, I am almost in shock. Why did Lou-before agree to this? How could he risk so much? I would like to grab him and shake him, but he is me now. I am his future, as he is my past. I am the light flung out in the universe, and he is the explosion from which I came.[6]

If 'Lou-before' is the character we have come to identify with throughout the novel, it is 'Lou-after' that we end with and, for all his clear happiness and accomplishments,[7] it is impossible not to feel troubled by a story which has, in effect, removed a central figure precisely at the point he most engages our sympathy.

Noting that the concept of the cure doesn't work in Moon's novel offers no particular insight into the wider debates about 'eradicating' autism. It does, however, remind us of two things that might help us to move on in the discussion. Firstly, *Speed of Dark* does, in the centrality with which it treats the idea of the cure, throw into relief all those other narratives which, as we have seen, offer ideas of cure by stealth – through ideas of love, or attainment, or compensation – and we would do well to see and understand how many of these stories actually perform notions of recovery and correction as they unfold. Secondly, the puzzling concern felt when the reader puts the novel down comes from the loss of Lou, and the realization that comes from this is that what has been of benefit up to this point in the story has precisely been the opportunity to *listen* to Lou as he describes his own life. In the argument above, between the NAS and Treating Autism, the different viewpoints on the ethics of disability evolved, as these debates often do, into opinions that increasingly left behind those who actually are autistic. There was not a lot of listening taking place.

Yet the benefits of listening are obvious. We might care less about causes if we knew exactly what it means to live with autism. We might be less sweeping in our assumptions about cures if we had a sense of what the condition entails. Conversely, we might *better* understand the links between autistic and non-autistic humanity if we approached the subject with less fear. To some degree, this book has shown that we try to banish this fear when we turn autism into narrative. By placing it within structures that we recognize, whether they are generic forms of fiction or the context of the family, we seek to blunt its difference, precisely because of the worries we sense such difference might contain. Such an outcome is always the product of situations which lack sufficient dialogue. Yet, even while this might be true, if we see more autism around us than at any time in history, and if we think of the consequences of knowing it to be a lifelong condition, then we can also admit that we have a greater opportunity for dialogue than has ever existed. Listening to those with autism has never been a more available option, and it is one that those who are in the business of making cultural representations of the condition need to take up.

So, the final category to which I find myself returning in this book is, indeed, one of care. This is not an instance of caring purely being seen in terms of 'looking after', though that will always be an undertaking that needs to be performed correctly; we make huge mistakes if we do not admit to the serious and profound difficulties that affect the lives of some people with autism. It is, rather, caring understood as a process of acknowledging, of thinking about, of admitting, debating, listening and sharing. This will take many forms across many locations, and I would like to think that this book is one of them, but it is a potential development and progression that is required at the present time if we are to properly discuss what autism means in the contemporary world. This is not, I would want to stress, an idea of care that is only a shorthand for an idea of liberal tolerance and acceptance. It has to be more aggressive, proactive and provocative than that. It has to demand that interventions are made, voices are listened to and even that texts are re-read in a fashion that has justice as its ultimate goal. There are still too many easy assumptions made, and casual stories told, about this condition. Caring about autism – what we know of it and how we put it in our narratives – is something from which all manner of people can and must benefit.

## Notes

1  Oliver Sacks, *An Anthropologist on Mars* (London: Picador, 1995), p. 181.
2  See, for example the claims from Tamara Mariea and George Carlo, of the Science and Public Policy Institute in Pennsylvania, that electromagnetic radiation, from sources such as wi-fi, cause heavy metals to be trapped in body cells, thus spreading toxins. Tamara J. Mariea and George L. Carlo, 'Wireless radiation in the etiology and treatment of autism: clinical observations and mechanisms', *Journal of the Australasian College of Nutritional & Environmental Medicine*, vol. 26, no. 2 (August 2007), pp. 3–7. Also available online at http://www.internalbalance. com/emr-autism-acnem.pdf. Accessed 2 December 2007.
3  See Ralph Smith's work at the 'Artisms and Autistry' website, http://www. sentex.net/~nexus23/art01.html. Accessed 25 November 2005.

4  Jane Asher, quoted in 'Autism: what are the ethics of treating disability?', *The Independent*, 16 November 2007.

5  Lara Hawkings, quoted in 'Autism: what are the ethics of treating disability?'

6  Elizabeth Moon, *Speed of Dark* (London: Orbit, 2002), p. 420.

7  In the conclusion, Lou becomes an astronaut, someone 'chasing the light', who asserts that 'now I get to ask the questions'. Moon, *Speed of Dark*, p. 424.

# Acknowledgements

All books incur debts, but it is my strong suspicion that this one has produced more than most. The idea for writing the book, or rather the knowledge that it would be possible, came very quickly, and surprisingly fully formed as something potentially achievable, as I sat in a workshop organized by the City of York Council for the parents of children newly diagnosed with autism. I have been very fortunate to work with some dedicated individuals in the fields of education and social care, and I am very grateful to all those who have shown me many aspects of autism that I might otherwise have missed.

The day-to-day work on the book largely took place in the School of English at the University of Leeds, and I am extremely fortunate to have colleagues who were willing to listen to my ideas, find space for conversations, and support me in my frequently unsure sense of where the work was going. As Heads of School when I began my research, David Lindley and Vivien Jones were understanding and supportive of the circumstances in which I started, and I am grateful to them and to Ed Larrissy, their successor, for giving me the right kind of space in which to think and write. Colleagues at Leeds – past and present – who may not have known the specifics of what I was working on would pass materials to me, or refer to films, television programmes or events, and I was made aware of many texts that might have eluded me as a result. For their help I would like to thank Frances Babbage, Sam Durrant, Anthea Fraser Gupta, Graham Huggan, Robert Jones, Ananya Kabir, John McLeod, Brendon Nicholls, Francis O'Gorman, Jay Prosser, Alistair Stead and John Whale. Because of the fact that she occupied an office next to mine, Katharine McGowran became one of my first audiences and I am very grateful for the enthusiasm – forced at times, I'm sure – with which she greeted my early thoughts. Both Bridget Bennett and Katy Mullin always understood the full extent of what was involved in this work, and I would like to thank both for always being available to talk. Mick Gidley gave me excellent advice on the issues involved surrounding photography, while Denis Flannery was vital in developing my ideas, whether on a road trip across New England or in a rushed conversation about the book's cover outside our offices. I owe Denis my thanks not least because, by example, he helped me keep this book the kind of study I always wanted it to be. Over the last four years by far the majority of conversations I have had about representing disability have been with Clare Barker, and her insight and friendship have been fundamental in the development of my thinking. Clare's own scholarship has ensured that this book is better than it would have been had I not had the opportunity to share many discussions with her.

Taking my ideas to the US changed everything, and here I am most indebted to Mark Osteen. Organizing firstly the panel on representations of autism at the 2004 Modern Language Association conference in Philadelphia and then (with other members of the Society of Critical Exchange) the 'Autism and Representation' conference at Case Western Reserve University in Cleveland in 2005, Mark's commitment to understanding how autism is figured in cultural narratives has been exemplary, and I owe him a great deal for both the opportunities which he provided and the ideas he shared. In Philadelphia, I had a very important conversation with Ralph Savarese and Kristina Chew, for which I am grateful, and Jim Fisher was the perfect host at Fordham University in New York in 2006 when he invited me to talk. I should also like to thank Tony Baker, James Berger, Martha Stoddard Holmes, Kristen Loutensock, Patrick McDonagh, Bruce Mills and Phil Schwarz for all the exchanging of ideas at various gatherings.

In the UK, I am grateful to audiences in Leeds, Liverpool, Manchester and Oxford for help in developing my thoughts. I would want to thank Lucy Burke in particular for her support and insight, and Michael Baron for his enthusiasm and detailed knowledge of the ways in which autism discussions have progressed over the decades. Over the last five years, many people have corresponded with me, or offered encouragement and assistance as the book developed, and I owe thanks to Larry Arnold, Anthony Bailey, Gerhard Beck, David Bolt, Jennifer Fleissner, Kat French, Suzi Ibbotson, Miranda Kemp, Chris Martinez, Ato Quayson, Irene Rose, Kathleen Seidel, Ralph Smith, Helen Tookey and others at *The Reader*, and Eric Zander. The staff at the Library of the National Autistic Society were welcoming and helpful during my research trip there, and I would also want to thank staff at the Brotherton Library in Leeds. In New Zealand in 2006, Jane Stafford, Lydia Wevers and Mark Williams were wonderfully encouraging and supportive, as they have been for nearly two decades now. To all those with autism who have written to me over the years, whether named or anonymous, I owe a great deal of thanks. They have given the book a dimension it would otherwise not have had. At Liverpool University Press, Anthony Cond has been the model of a supportive editor, and I wish to thank him for his continued support in this project and belief in my writing. Thanks, too, to Ralph Footring for the care with which he helped me produce the final text.

As anyone connected in any way to autism will know, families and friends make life possible. Regardless of intellectual or institutional life, there would have been no book at all without the often unquestioning support that came from those closest to me. Kevin, Marion and Tim McLoughlin provided both a space to write when writing was imperative, and encouragement and assistance at every point. Alison Murray has cared across distances and changes in both our lives. To Kirsty Bennett, Jan Hartwell, Stephanie Rains, Catherine Smallwood, Lisa Solanki and Valérie Steunou foremostly and especially, I owe sincere thanks for all that which sometimes goes unnoticed but is not ever forgotten. Antoine and Yann have never once asked me why we live our lives the way that we do, never complained that things are not fair or should change. Their love and support has always been total, and words here cannot express how much I owe them. Megan has made so much possible, and reminded me that there is much, much more to even the busiest of lives than the writing of books. I thank her for all her love and for all the time we are together.

Ultimately, this book was a gift to me from Lucas, an extraordinary act that I am not sure I will ever fully understand. I do know, however, that I will always marvel at everything he continues to be. The central irony is not lost on me: someone supposedly lacking in so many things has taught me more about being human than any person on the planet. He is in every word of these pages, and he is always singing his own song.

Stuart Murray
*Leeds, February 2008*

# Select bibliography

Adams, Sarah, 'A curious phenomenon', *Guardian*, 7 December 2005.

American Psychiatric Association, *Diagnostic and Statistical Manual of Mental Disorders*, fourth edition (*DSM–IV*) (Washington, DC: American Psychiatric Association, 1994).

Andrews, Jonathan, 'Begging the question of idiocy: the definition and socio-cultural meaning of idiocy in early modern Britain. Part 1', *History of Psychiatry*, vol. 9, no. 33 (1998), pp. 65–95.

Armitage, Simon, *Little Green Man* (London: Penguin, 2002).

Ashton, Maxine, *The Other Half of Asperger Syndrome: A Guide to Living in an Intimate Relationship with a Partner Who Has Asperger Syndrome* (London: National Autistic Society, 2001).

——, *Aspergers in Love* (London: Jessica Kingsley, 2003).

Asperger, Hans, '"Autistic psychopathy" in childhood', in Uta Frith (ed. and trans.), *Autism and Asperger Syndrome* (Cambridge: Cambridge University Press, 1991), pp. 37–92.

Baggs, A. M., 'In My Language', http://www.youtube.com/watch?v=JnylM1hI2jc. Accessed 31 May 2007.

——, 'Ballastexistenz', http://ballastexistenz.autistics.org/?page_id=2. Accessed 4 June 2007.

Balsamo, Thomas, and Sharon Rosenbloom, *Souls: Beneath and Beyond Autism* (New York: McGraw-Hill, 2004).

Barker, Clare, 'From narrative prosthesis to disability counternarrative: reading the politics of difference in *Potiki* and *the bone people*', *Journal of New Zealand Literature*, vol. 24, no. 1 (2006), pp. 130–47.

Baron-Cohen, Simon, *Mindblindness: An Essay on Autism and Theory of Mind* (Cambridge, MA: Bradford/MIT Press, 1995).

——, *The Essential Difference: Men, Women and the Extreme Male Brain* (London: Penguin/Allen Lane, 2003).

Barron, Judy and Sean Barron, *There's a Boy in Here: Emerging from the Bonds of Autism* (Arlington, TX: Future Horizons, 2002).

Bazelon, Emily, 'What autistic girls are made of', *New York Times*, magazine, 5 August 2007. Available online at http://www.nytimes.com/2007/08/05/magazine/05autism-t.html. Accessed 3 December 2007.

Berger, Maurice, Brian Wallis and Simon Watson (eds), *Constructing Masculinity* (New York: Routledge, 1995).

Bérubé, Michael, *Life As We Know It: A Father, a Family and an Exceptional Child* (New York: Vintage, 1998).

Bettelheim, Bruno, *The Empty Fortress: Infantile Autism and the Birth of the Self* (New York: Free Press/Macmillan, 1967).

Biklen, Douglas, *Autism and the Myth of the Person Alone* (New York: New York University Press, 2005).

Birkett, Dea, 'See it my way', *Guardian*, 'Weekend', 23 November 2002, pp. 32–42.

Bissonnette, Larry, 'Beyond questions and answers: free expression through art and words', http://suedweb.syr.edu/thefci/7-3bis.htm. Accessed 30 August 2007.

Bleuler, Eugene, 'Die prognose der Dementia Praecox (Schizophreniegruppe)', *Allgemeine Zeitschrift fur Psychiatrie und Psychisch-Gerichtliche Medizin*, no. 65 (1908), pp. 436–64.

Bradshaw, Peter, 'Does Control's take on disability mark a new dawn?', http://blogs.guardian.co.uk/film/2007/10/does_controls_take_on_disabili.html. Accessed 3 October 2007.

Buten, Howard, *Through the Glass Wall: Journeys into the Closed-Off Worlds of the Autistic* (New York: Bantam, 2004).

Cahir, Linda Constanza, *Solitude and Society in the Works of Herman Melville and Edith Wharton* (Westport, CN: Greenwood Press, 1999).

Cassuto, Leonard, 'Oliver Sacks and the medical case narrative', in Sharon L. Snyder *et al.* (eds), *Disability Studies: Enabling the Humanities* (New York: Modern Language Association, 2002), pp. 118–30.

Coetzee, J. M., *Life & Times of Michael K* (1983; London: Vintage, 2004).

Collins, Paul, *Not Even Wrong: A Father's Journey into the Lost History of Autism* (London: Bloomsbury, 2004).

Conrad, Joseph, *Tales of Unrest* (London: Eveleigh, Nash & Grayson, n.d. but 1898).

——, *The Secret Agent* (1907; London: Penguin, 1994).

Darke, Paul, 'Understanding cinematic representations of disability', in Tom Shakespeare (ed.), *The Disability Reader: Social Science Perspectives* (London: Continuum, 1998), pp. 181–97.

Davidson, Joyce, '"In a world of her own": re-presenting alienation and emotion in the lives and writings of woman with autism', *Gender, Place and Culture*, vol. 14, no. 6 (December 2007), pp. 659–77.

Davis, Bill (as told to Wendy Goldband Schunick), *Breaking Autism's Barriers: A Father's Story* (London: Jessica Kingsley, 2001).

Davis, Lennard J., *Enforcing Normalcy: Disability, Deafness and the Body* (London: Verso, 1995).

——, *Bending Over Backwards: Disability, Dismodernism and Other Difficult Positions* (New York: New York University Press, 2002).

Delacato, Carl H., *The Ultimate Stranger: The Autistic Child* (Novato, CA: Arena, 1984).

Desai, Anita, *Clear Light of Day* (Harmondsworth: Penguin, 1980).

Dickens, Charles, *Barnaby Rudge: A Tale of the Riots of 'Eighty* (1841; London: Penguin, 2003).

——, with W. H. Wills, 'Idiots' and 'A curious dance round a curious tree', in Harry Stone (ed.), *Charles Dickens' Uncollected Writings from* Household Works *1850–1859, Vol. II* (Bloomington, IN: Indiana University Press, 1968).

Dickinson, Hilary, 'Idiocy in nineteenth-century fiction compared with the medical perspectives of the time', *History of Psychiatry*, vol. 11, no. 3 (2000), pp. 291–309.

Donnellan, A. M. (ed.), *Classic Readings in Autism* (New York: Teachers College, Columbia University, 1985).

Emerson, Ralph Waldo, 'Self-Reliance', in Nina Baym *et al.* (eds.), *The Norton Anthology of American Literature*, third edition (New York: Norton, 1979), vol. 1, pp. 956–72.

Ernst, Waltraud (ed.), *Histories of the Normal and the Abnormal: Social and Cultural Histories of Norms and Normativity* (London: Routledge, 2006).

Farrell, G. Patrick, 'Autism in literature', *Journal of Autism and Developmental Disorders*, vol. 15, no. 4 (December 1985), pp. 441–2.

Faulkner, William, *The Sound and the Fury* (1929; Harmondsworth: Penguin, 1964).

Fitzgerald, Michael, *Autism and Creativity: Is There a Link Between Autism in Men and Exceptional Ability?* (Hove: Brunner-Routledge, 2004).

——, *The Genesis of Artistic Creativity: Asperger's Syndrome and the Arts* (London: Jessica Kingsley, 2005).

Fitzpatrick, Michael, *MMR and Autism: What Parents Need to Know* (London: Routledge, 2004).

Fling, Echo R., *Eating an Artichoke: A Mother's Perspective on Asperger's Syndrome* (London: Jessica Kingsley, 2000).

Freak Parade, 'The Hollywood B list and autism', http://ourfreakparade.com/2007/10/05/the-hollywood-b-list-and-autism. Accessed 8 October 2007.

Frith, Uta, *Autism: Explaining the Enigma* (Oxford: Basil Blackwell, 1989; second edition 2003).

—— (ed.), *Autism and Asperger Syndrome* (Cambridge: Cambridge University Press, 1991).

Furlani, Andre, 'Bartleby the Socratic', *Studies in Short Fiction* (summer 1997). Available online at http://findarticles.com/p/articles/mi_m2455/is_3_34/ai_59211541. Accessed 24 July 2007.

Garland-Thomson, Rosemarie, *Extraordinary Bodies: Figuring Physical Disability in American Culture and Literature* (New York: Columbia University Press, 1997).

——, 'The politics of staring: visual rhetorics of disability in popular photography', in Sharon L. Snyder *et al.* (eds), *Disability Studies: Enabling the Humanities* (New York: Modern Language Association, 2002), pp. 56–75.

——, 'Review of *Monsters: Human Freaks in America's Gilded Age* and *Extraordinary Exhibitions*', *Disability Studies Quarterly*, vol. 25, no. 4 (2005).

——, 'Ways of staring', *Journal of Visual Culture*, vol. 5, no. 2 (August 2006), pp. 173–92.

Gottlieb, Eli, *The Boy Who Went Away* (London: Jonathan Cape, 1997).

Grandin, Temple, *Animals in Translation: Using the Mysteries of Autism to Decode Animal Behavior* (London: Bloomsbury, 2005).

——, *Thinking in Pictures, And Other Reports from My Life with Autism*, second edition (London: Bloomsbury, 2006).

—— and Margaret M. Scariano, *Emergence: Labeled Autistic – A True Story*, second edition (New York: Warner Books, 2005).

Grant, Brian (ed.), *The Quiet Ear: Deafness in Literature* (London: André Deutsch, 1987).

Griffiths, Niall, *Runt* (London: Jonathan Cape, 2007).

Grinker, Roy Richard, *Unstrange Minds: Remapping the World of Autism* (New York: Basic Books, 2007).

Groom, Winston, *Forrest Gump* (Garden City, NY: Doubleday, 1986).

Hacking, Ian, *The Social Construction of What?* (Cambridge, MA: Harvard University Press, 1999).

——, 'What is Tom saying to Maureen?', *London Review of Books*, vol. 28, no. 9 (11 May 2006), pp. 3–7.

Haddon, Mark, *The Curious Incident of the Dog in the Night-Time* (London: Jonathan Cape, 2003).

Halliwell, Martin, *Images of Idiocy: The Idiot Figure in Modern Fiction and Film* (Aldershot: Ashgate, 2004).

Hayes, Michael T., and Rhonda S. Black, 'Troubling signs: disability, Hollywood movies and the construction of a discourse of pity', *Disability Studies Quarterly*, vol. 23, no. 2 (spring 2003), pp. 114–32.

Hermelin, Beate, *Bright Splinters of the Mind: A Personal Story of Research with Autistic Savants* (London: Jessica Kingsley, 2001).

Hornby, Nick, *About A Boy* (London: Penguin, 2000).

——, *31 Songs* (London: Penguin, 2003).

Howe, Michael, J. A., *Fragments of Genius: The Strange Feats of Idiots Savants* (London: Routledge, 1989).

Hughes, Robert, *Running with Walker: A Memoir* (London: Jessica Kingsley, 2003).

Hulme, Keri, *the bone people* (1983; London: Picador, 1986).

Jackson, Luke, *Freaks, Geeks and Asperger Syndrome: A User Guide to Adolescence* (London: Jessica Kingsley, 2002).

——, *A User Guide to the GF/CF Diet for Autism, Asperger Syndrome and AD/HD* (London: Jessica Kingsley, 2002).

——, *Crystalline Lifetime: Fragments of Asperger Syndrome* (London: Jessica Kingsley, 2006).

Jacobs, Barbara, *Loving Mr Spock* (London: Michael Joseph, 2003).

Jordan, Thomas E., *The Mentally Retarded* (Columbus, OH: Charles E. Merrill, 1961).

Jurecic, Ann, 'Mindblindness: autism, writing, and the problem of empathy', *Literature and Medicine*, vol. 25, no. 1 (spring 2006), pp. 1–23.

Kalliney, P. J., *Cities of Affluence and Anger* (Charlottesville, VA: University of Virginia Press, 2006).

Kanner, Leo, 'Autistic disturbances of affective contact', *Nervous Child*, no. 2 (1943), pp. 217–50.

——, 'Early infantile autism', *Journal of Pediatrics*, no. 25 (1944), pp. 211–17.

Kaplan, E. Ann, *Looking for the Other: Feminism, Film and the Imperial Gaze* (New York: Routledge, 1997).

Kaufman, Barry Neil, *To Love Is To Be Happy With: The Miracle of One Autistic Child* (London: Souvenir Press, 1976).

——, *A Miracle to Believe In* (New York: Fawcett Crest, 1981).

——, *Son-Rise: The Miracle Continues* (Tiburon, CA: H. J. Kramer/New World Library, 1994).

Kelly, Wyn, *Melville's City: Literary and Urban Form in Nineteenth-Century New York* (Cambridge: Cambridge University Press, 1996).

Kephart, Beth, *A Slant of Sun: One Child's Courage* (New York: Quill, 1999).

Keyes, Daniel, *Flowers for Algernon* (1966; New York: Harvest/Harcourt, 2004).

Kirby, David, *Evidence of Harm – Mercury in Vaccines and the Autism Epidemic: A Medical Controversy* (New York: St Martin's Press, 2005).

Lasalle, Barbara, *Finding Ben: A Mother's Journey Through the Maze of Asperger's* (New York: McGraw-Hill, 2003).

Lea, Daniel, and Berthold Schoene (eds), *Posting the Male: Masculinities in Post-war and Contemporary British Literature* (Amsterdam: Rodopi, 2003).

Lee, Hermione, *Virginia Woolf* (London: Chatto & Windus, 1996).

Leimbach, Marti, *Daniel Isn't Talking* (London: Fourth Estate, 2006).

Levine, Robert S. (ed.), *The Cambridge Companion to Herman Melville* (Cambridge: Cambridge University Press, 1998).

Livesey, Margot, *Banishing Verona: A Novel* (New York: Henry Holt, 2004).

Lodge, David, *Thinks* (London: Penguin, 2002).

Lovell, Ann, *In a Summer Garment: The Experience of an Autistic Child* (London: Secker & Warburg, 1978).

McCracken, Scott, *Pulp: Reading Popular Fiction* (Manchester: Manchester University Press, 1998).

McDonagh, Patrick, 'Barnaby Rudge, "idiocy" and paternalism: assisting the "poor idiot"', *Disability & Society*, vol. 21, no. 5 (August 2006), pp. 411–23.

McGovern, Cammie, *Eye Contact* (London: Viking, 2006).

McGrath, James, 'Reading autism', *Interdisciplinary Literary Studies*, vol. 8, no. 2 (spring 2007), pp. 100–13.

Maltby, Richard, *Hollywood Cinema: An Introduction* (Oxford: Blackwell, 1995).

Mann, Lisa Barrett, 'Oscar nominee: documentary or fiction?', *Washington Post*, 22 February 2005, p. HE01.

Melville, Herman, 'Bartleby the Scrivener', in Harrison Hayford *et al.* (eds.), *The Writings of Herman Melville, Vol. 9: The Piazza Tales and Other Prose Pieces, 1839– 1860* (Evanston, IL: Northwestern University Press/Newberry Library, 1987).

Melville, Pauline, *The Ventriloquist's Tale* (London: Bloomsbury, 1997).

Mitchell, David T., and Sharon L. Snyder, 'Introduction: disability and the double bind of representation', in David T. Mitchell and Sharon L. Snyder, *The Body and Physical Difference: Discourses of Disability* (Ann Arbor, MI: University of Michigan Press, 1997), pp. 1–31.

—— and ——, *Narrative Prosthesis: Disability and the Dependencies of Discourse* (Ann Arbor, MI: University of Michigan Press, 2000).

Moon, Elizabeth, *Speed of Dark* (London: Orbit, 2002).

Moore, Charlotte, *George and Sam* (London: Viking, 2004).

Mukhopadhyay, Tito Rajarshi, *Beyond the Silence: My Life, the World and Autism* (London: National Autistic Society, 2000).

——, *The Mind Tree: A Miraculous Child Breaks the Silence of Autism* (New York: Arcade Publishing, 2003).

——, *How Can I Talk If My Lips Don't Move? Inside My Autistic Mind* (New York: Arcade Publishing, 2008).

——, with Soma Mukhopadhyay, *The Gold of the Sunbeams, and Other Stories* (New York: Arcade Publishing, 2005).

Murray, Stuart, 'Autism and the contemporary sentimental: fiction and the narrative fascination of the present', *Literature and Medicine*, vol. 25, no. 1 (spring 2006), pp. 24–45.

Nadesan, Majia Holmer, *Constructing Autism: Unravelling the 'Truth' and Understanding the Social* (New York: Routledge, 2005).

Nazeer, Kamran, *Send in the Idiots: Stories from the Other Side of Autism* (London: Bloomsbury, 2006).

Neale, Steve, and Murray Smith (eds), *Contemporary Hollywood Cinema* (London: Routledge, 1998).

Norden, Martin, F., *The Cinema of Isolation: A History of Physical Disability in the Movies* (New Brunswick, NJ: Rutgers University Press, 1994).

Ockelford, Adam, *In the Key of Genius: The Extraordinary Life of Derek Paravicini* (London: Hutchinson, 2007).

O'Gorman, Gerald, *The Nature of Childhood Autism* (London: Butterworths, 1967).

Osteen, Mark (ed.), *Autism and Representation* (New York: Routledge, 2008).

Paradiz, Valerie *Elijah's Cup: A Family's Journey into the Community and Culture of High-Functioning Autism and Asperger's Syndrome* (New York: Free Press, 2002).

Park, Clara Claiborne, *The Siege: A Family's Journey into the World of an Autistic Child* (Boston, MA: Little, Brown, 1967).

Pease, Bob, *Recreating Men: Postmodern Masculinity Politics* (London: Sage, 2000).

Peek, Fran, *The Real Rain Man* (Salt Lake City, UT: Harkness Publishing, 1996).

Pell, Angela, 'Rain and snow', *Communication*, vol. 40, no. 3 (autumn 2006), pp. 20–1.

Perry, Natalie, *Teaching the Mentally Retarded Child* (New York: Columbia University Press, 1960).

Quayson, Ato, *Aesthetic Nervousness: Disability and the Crisis of Representation* (New York: Columbia University Press, 2007).

Reed, Naomi C., 'The specter of Wall Street: "Bartleby the Scrivener" and the language of commodities', *American Literature*, vol. 76, no. 2 (June 2004), pp. 247–73.

Revill, Jo, 'The view from in here', *Observer Magazine*, 28 October 2007, pp. 36–46.

Rexer, Lyle, *Jonathan Lerman: Drawings by an Artist with Autism* (New York: George Braziller, 2002).

Rose, Irene, 'Autistic autobiography – introducing the field' (October 2005), http://www.case.edu/affil/sce/Texts_2005/Autism%20and%20Representation%20Rose.htm. Accessed 7 September 2006.

Sacks, Oliver, *The Man Who Mistook His Wife for a Hat* (London: Pan Books, 1986).

——, *An Anthropologist on Mars* (London: Picador, 1995).

Savarese, Ralph James, *Reasonable People: A Memoir of Autism & Adoption* (New York: Other Press, 2007).

Schonell, Fred J., *Backwardness in the Basic Subjects* (Edinburgh: Oliver and Boyd, 1942).

Schreibman, Laura, *The Science and Fiction of Autism* (Cambridge, MA: Harvard University Press, 2005).

Shakespeare, Tom, 'Art and lies? Representation of disability on film', in Mairian Corker and Sally French (eds), *Disability Discourse* (Buckingham: Open University Press, 1999), pp. 164–72.

Showalter, Elaine, *Hystories: Hysterical Epidemics and Modern Culture* (New York: Columbia University Press, 1997).

Shull, Rich, *Autism, Pre Rain Man* (New York: iUniverse, 2003).

Siegel, Bryna, *The World of the Autistic Child: Understanding and Treating Autistic Spectrum Disorders* (New York: Oxford University Press, 1996).

Snyder, Sharon L., and David T. Mitchell, *Cultural Locations of Disability* (Chicago, IL: University of Chicago Press, 2006).

Stokes, Melvyn, and Richard Maltby (eds), *Identifying Hollywood's Audiences: Cultural Identity and the Movies* (London: British Film Institute, 1999).

Sullivan, William P., 'Bartleby and infantile autism: a naturalistic explanation', *Bulletin of the West Virginia Association of College English Teachers*, no. 3 (1976), pp. 170–87.

Swarup, Vikas, *Q&A* (London: Doubleday, 2005).

Tammet, Daniel, *Born on a Blue Day: A Memoir of Asperger's and an Extraordinary Mind* (London: Hodder & Stoughton, 2006).

Taylor, Debbie, 'The dark side of mothering', *The Times*, 23 April 2006. Available online at http://www.timesonline.co.uk/tol/news/article708206.ece. Accessed 11 December 2007.

Vizenor, Gerald, *Fugitive Poses: Native American Scenes of Absence and Presence* (Lincoln, NE: University of Nebraska Press, 1998).

Wakefield, A. J., *et al.*, 'Illeal–lymphoid–nodular hyperplasia, non-specific colitis, and pervasive developmental disorder in children', *Lancet*, vol. 351, no. 9103 (February 1998), pp. 637–41.

Waltz, Mitzi, 'Reading case studies of people with autistic spectrum disorders: a cultural studies approach to issues of disability representation', *Disability & Society*, vol. 20, no. 4 (June 2005), pp. 421–35.

Webster, C. D., 'Conrad's "The Idiots": case examples of autism?', *Journal of Autism and Developmental Disorders*, vol. 14, no. 3 (September 1984), pp. 346–7.

Weinstein, Cindy, 'Melville, labor, and the discourses of reception', in Robert S. Levine (ed.), *The Cambridge Companion to Herman Melville* (Cambridge: Cambridge University Press, 1998), pp. 202–23.

Williams, Donna, *Nobody Nowhere: The Extraordinary Autobiography of an Autistic* (New York: Times Books, 1992).

——, *Somebody Somewhere: Breaking Free from the World of Autism* (New York: Times Books, 1994).

——, *Like Color to the Blind* (New York: Times Books, 1996).

——, *Autism – An Inside-Out Approach* (London: Jessica Kingsley, 1996).

——, *Exposure Anxiety: The Invisible Cage – An Exploration of Self-Protection Responses in the Autistic Spectrum* (London: Jessica Kingsley, 2002).

——, *Everyday Heaven: Journeys Beyond the Stereotypes of Autism* (London: Jessica Kingsley, 2004).

——, *Not Just Anything: A Collection of Thoughts on Paper* (London: Jessica Kingsley, 2004).

——, 'Putting autism on trial: an interview with Amanda Baggs by autistic author Donna Williams', *American Chronicle*, 5 July 2007. Available online at http://www.americanchronicle.com/articles/viewArticle.asp?articleID=31329. Accessed 9 July 2007.

Wing, Lorna, 'The history of ideas on autism: legends, myths and reality', *Autism: The International Journal of Research and Practice*, vol. 1, no. 1 (July 1997), pp. 13–23.

Wiseman, Nancy D., *Could It Be Autism? A Parent's Guide to the First Signs and Next Steps* (New York: Broadway Books, 2006).

Zelan, Karen, *Between Their World and Ours: Breakthroughs with Autistic Children* (New York: St Martin's Press, 2003).

# Index

Note: page numbers in bold refer to figures.